Ontario

Commission of Inquiry
Into Unregulated Residential
Accommodation

76 College Street
6th Floor
Toronto, Ontario
M7A 1N3

416/327-2427
Fax:
416/327-2425

Commission d'enquête
sur les Établissements
résidentiels non-réglementés

76, rue College
6e étage
Toronto (Ontario)
M7A 1N3

416/327-2427
Télécopieur
416/327-2425

To His Honour
The Lieutenant-Governor of the
Province of Ontario

Dear Sir:

I am pleased to submit herewith the Report of the
Commission of Inquiry Into Unregulated Residential
Accommodation.

Ernie Lightman, PhD
Commissioner

May 1, 1992

Ernie S. Lightman, PhD Commissioner/Commissaire

A Community of Interests

THE REPORT OF THE COMMISSION OF INQUIRY
INTO UNREGULATED RESIDENTIAL
ACCOMMODATION

ERNIE S. LIGHTMAN, PH.D.
Commissioner

JOHN KENEWELL, LL.B.
Director of Policy and Research

Ce rapport est aussi disponible en français

Copies of this document are available from:

Publications Ontario Bookstore

800 Bay St.

Toronto, Ontario

M7A 1N8

Tel: (416) 326-5300

Toll-free: 1-800-668-9938

Out-of-town residents write to:

Publications Ontario Mail Order Service

800 Bay St., 5th Floor

Toronto, Ontario

M7A 1N8

Credits:

Design: Peter Maher

Cover Illustration:

    Jeremy Smith

    Stairway to Gilmour Street, 1982

    Pencil on paper board mounted on wood

    43 in. x 35 in. (109 cm x 89 cm)

    Collection of Imperial Oil, Toronto

    Photo Courtesy of Mira Godard Gallery

Editor: Charis Wahl

Copy Editor/Proofreader: Alison Reid

Production Consultant: Paula Chabanais & Associates Limited

Contents

PART II: **THE REST HOME AS HOME**

PART III: **EMPOWERING AND PROTECTING VULNERABLE ADULTS**

PART IV: **RELATED ISSUES**

Acknowledgements

The Commission wishes to thank the many individuals, groups, and agencies who contributed to our work in so many ways:

most particularly, the residents of rest homes across Ontario, who shared with us their experiences and opinions, both publicly and in confidence;

the rest-home operators and their associations, who supported our activities and facilitated our site visitations with courtesy and grace;

the many community groups and agencies who made submissions, assisted in the organization of our public consultation process, and challenged our ideas;

the professionals in many fields who talked and wrote of their concerns and their suggestions for reform, often based on years of practical experience;

the government ministries and departments, both provincial and municipal, who aided and accelerated our research inquiries, and provided information and advice;

everyone at the Office of Seniors' Issues, Ministry of Citizenship, who welcomed our staff into their crowded quarters and provided administrative backup and support with warmth and efficiency;

Charis Wahl, who once again has brought her amazing editorial skills to bear on a very long manuscript.

Commission Staff

Ernie S. Lightman, Commissioner, received his Ph.D. in economics and is a professor of social policy at the University of Toronto.

John Kenewell, Director of Policy and Research, is a member of the Ontario Bar and was seconded to the Commission by the Ministry of Community and Social Services, where he is a Senior Policy Adviser.

Janet Cornfield, Policy Analyst, holds a diploma in nursing and is completing the Gerontology Certificate program at Ryerson Polytechnical Institute.

Millinese Vaughan, Project Manager, has held a variety of senior administrative and managerial positions.

Executive Summary

This Commission was created following the death of Joseph Kendall, a resident of Cedar Glen, an unregulated boarding home near Orillia, Ontario. The coroner's inquest into Mr. Kendall's death was the longest in Canadian history and produced more than eighty recommendations; key among these was that a Commission be appointed to inquire into unregulated residential accommodation in which vulnerable adults reside.

This Commission was appointed two days after the coroner's report was filed, in November 1990, and began its work on January 1, 1991, under the *Public Inquiries Act*. The Commission produced a widely circulated Discussion Paper in March 1991, which defined certain parameters for the Inquiry and raised several central questions for examination. The Commission consulted extensively, travelled to several communities across Ontario, visited a great variety of boarding, rest, and retirement homes, and met with residents, members of the public, and interest groups. We received some 230 written submissions.

Many vulnerable adults in Ontario live in unregulated settings, from luxury retirement homes to boarding/lodging/rest homes in which residents' only source of income may be social assistance [Family Benefits/GAINS(D) or General Wel-

1 Other than fire, public health, and construction standards that apply to all premises.

fare Assistance (GWA)], or Old Age Security (and its supplements). The accommodation is "unregulated" because there are no provincial licensing, standards[1] or inspection; nor are there other viable protections for the lives and well-being of residents.

All premises within the scope of this Inquiry offer residents housing and limited care services (assistance with the activities of daily living); often some or all meals are provided. Virtually all are operated on a commercial or for-profit basis. Some are very small; one facility has 450 beds. Research conducted for the Commission uses census data to estimate there are 47,500 vulnerable adults living in unregulated accommodation in Ontario.

Some of the settings visited by the Commission appear to be exemplary: residents seem well cared for and content. Other premises revealed inadequate physical environments and unacceptably low-quality care: abuse of residents—physical, emotional, financial, and sexual—may occur with great regularity.

It is our general view that any setting in which both accommodation and care are supplied by operators creates a power imbalance between sellers and buyers, and the potential for abuse of this power.

The principal aim of this Inquiry has been to redress these structural imbalances, to empower vulnerable adults who live in unregulated settings, and to assist them to assume control of their lives to the maximum extent possible. Such control includes making decisions about where, how, and with whom to live. An allied goal of the Inquiry is to offer protection to those residents of rest homes who wish it.

The Commission considered two broad approaches:

1. Comprehensive regulation by the government of Ontario, on the nursing-home model, or by municipalities through municipal by-laws.
This approach would involve mandatory minimum stan-

dards set by government (provincial or municipal); government inspection; and, possibly, government funding to ensure these standards can be met. The rest home would be viewed as an institution, part of a continuum of institutional care—in effect, a low-level, care-providing commercial nursing home.

2. An empowerment approach, in which residents are given rights and the means to ensure that these rights are respected, combined with limited regulation to attain minimum standards in areas where a rights-based approach is unlikely to be effective.

This approach considers the rest home to be a permanent community residence rather than a place of temporary sojourn or a first-stage, low-level nursing home.

The Commission rejects the first alternative. The protections promised by comprehensive regulation are uncertain, the empowerment of residents modest or non-existent. This approach would also be costly to deliver and enforce; experience in other areas—particularly the nursing-home sector— also suggests there are many technical and operational obstacles to effective regulation.

The Commission recommends the second alternative, which should better achieve empowerment and protection, at lower overall cost.

To view the rest home as a form of permanent community housing is compatible with recent government directions: the development of new care-giving institutions is not being contemplated today. Instead, the goal is community care: to serve care needs in the community whenever possible; to lower the rate of institutionalization; and to limit institutional beds to those whose care needs are so high that they cannot be met in the community. As well, recent initiatives favour delinking (or separating) accommodation from the provision of care. The former would be provided by landlords and the latter delivered by non-profit community-based agencies to people in their own homes. Those for whom rest homes are home would then be fully eligible for all in-home services now available or developed in future under the long-term-care initiative.

We define "rest homes," whether retirement or boarding homes, as residences in which owners/operators provide or are paid to provide care services, or cause others to understand that they provide care.

We call for mandatory registration of all rest homes with the municipality. Registration merely makes rest-home operators known to municipal authorities: it is not dependent on meeting particular standards; and registrations, unlike nursing home licences, cannot be bought or sold. Registration will end the current practice by which rest homes may operate totally unknown to any level of government.

The Commission recommends a multi-faceted approach to empowerment while offering protection to rest-home residents. Specific elements include the following:

1. a Rest Home Residents' Bill of Rights, which contains protections and entitlements regarding the physical accommodation and the quality of care;

2. a Rest Homes Tribunal (RHT), through which residents, with assistance as desired, will seek enforcement of the protections and entitlements set out in the bill of rights; the RHT is premised on adequate advocacy supports, both informal—by relatives and friends—and those to be created under Bill 74, the proposed *Advocacy Act, 1991*;

3. mandatory reporting of abuse in rest homes;

4. a police check of operators through the Canadian Police Information Centre to determine any criminal record, prior to registration;

5. clarification of minimum safety standards regarding health, fire, and the physical environment, including the Building Code and municipal occupancy by-laws. (In considering minimum standards, the Commission has been particularly concerned to avoid the loss of low-income

housing that might follow from standards—and costs—that are too high.)

The Commission also proposes to increase the accountability of local inspectors to residents for non-response or delayed/inadequate response to residents' complaints. No inspection visit should be announced in advance;

6. mandatory minimum staff-to-resident ratios in all rest homes at all hours. These ratios will be premised on a safety function, i.e., in case of emergency, staff will be expected to obtain appropriate assistance expeditiously. The ratio is not premised on staff providing ongoing care to residents;

7. a minimum "competence" standard for all staff who assist with medications. Operators should not be required to assist residents with medications; however, should they choose to do so, staff must bc adults, able to read and follow prescribed directions, and able to identify and communicate with each resident. They will not be required to have any medical training.

Following directly from our view of the rest home as permanent residential accommodation, the Commission also recommends:

1. coverage of all rest homes under Part IV of the *Landlord and Tenant Act* (*LTA*);
2. coverage of all rest homes under the proposed *Rent Control Act* (*RCA*).

These coverages should address many of residents' most commonly expressed problems, including capricious temporary or permanent eviction; failure to respect residents' privacy; denial of access to visitors; and sudden steep rises in costs.

We have also recommended criteria for *LTA* coverage for group homes, supportive housing, and rehabilitative and therapeutic residences.[2]

Amendments to the *LTA* and proposed *RCA* are necessary

2 Accommodation exempted from the *LTA* based on these criteria will also be exempted from our definition of a "rest home."

to accommodate the special nature of rest homes. For example, eviction of a tenant can be time-consuming and difficult under the *LTA*; yet in some cases, particularly where accommodation is shared and living is communal, rapid departure is essential. Residents' care needs may suddenly exceed those that can be met in a rest home (either with operator- or community-supplied services); the result may be severe disruption of the residence and even physical danger to operators and other residents.

The Commission is satisfied there are sufficient grounds for eviction under the *LTA*, but timeliness is a problem. We recommend a new "fast-track" procedure under *LTA* through which operators will be able to obtain interim orders to temporarily remove residents from the premises when the behaviour of those residents likely meets existing grounds for eviction, and when delay is likely to cause serious harm to the person or property of operators or other residents.

Our approach to rent control differs from that of the February 1991 Ministry of Housing Green Paper on Rent Control. That document would have required operators to "debundle" (i.e., sell separately) accommodation and care services; all care would be sold as optional extras. We recommend that operators be permitted to sell a mandatory package including accommodation, meals, and care services. However, whatever is sold on a mandatory basis must be fully subject to rent control. The prices of optional care services will not be controlled; however, the timing of increases will be restricted, access to alternative providers must be available, and residents must have the opportunity to move out when prices of optional services rise.

With respect to retirement homes, whose residents have relatively high incomes, government's primary interest is to ensure that the market works as it should: operators must provide full pricing information to all potential residents, including a posted "rate sheet" and history of recent price increases. (They must also describe, in writing, any emergency-response system, including details of any commitment to a particular response; any staffing levels above legal requirements; and any internal complaint procedures.)

The Commission recommends that domiciliary hostels—rest homes in which residents are funded through GWA—be phased out as rapidly as possible. Currently, private operators may be paid a per diem (up to $1,015 per month) to provide accommodation, meals, and care services for each of about 4,500 vulnerable adults, most of whom have psychiatric and/or developmental disabilities. Accountability of operators is often limited or non-existent. In our view, operators of hostels should not be funded through a per diem to assess and meet care needs of residents; as quickly as possible, they should come to approximate traditional landlords.

We recommend that hostel residents who so desire should be assisted in leaving the hostels and reassigned to an appropriate category of social assistance. This will usually involve a shift from municipally administered GWA to provincially administered Family Benefits, potentially saving a municipality as much as $203 per resident per month.

The difference between current funding to operators and social assistance should be made available for the development and delivery of community-based care services. Residents should have a primary role in identifying, arranging, and, when possible, delivering these care services. Additional funding of about $1,000 per resident per year should be provided to approximate the cost of comparable community services currently provided to similar populations.

As interim measures, we recommend that all hostel contracts under GWA be limited to one-year renewable terms; and that the province set a maximum total-bed capacity for each domiciliary hostel. We also believe that operators should be prohibited from involvement in the distribution of the personal-needs allowance (PNA) to hostel residents.

The Commission also recommends:

1. that coverage of rest homes under the *Workers' Compensation Act* and *Hospital Labour Disputes Arbitration Act* (*HLDAA*) be consistent with the definition of rest homes as residential settings, not institutions;

2. that the *Planning Act* be amended to make accessory apartments and rooming, boarding, and lodging houses an as-of-right use in all zones where residential uses are permitted;

3. that a pilot project be considered, as resources permit, to implement full community-based services in one or more communities; and that Windsor be considered for inclusion in such a pilot project;

4. that the Residential Services Branch develop a precise legal definition of a nursing home, and that rest homes that offer high levels of care and serve, in effect, as "bootleg" nursing homes without nursing-home licences, cease offering nursing-home levels of care;

5. that the Ministry of Health investigate the quality of medical care delivered to residents in rest homes, and the billing practices of doctors (including "house doctors") who regularly claim for multiple and sequential home visits in rest homes.

In an Appendix to the Report, the Commission also suggests that the announced intention of the government of Ontario to eliminate the funding differential between nursing homes and homes for the aged be deferred pending clear evidence of effective accountability to residents in nursing homes.

Much of this Report focuses on residents' day-to-day problems and quality of life. We argue that the protections promised by comprehensive regulation would not be effective. Instead, a variety of remedies and avenues for redress should be available to residents; we believe that, overall, such measures will be more powerful and more accountable:

1. violations of the residents' bill of rights may be pursued

through the Rest Homes Tribunal, which will have available a wide array of remedies from mild reprimands, through orders to do or cease doing something, to permanent closure of premises and banning of individual operators from the industry;

2. the *LTA* and/or rent control may offer remedies for violations of the terms of the lease (mandatory package), including permanent or temporary abatement of rent and termination of lease; and

3. violations with respect to commercial contracts for optional services may be pursued through the courts.

In summary, this Report has placed before the people and government of Ontario a number of responses to the many problems identified in rest homes. To do nothing is unacceptable: abuses continue to be identified, and the quality of residents' lives in too many cases is frankly appalling. To regulate comprehensively, creating, in effect, a new set of care-giving institutions would be costly, and the outcome very uncertain.

An approach based on empowerment, which we endorse, has the potential to do more, and at less cost. However, the empowerment must be practical and operational, not merely theoretical—and this, ultimately, is the greatest challenge Ontarians face.

Prologue

*We regulate cars, guns, repair shops, and just about
every other kind of business practice; but when it comes
to the people that least can protect and help themselves
we turn the other way.*

Written submission from Hamilton, Ontario

Many vulnerable adults in Ontario live in conditions that we associate with the poor of Victorian England, not with residence in late-twentieth-century Canada. Today, Ontarians with psychiatric histories are living six or more to a room, sleeping in bunk beds or on floors, with few protections from exploitation, abuse, and capricious behaviour by landlords, staff, and sometimes complete strangers. Frail seniors lie bedridden and ignored, ofttimes in dirty, foul-smelling wards, sometimes in luxurious private suites. The Commission met one woman with developmental disabilities who was paying $675 monthly room and board. Her social-assistance cheque totalled $638; the balance came from handing over her sheltered-workshop earnings and by doing chores around the residence.

These vulnerable adults are not being accommodated; they are being warehoused, conveniently out of sight and mind of the people of Ontario.

Some thirty-five years ago, we as a society began to close our large psychiatric hospitals and return patients to the community. In doing so, we did everything wrong that could possibly be done wrong: we discharged people from institutions, gave them inadequate incomes, and essentially abandoned them.

Nor did we create supportive housing, group homes, or independent-living options sufficient for people with developmental disabilities. As children, they are relatively protected; as soon as they reach the age of majority, far too many are given a welfare cheque and little social support.

We talk much of the aging of Canada's population, yet we have done little to meet the needs of our growing numbers of seniors. Public policy still takes for granted nuclear families and the unpaid labour of women as primary care-givers. Even elderly persons with adequate resources who choose to enter retirement homes may be victimized by unscrupulous operators and the abuses that respect neither income nor economic class. Many frail elderly persons without private means can expect only inadequate care in whatever accommodation they can find.

Each of these three population groups—persons with psychiatric histories, adults with developmental disabilities, and frail elderly persons—experiences different problems and is subject to different pressures. However, far too often, all have been neglected or substantially abandoned by our society. They may be provided with an income inadequate to their basic needs; otherwise they are, for the most part, left on their own.

This societal neglect is most clearly visible in the area of housing. Everyone must have somewhere to live, and accommodation often represents a person's largest single expense. Moreover, as vulnerability grows, people become increasingly dependent on their housing, which should be—but often is not—a stable refuge in an ever more turbulent and threatening environment.

We did not set out to create a system of rental housing in which the most vulnerable members of society are the least protected; but that has certainly been the outcome, for often they live in accommodation that is uninspected and outside the protection of rent control, the *Landlord and Tenant Act* (*LTA*), and other regulatory legislation. Through our indifference and neglect, those with the greatest needs often receive the least from our programs and services.

Within a psychiatric hospital, patients are formally protected by extensive rules and regulations; when they pass through the gates into the community, our collective responsibility largely ends and individuals are at the mercy of a cruelly indifferent society. Our obligations to persons with developmental disabilities often seem to end at the age of majority; these adults, too, can be left to find whatever housing they can.

The number of beds in licensed and regulated premises for elderly persons, such as homes for the aged or nursing homes and community-based supports for independent living, have not increased as the population ages; many elderly persons are left to languish, virtually ignored, in unregulated accommodation.

This Commission of Inquiry arose as a result of a death at Cedar Glen, an unregulated boarding home near Orillia, and the subsequent coroner's inquest, the longest in Canadian history. It might have been initiated equally well in response to any number of deaths, abuses, and cases of neglect in similar residential settings across the province. Throughout the Commission's work, one question has been our touchstone: "Would this [approach/recommendation] have prevented Cedar Glen?" The answers determine the efficacy of our work.

We do not know how many deaths each year in Ontario are attributable to improper treatment or neglect of residents in rest and boarding homes. We do not know how many instances of abuse—physical, emotional, and sexual—occur daily. We cannot determine what proportion of these vulnerable populations receive adequate or excellent accommodation, and how much is barely acceptable or utterly intolerable. Indeed, we have only a rough idea of how many unregulated premises operate in this province, as there is no obligation for them to make themselves known to any governmental body. We have even less knowledge of how many people live in such settings.

We are dealing with a profound public-policy void.

The purpose of this Inquiry has not been to determine guilt, or identify villains. Rather, the focus has been on the residents of rest homes, on the quality of their daily lives, and on how the government of Ontario can help create an environment in which the best quality of life is possible. Sadly, a Commission of Inquiry would have been warranted solely to investigate the quality of life experienced on a daily basis by many vulnerable residents in unregulated housing, quite apart from any concerns about death and abuse.

This Commission has heard from operators and visited rest homes in which the services provided are exemplary and the needs of residents uppermost. We have seen retirement homes where the residents are content and well cared for, in environments that are clean and cheerful, with creative programming and staff who are well trained and conscientious. We have heard from people for whom it was a spiritual obligation to care for vulnerable adults, regardless of the personal or financial sacrifice.

We wish at the outset of this Report to commend such homes and individuals, and to express our respect for and admiration of their ability to perform a very difficult job under circumstances that are trying at best. These individuals, often motivated by a personal ethical commitment, are doing society's work and dealing with significant social issues that too many of us simply refuse to face.

PART I

Where You Live Can Make You Vulnerable

1
An Introduction

n May 1985, Joseph Kendall was discharged from the Queen Street Mental Health Centre in Toronto to Cedar Glen Boarding Home, Orillia, a privately run home for ex-psychiatric patients and people with developmental disabilities. In November 1987, Mr. Kendall died in hospital after being assaulted by another resident at Cedar Glen. A police investigation into allegations of abuse at Cedar Glen led to a coroner's inquest into Mr. Kendall's death; the inquest ran from August 8 until November 27, 1990.

The jury's report contained more than eighty recommendations; key among these was that "the Premier of Ontario should immediately appoint a Public Provincial Commission to inquire into unregulated residential facilities in the province and conduct a census of the vulnerable adults housed in these facilities." Two days after the report was filed, the establishment of this Commission was announced in the Ontario Legislature by the Hon. Elaine Ziemba, Minister of Citizenship with Responsibility for Human Rights, Disability Issues, Seniors' Issues, and Race Relations.

The terms of reference for this Commission of Inquiry were, in part, "to examine, study, inquire into and to report upon the level of care and living conditions of physically, developmentally, socially or psychiatrically disabled adult persons, as well as frail or cognitively impaired elderly persons

1 Order in Council under the *Public Inquiries Act* issued by the lieutenant-governor on December 20, 1990.

2 *Doing the Right Thing Right: An Analysis of the Community Mental Health Services Legislation Consultation Undertaken by the Ontario Ministry of Health*, by David Reville, MPP (1990).

3 *You've Got a Friend, the Report of the Review of Advocacy for Vulnerable Adults* (1987) used the term "vulnerable" to describe specific groups of adults: frail elderly; physically disabled; psychiatrically disabled; and developmentally handicapped. The report (p.55) defined vulnerable adults as "people with some type of physical, emotional or cognitive impairment."

who reside in unregulated residential accommodation in Ontario."[1]

This Commission began its work on January 1, 1991, with a request for submissions; more than 230 written presentations were received, from handwritten notes to formal documents.

A Discussion Paper, released in March 1991 and widely distributed, established the framework and identified key questions for public consultations in April and May 1991 in seven communities around the province. We also met privately with numerous stakeholders, interest groups, and concerned individuals between January and May 1991.

Of particular importance to the Commission were sessions organized by consumer/survivors in three communities: we are indebted to the powerful report *Doing the Right Thing Right*[2] by David Reville, which emphasized for us the necessity to conduct consultations involving vulnerable populations on terms set by and familiar to the respondents, rather than on grounds convenient to the Commission.

Basic Definitions

THE MEANING OF "VULNERABLE"

The term "vulnerable" was used in the O'Sullivan Report[3] to describe the population groups of interest to this Commission. More recently, the proposed *Advocacy Act, 1991* (Bill 74, section 2) defines "vulnerable persons" in the following way:

"vulnerable person" means a person who, because of a mental or physical disability, illness or infirmity, whether temporary or permanent, has difficulty in expressing or acting on his or her wishes or in ascertaining or exercising his or her rights.

Many presentations before the Commission questioned the applicability of the term "vulnerable" to specific groups or particular individuals. Some argued that when we label people "vulnerable," we create a self-fulfilling prophecy rather than a starting point for assistance. At least one agency for persons with physical disabilities expressed concern that classifying its population as "vulnerable" would conflict with the philosophy of independent living that it promotes.

Some operators and residents of luxury retirement homes have taken exception to their inclusion in this Inquiry; they have indicated that the term "vulnerable" does not accurately reflect the status or the needs of the "well elderly." Neither do they accept that the concept of "vulnerability" can or should apply to persons who choose to spend their own money on a particular type of accommodation. They argue that the state has no right to interfere in these private financial transactions by competent adults, although they acknowledge that private financial transactions in many other commercial areas are extensively regulated.

Other people have noted, as did the O'Sullivan Report (p.57), that institutions by their very nature create vulnerability and dependence. Some presenters argued that all rest homes should be considered institutions, as should any setting in which a person's right to autonomous decision-making is eroded or removed in favour of rules and conditions set by and serving the interests of the owners/operators/staff.

We wish to distinguish between two types of vulnerability that, incidentally, correspond to two types of advocacy set out in Bill 74, the *Advocacy Act, 1991*: individual vulnerability, and collective vulnerability.

This distinction is important, for each type of vulnerability calls for a different societal response. In the first case, we must focus on reinforcing individual capability so that individ-

4 To illustrate, the *Landlord and Tenant Act* (*LTA*) was intended to redress the inherent power imbalances between landlords and tenants, particularly in a tight housing market: tenants are seen as collectively vulnerable, regardless of any individual vulnerability due to membership in a particular group.

uals disadvantaged by personal characteristics have access to means of enhancing their functioning, a process described as "empowerment."

Collective vulnerability, however, reflects systemic power imbalances within society; redress cannot be on the individual level. Rather, it is necessary to focus on the social structures that created the vulnerability or dependence.[4]

In broad terms, the Commission views many of the problems experienced by residents of rest homes to be the result of both individual vulnerability and systemic power imbalances.

THE MEANING OF "ACCOMMODATION"

The types of housing examined by this Inquiry vary widely, but are generally associated with the provision of three services: accommodation; some or all meals; and limited care, such as supervision or help with bathing or assistance with medications. The housing includes rest homes (also known as "boarding" or "lodging" homes), for which rates are often determined by social-assistance levels, as well as luxury retirement homes, for which charges are determined by open-market forces. Virtually all are operated on a for-profit or commercial basis; tenancy is usually privately negotiated between the operators and potential residents (or, in the case of those with low incomes, the municipality acting on behalf of the residents). The premises may be ordinary former single-family homes or huge complexes. (The largest, in Windsor, has approximately 450 beds.) At the lower end of the market, most residents are men, typically with psychiatric histories or developmental disabilities; in the retirement homes, the vast majority of residents are women.

Residents may have their own rooms or apartments, or they may sleep several to a room, and at least some meals will be taken communally; but it is the delivery of care services by the operators that distinguishes rest homes from traditional apartments or room-and-board settings.[5]

In the wide range of rest-home settings, variable amounts of care are delivered, according to individuals' needs and ability to pay. In some luxury retirement homes catering to the "well elderly," care services may be limited to a registered nurse or registered nurse's aide on the premises and/or a twenty-four-hour, emergency call bell in each unit. Other premises function as de facto or "bootleg" nursing homes, in which high levels of care are given to residents. For those with low incomes, the extent and quality of care expected by residents and delivered by operators are often problematic.

Nomenclature can be confusing: accommodation with care services is typically referred to as a "second-level lodging home" in the Hamilton area, a "rest home" in Windsor, and a "boarding home" in the Toronto area, though this latter term sometimes describes room-and-board situations only. Accommodation for seniors with high incomes is widely referred to as a "retirement home."

In this Report, "rest home" will be used generically to include boarding homes, lodging homes, rest homes, and retirement homes as set out above. When the reference is solely to the lower end of the market, "boarding home" may be used; upper-income accommodation with care for elderly persons will typically be referred to as a "retirement home." The intended use will, however, always be clear from the context. Unless indicated otherwise, all terms refer to settings in which care is delivered.[6]

THE MEANING OF "REST HOME"

"Rest homes" as we define them are nowhere defined in law; the meaning of the term is ambiguous. It is easiest to set out what they are *not*: they are not nursing homes—although the public often confuses the two—for nursing homes are subject

5 "Retirement communities" and "seniors-only" apartment buildings, condominiums, etc., that offer housing only, whether based on equity or rental, are excluded from this Inquiry, as there is no care-services component.

6 "Room and board" in this Report indicates the absence of care services.

7 "Residential premises" as used here is defined in the *LTA*, clauses 1 (c), (i) and (ii). The specification of three or more residents is arbitrary, but the *Municipal Act* (section 236) uses a three-person minimum in its definition of a group home.

For the purposes of this Report we do not distinguish between owners and operators, although these may be different persons. The owners of the premises in which a "rest home" is situated may rent the premises to the operators. The operators provide accommodation and services on the premises and are entitled to the income from the rest home. Some of the Commission's recommendations may be relevant to only one or the other when owners and operators are not the same persons.

8 No disclaimer in the contract or elsewhere is relevant in determining whether the conditions are satisfied. Though some or all meals are normally provided in a rest home, they are not seen as essential to the definition.

9 The definition is intended to include premises where care is promised or provided, regardless of whether there is an agreement that the care is being paid for.

10 Assistance, care or treatment provided by any person subject to the proposed *Regulated Health Professions Act, 1991*, Bill 43, should fall within the definition of "care."

to provincial licensing, standards, and per diem funding. Rest homes are not so subject. They are also not "room-and-board" settings, in which individuals purchase accommodation and meals only; nor are they rooming houses, which offer accommodation only.

We are therefore left to develop a definition:

RECOMMENDATION 1: That a "rest home" be defined as any residential premises in which three or more persons unrelated to the owner/operator reside,[7] and in which one or more of the following conditions is satisfied:[8]

1. the operator is paid for caring for residents, whether or not this care is actually received;

2. the operator makes public or gives others, such as hospital discharge planners, to understand that care to residents is provided by the operator; and/or

3. care is regularly provided by the operator to residents.[9]

For the purposes of this definition, "care" includes the following:

1. any assistance with the activities of daily living (including, for example, bathing and washing, grooming, dressing, personal hygiene, toileting, rising and retiring, dining);

2. the provision of any health care (for example, care provided by nurses or therapists);[10] and

3. staff on the premises to assist with medications, supervise the activities of residents, and/or respond to personal emergencies (for example, a call bell or intercom that will call staff, who will summon help from within or outside the residence).

This list is not comprehensive, although it is intended to exclude residences in which household cleaning and meals are the only services provided. As well, some accommodation that would otherwise fall within the above definition must be specifically exempted, for example, short-term accommodation provided as emergency shelter.[11]

THE MEANING OF "COMMERCIAL" AND "NON-PROFIT"

Virtually all the accommodation described above is operated by private entrepreneurs on a commercial or for-profit basis. Thus, at the outset, we assumed that group homes and other accommodation run by non-profit agencies would be excluded from our mandate. However, this proved unacceptable to many who argued that the only relevant criterion for inclusion in the Commission's mandate was whether premises were regulated, that commercial or non-profit status was irrelevant. There are many government-supported group homes[12] across the province that are not subject to regulation in law or practice. Other group homes are completely "free-standing," operated without government regulation or financial support.

A large number of submissions argued that vulnerable adults in non-profit unregulated accommodation are as much in need of protection as are residents of commercial rest homes: non-profit status does not guarantee protection of the rights and interests of vulnerable adults. The debate was most heated when dealing with the issue of bringing group homes under the *LTA* and its provision of security of tenure for residents.

The Commission became convinced that non-profit unregulated accommodation should, indeed, be included in our mandate. Granted, the particular problems we were asked to consider involved primarily the commercial sector; however, our formal terms of reference did not exclude the non-profit sector, and we are satisfied that many of the concerns raised—particularly regarding the protection of residents—were relevant to all rest homes, irrespective of their

11 This issue is examined in more detail in the context of the *Landlord and Tenant Act*, in chapter 5.

12 The term "group home" is not defined in legislation. Group homes funded by government operate under a variety of statutes. Some are funded under the *Ministry of Community and Social Services Act* or the *Ministry of Health Act*. Neither statute identifies standards, conditions, or terms that may be attached to the receipt of government money, nor is either regulatory in scope.

13 An alternative way to define "regulated" accommodation would be to identify statutes that refer to specific types of accommodation—such as the *Nursing Homes Act* or the *Public Hospitals Act*—and to assume that coverage under these statutes, by definition, constitutes regulation. For reasons made clear in the next part of this Report, the Commission does not accept this approach.

commercial or non-profit status.

Our definition of a rest home, then, is intended to include for-profit and non-profit accommodation. As well, unless otherwise exempted by criteria the Commission will present later, group homes are rest homes. (See discussion in chapter 5.)

THE MEANING OF "UNREGULATED"

"Regulated" accommodation is typically considered to be that in which the provincial government licenses operators, sets standards, and inspects for compliance with the standards; "unregulated" accommodation usually comprises everything else.[13]

No residential accommodation in Ontario is completely unregulated, for the *Fire Marshals Act* and the *Public Health Act* are universally applicable. Legislation such as the *Homes for Special Care Act* sets out (in the regulations) standards for the physical plant in this accommodation, on matters such as fire safety. However, neither the Act nor its regulations prescribe standards of care for residents. Thus, certain aspects of Homes for Special Care are regulated, while others are unregulated. Such homes could fall, in part, within the scope of this Inquiry.

A clear distinction between "regulated" and "unregulated" accommodation has proven difficult to make, as a particular type of accommodation can be regulated with respect to only specific considerations.

Many submissions were made to the Commission requesting inclusion of various types of accommodation for vulnerable persons within our mandate on the grounds that the forms of regulation were in place, but enforcement was sporadic and inadequate. For all practical purposes, the presenters argued, the housing was "unregulated." A number of presentations suggested that even nursing homes—perhaps the most comprehensively regulated accommodation in Ontario—

should be included because inspections and protection of vulnerable adults were considered inadequate:[14] for example, if residents of rest homes are to be provided with security of tenure, under *LTA* or in other ways, residents of nursing homes should be equally protected.[15]

Using effective regulation as the criterion to exclude accommodation from this inquiry is fraught, as many additional types of settings might then fall within our net. In 1987, for example, the provincial auditor examined Homes for Special Care and found consistent provincial standards across Ontario were wanting. Although the Ministry of Health (MoH) is now developing such standards, one might well argue—as some have done—that regulation in these settings is deficient and therefore they should be part of this Inquiry.

Similarly, in 1990, the provincial auditor examined the *Developmental Services Act*, looking at three of the eleven large provincial institutions (Schedule 1 facilities) and three smaller group homes (Schedule 2 facilities) for persons with developmental disabilities.[16] In each case, the auditor found that Ministry of Community and Social Services (MCSS) monitoring did not ensure that funds were well spent, or that persons with developmental disabilities were receiving adequate care and services. Once again, one might well argue that existing regulation is ineffectual.

Thus, like a snowball rolling down a hill, the types of accommodation included within our mandate could grow until we would examine virtually all housing in which vulnerable people reside. Such an approach would, however, be impractical.

The Commission has previously presented its definition of a rest home. Unless exempted, any accommodation that fits within the definition is subject to the recommendations of this Report. In the next part of this Report, the Commission sets out criteria for making exemptions from our definition of a rest home. Our discussion of what should be exempted indicates the line the Commission draws between "regulated" and

14 The Ministry of Health's monitoring of quality of care in nursing homes "required significant improvement," according to the *1990 Annual Report* of the provincial auditor, p. 139.

15 Notwithstanding nursing home operators' obligation to locate alternative premises before discharging residents.

16 Office of the Provincial Auditor, *1990 Annual Report.* Queen's Printer for Ontario.

17 A person with identical needs would, in many cities in the southern part of the province, be housed in a rest home, where the operators might be directly compensated by the municipality for providing identical care. The for-profit rest home as understood in Southern Ontario is virtually non-existent in Northern Ontario.

"unregulated" accommodation where care is provided.

The Commission acknowledges that many types of "regulated" accommodation are, in practice, regulated only minimally or not at all. Many of the Commission's recommendations might well apply to such accommodation. In considering implementation of the Commission's recommendations, the government of Ontario should examine the desirability of their wider application to other types of housing for vulnerable adults in which regulation is inadequately effective.

Informal Care Services

We have included within our definition of a rest home the condition that care is regularly provided by the operators. It is not the Commission's intention to consider premises in which care services are offered to residents only on an informal or occasional basis.

In Northern Ontario cities, accommodation-only premises ("rooming houses") are the norm for persons discharged from psychiatric hospitals; care services may be offered, on an informal and unpaid basis, by the operators or other residents.[17] When operators provide such assistance on a regular basis—whether compensated or not—the home is a de facto rest home, regardless of any stated mandate. As such, it must be fully subject to the Commission's recommendations.

Should higher standards be imposed on care-giving premises only, operators might withdraw from the provision of care in order to be exempt from the standards and associated costs, particularly if the care is offered on an unpaid basis. This would result in a loss of accommodation offering low levels of care, or loss of care in the settings that remain. The Commission deems this outcome regrettable; however, accommodation offering care must be treated as a rest home, and the same protections should be offered to vulnerable residents in all cases where operators regularly provide care.

2
Who Are Vulnerable Adults?

One of the Commission's first tasks, as set out in its terms of reference, was to "conduct a census [survey] of vulnerable adults [in unregulated accommodation] in Ontario." In developing over-all estimates of this population and data on par-ticular groups and their housing, we have used the 1986 census, and the Health and Activity Limitation Survey (HALS), conducted in conjunction with the 1986 census. The data are projected forward to a 1991 base.

The advantages of using the census are those of economy, speed, and efficiency. It was not feasible to develop a primary survey in the time available to this Inquiry; moreover, we doubt that the quality of such data would have equalled that of the census.

The obvious difficulty of using secondary data, however, is that one cannot design the questions; therefore, we developed operational definitions of "vulnerable adult" and "unregulated accommodation" using the available census categories. Neither definition corresponds precisely to those used elsewhere in this Report, but they are reasonable approximations; taken together, the definitions should yield an estimate of "vulnerable adults" in "unregulated accommodation" in Ontario. (The Commission contracted with the G. Allan Roeher Institute [Canadian Association for Community Living] at York University to estimate the

1 *Vulnerable Adults in the Province of Ontario: A Report Submitted to the Commission of Inquiry into Unregulated Residential Accommodation by the G. Allan Roeher Institute*, prepared by Cameron Crawford, assistant director, June 1991. Copies of the full report are available from the Roeher Institute. All numbers reported in this section are drawn from that report.

A survey was also conducted for this Commission in the spring of 1991 by Louise Doyon of the Office for Seniors' Issues, with the assistance of the Ontario Municipal Social Service Association (OMSSA). Information was sought on the quantity of unregulated accommodation existing in the municipalities. Though the overall response rate was high (over 80 percent), the Commission was able to determine, through comparison with other existing data, that the reported results were generally not valid. They are, therefore, not presented here.

2 The "long" form of the census questionnaire administered to individuals posed the following question: "Are you limited in the amount of activity that you can do because of a long-term physical condition, mental condition, or health problem?" Answers to a number of specific question items on the HALS survey were aggregated to form three categories: "mild," "moderate," and "severe" disability.

3 The definition has been broadened slightly to include all persons residing in unregulated special-care homes (described later in this sec-

number of vulnerable adults in Ontario who live in unregulated settings.)[1]

CENSUS ESTIMATES OF VULNERABLE ADULTS

The most commonly used estimate of vulnerable adults is derived from the HALS Survey.[2] The survey found that 1,164,000 adults in Ontario (16 percent of the adult population) had some type of physical or mental disability. Of these, 359,000 reported a "moderate" disability; 279,000 were reported as "severely" disabled. These two groups comprise more than 600,000 persons.

For the purposes of this Inquiry, this estimate of 600,000 must be reduced to those who live in unregulated accommodation. In addition, the automatic exclusion of those with mild disabilities and the automatic inclusion of all persons with moderate or severe disabilities appears to be somewhat arbitrary. We are unwilling on a priori grounds to exclude all persons having mild disabilities. As well, some persons are categorized as having severe disabilities because of a high score on a single survey question; yet they are able to get on with their lives reasonably well, perhaps because they have sufficient income.

The Roeher Institute study has provided us with an alternative definition that we feel is more precise and more useful for our purposes. Based on the Roeher definition, three conditions (derived from the census responses) must be satisfied for people to be considered vulnerable:

1. they must be poor[3] (with incomes below $15,000[4] in 1986);
2. they must have disabilities and not be living with family members; and
3. they are characterized by one or more of the following traits:

(a) because of their disability, they require help from others in one or more area of daily living, but are receiving less help than they need;

(b) in the event that they are refused housing or employment because of their disability, they do not know where to go to find information about their rights; and

(c) they have learning or psychiatric disabilities, developmental disabilities and/or physical conditions that have resulted in emotional or nervous problems.

Based on this definition, our estimate is that in 1991[5] there were in Ontario some 196,000 non-institutionalized vulnerable adults living alone or with non-relatives. Of these, about 150,000 live alone, two-thirds of them in rented premises. About 120,000 vulnerable adults are sixty-five years of age or older.

CENSUS ESTIMATES OF UNREGULATED ACCOMMODATION

The number of vulnerable persons living in unregulated accommodation was calculated by totalling the number of those living in the following types of housing, as categorized by the census:

1. "Unattached with non-relatives"
This includes persons living with others to whom they are not related, often as lodgers, room-mates, or employees. They may also be unrelated adults in shared living arrangements, though usually not a group home. The dwellings are privately owned, but none of the residents need be the owner.

About 24,500 vulnerable adults reside with non-relatives in shared living arrangements.[6]

tion), who are presumed to be vulnerable adults. This would include some persons in upper-income retirement homes.

The Commission is aware that vulnerability is not solely or necessarily an income-based concept. Seniors, in particular, become increasingly vulnerable with age, irrespective of income level. Therefore, elsewhere in this Report a person need not have a low income to be classed as vulnerable.

4 The cutoff figure is arbitrary and above the Statistics Canada low-income cutoffs; but it is based in part on the substantial out-of-pocket expenses typically incurred by persons with disabilities.

5 The 1986 census figures are projected forward to produce 1991 estimates. In these forward projections, allowance was made for shifts in family types (e.g., living with non-relatives, etc.). It was assumed that the proportion of persons with disabilities to persons without disabilities has remained constant within the fifteen-to-sixty-four and sixty-five-plus age categories respectively: given the general aging of the population, this assumption probably results in an underestimate of the number of vulnerable older people in Ontario in 1991.

6 Slightly more than 13,000 of these individuals are the only person with disabilities in the setting; the remaining 11,000 reside with one or more other persons with disabilities. Presumably, many vulnerable adults living with

non-relatives are in small, informal boarding arrangements. Most vulnerable adults living with non-relatives live with one to four other persons. These estimates include both premises where care is and is not given.

7 Those over sixty-five years tend to live in premises where there are ten or more other persons, while about half of those under sixty-five live in premises with five to ten other persons.

8 The census category of "special-care homes" is generic and less well defined than Homes for Special Care, a particular type of Ontario Ministry of Health–licensed and–regulated accommodation. Persons resident in Ministry of Health Homes for Special Care would not be included in the category of "unregulated special-care homes," because their accommodation is considered for census purposes to be regulated.

9 Derived from *Health Reports, Supplement, Residential Care Facilities, 1986-87*, Volume 1, Number 1, 1989, Table 1. Statistics Canada simply reports data provided by the provinces and territories. It provides general criteria (licensed, approved, regulated, or funded, and providing care); the provinces and territories then determine those premises to be included in the data. The category "providing care" may include some units that should be excluded for our purposes (e.g., independent apartments visited occasionally by a social worker).

2. "Service collective dwellings"

This category comprises four census categories of non-institutional accommodation: hotels, motels, and tourist homes; lodging and rooming houses; work camps; "other" collective dwellings (primarily YM/YWCAs, missions, and camp grounds).

More than 7,600 vulnerable adults live in these settings, the vast majority in lodging/rooming houses, and YM/YWCAs and missions.[7]

3. "Non-regulated special-care homes"

The numbers in this category have been calculated as follows: from the total number of persons residing in the census category of "special-care homes[8] and institutions for the elderly and chronically ill" we subtracted the number of residents in approved, funded, regulated, or licensed special-care[9] premises. The difference—more than 15,300—represents the number of residents in unregulated special-care homes.[10]

In total, some 47,500 vulnerable adults live neither alone nor with family members, in unregulated accommodation in Ontario. Of these, some 32,300 are between the ages of fifteen and sixty-four; 15,200 are sixty-five years of age or older.

This estimate of 47,500 persons represents our single best estimate of the number of vulnerable adults living in unregulated residential accommodation in Ontario in 1991.

Table 1 presents detailed information on vulnerable adults in Ontario for 1991. The table also includes two other empirical indicators of vulnerability:

1. "poor with a disability": all persons with disabilities whose incomes (in 1986) were below $15,000;
2. "at risk": all persons "poor with a disability" as well as

Table 1
Adults Living with Non-Relatives in Various Arrangements — Ontario 1991

	Total	Living Alone	Living Not Alone (Unregulated Accommodation)			
			Unattached with Non-Relatives	Service Collective Dwellings	Non-Regulated Special-Care Homes	Total Not Alone
Vulnerable Adults						
15-64	77,800	45,496	20,283	5,600	6,421	32,304
65 +	118,898	103,688	4,185	2,062	8,963	15,210
Total	196,698	149,184	24,468	7,662	15,384	47,514
Poor and Disabled						
15-64	77,198	49,626	21,827	5,745	—	27,572
65 +	139,039	129,466	7,431	2,142	—	9,573
Total	216,237	179,092	29,258	7,887		37,145
"At Risk"						
15-64	180,653	137,916	28,248	8,068	6,421	42,737
65 +	214,707	194,555	9,005	2,184	8,963	20,152
Total	395,360	332,471	37,252	10,251	15,385	62,889

10 Slightly more than half of these are sixty-five years of age or older. Persons living in unregulated special-care homes (which may include some upper-income retirement homes) are automatically presumed, in the Roeher Institute report, to be vulnerable adults.

11 The Roeher Institute study also generated the following demographic data on vulnerable adults in Ontario: of the 103,000 vulnerable persons aged sixty-five and older who live alone, 86 percent (more than 89,000) are women. In urban centres outside Toronto, the rate of vulnerable adults living alone is more than twice that of the general population. In rural areas, it is nearly 2.6 times that of the general population. The rate of vulnerable adults in urban centres living in service-collective dwellings such as hotels, rooming and lodging houses, shelters, YM/YWCAs, etc. is more than three times that of the general population.

12 There is a range of government-funded institutions and alternative group- and independent-living arrangements in the community for each of the population groups of interest to this Inquiry. At least two ministries—MCSS and MoH—which have traditionally held bureaucratic responsibility for these groups—have exercised variable conceptions of and commitments to non-institutional forms of living and care for vulnerable adults.

those who were poor, did not have disabilities, and lived with one or more persons with disabilities.

Depending on the definition used, the numbers of vulnerable adults living in unregulated accommodation with others is between 37,000 and 63,000.[11]

Rest-Home Residents

Having determined the number of those living in rest homes, we turned our attention to the residents themselves and the needs that the rest homes are intended to meet.

Rest homes evolved in Ontario as a private-sector response to social needs for accommodation and care that were otherwise not being met. They are the product of limited and decreasing institutional accommodation and our society's ambivalent commitment to community-based alternatives.

The rest home is a "spillover," a symptom of the failure of government to provide adequately in the community for those not in institutions or being cared for at home by their families.[12]

Government policy towards those with psychiatric histories and developmental disabilities has been dominated by the closing of institutions, yet our practice towards elderly persons has focused excessively on institutionalization. In each case, the result has been fundamentally unacceptable. In closing provincial institutions, we usually failed to follow through: closing beds became an end in itself. In institutionalizing our seniors, we have revealed the principle itself to be wrong-headed.

What this Commission—and the community—is being called upon to do is to begin again. But this time we must do it right.

Let us briefly look at each vulnerable group in turn.

SENIORS

Ontario has one of the highest rates of institutionalization of seniors in the developed world. We place too many elderly people in institutional settings that can be impersonal, dehumanizing, costly and, at times, dangerous, even though the evidence suggests that many would live better and longer if they were given adequate supports to remain in the community.

In 1975, Ontarians sixty-five years and older comprised just less than 9 percent of the province's population; in 1990, their numbers had risen to 11.7 percent, and by the year 2011, seniors will comprise more than 15 percent of the population. Between 1975 and 2011, the seniors population will grow more than three times as fast as the total population (147 percent compared to 46 percent for the total population). Between 1990 and 2011, the growth rates will be 59 percent for seniors, 22 percent for the total population.

As the average lifespan continues to increase, the number of older seniors grows. Persons eighty-five years of age and older comprised just more than 8 percent of the elderly population between 1975 and 1990. However, by the year 2000, those eighty-five and older will comprise nearly 11 percent of the seniors population; by 2011, they will account for nearly 14 percent.[13] Put another way, in less than twenty years, persons eighty-five years and over will increase from about one in twelve of all seniors to almost one in seven. Those eighty-five and over, slightly more than 1 percent of the total population in 1990, will become 2.1 percent by the year 2011.[14]

Our fiscal capacity to care for this aging population in institutions will be severely strained: between 1980 and 1989, the number of nursing-home residents in Ontario increased by 18 percent; the number of extended-care residents in homes for the aged grew by 22 percent;[15] and the total number of residents in these settings grew by 19 percent, from 35,244 to 42,049.

Table 2 indicates there are currently about 70,000 institu-

13 This represents growth of 110 percent in the number of persons sixty-five to seventy-four between 1975 and 2011, 176 percent for those seventy-five to eighty-four and 316 percent for persons eighty-five and older.

14 Two-thirds (68 percent) of the older elderly in 1975 were women. Three-quarters (75 percent) of the older elderly by 2011 will be women.

15 In addition to extended-care beds in homes for the aged, there are also residential-care beds, which are not included here.

Table 2
Health and Social-Service Institutions for Long-Term Care in Ontario

	Number	Beds	Funding
Homes for the Aged[1]			
Municipal	94	18,720	$325.6m[3]
Charitable	88	9,496	$ 77.1m[3]
Total	182	27,966[2]	$402.7m
Satellite Beds[4]	38	858	
Nursing Homes[6]	336[3]	30,489[3]	$395.1m[5]
Homes for Special Care[7]			
Residential	199	1,678	
Nursing	174	2,004	$ 77.3m[3]
Total	373	3,682	
Chronic-Care Hospitals[8]	221	11,436[9]	$743.5m[5]

Notes
1. Homes for the Aged are operated either by municipalities or charitable organizations on a non-profit basis; the Ministry of Community and Social Services is the ministry responsible for ensuring standards.
2. As of April 1991. Includes both residential and extended-care beds.
3. 1990/91.
4. These are beds in community residences or facilities contracted for by municipal Homes for the Aged. They are subject to regulation under the *Homes for the Aged and Rest Homes Act*. Size range is from four to 120 beds. These beds may be in nursing homes or in unregulated rest homes.
5. 1988/89.
6. Most nursing homes are operated on a for-profit basis and are licensed and regulated by the Ministry of Health. Some nursing homes also provide "satellite-home" beds under contract with municipal Homes for the Aged. There are no official figures, but it is estimated that seventy-one nursing homes have a total of approximately 3,000 unregulated rest-home beds. See chapter 3.
7. Provides nursing and supervised accommodation for both discharged patients from provincial psychiatric hospitals and residents with developmental disabilities from regional centres for persons with developmental disabilities.
   Provided in residential homes and in nursing homes. There are 199 residential homes with 1,678 beds and 174 nursing homes have 1,951 extended-care beds and fifty-three intermediate beds. These 2,002 beds are also reflected in the nursing-home totals above.
8. Chronic-care hospitals are part of the hospital system regulated by the Ministry of Health. Twenty-two of these hospitals provide only chronic care; the others are general hospitals.
9. As of September 1990.

tional beds for seniors in Ontario (including residential, extended, and chronic care, but excluding private rest homes). This yields an institutionalization rate of 5.9 percent (fifty-nine beds per thousand population) among persons aged sixty-five years and older.

PERSONS WITH PSYCHIATRIC HISTORIES

Our practices towards persons with psychiatric histories have come in for well-deserved criticism:

> if by deinstitutionalization we mean a clearcut policy directed toward reducing the population of provincial psychiatric hospitals and establishing community services to receive discharged patients, then no such policy ever existed in Ontario. However if by deinstitutionalization we mean a deliberate policy of reducing the long-stay population of the large mental hospitals regardless of what happened to the patients afterward, then deinstitutionalization began in 1960.[16]

Deinstitutionalization in favour of community-based care for persons with psychiatric histories has always been marked by a fundamental ambivalence of purpose: the lure of saving money by shutting large and inhumane institutions has been omnipresent in government decision-making; the commitment to develop true community care has been far weaker. (See Table 3.)

Between 1961 and 1970, the number of patients in provincial hospitals decreased by 52 percent, from 18,292 to 8,838. This process was largely a matter of "skimming off" the easy cases. Many of the people discharged should not have been in institutions in the first place and were able to cope on the outside relatively well. These early discharges were strictly for financial reasons; the idea that people would live better in the

16 Harvey G. Simmons, *Unbalanced: Mental Health Policy in Ontario, 1930-1989.* (Toronto: Wall and Thompson, 1990), p.160.

17 Neuroleptic drugs are major tranquillizers, also commonly referred to as anti-psychotics.

18 *Building Community Support for People: A Plan for Mental Health in Ontario* (The Provincial Mental Health Committee, Robert Graham, chairman, July 28, 1988).

19 This Commission is indebted to the work of the Graham Committee. It is from them that we have drawn the phrase "consumer/survivor" to describe those who have used psychiatric services, and it is from Graham's extensive consultations around Ontario that we learned much about conducting hearings with disempowered groups. The consumer-centred approach of Graham's work is the central principle on which this Report is founded.

20 A patient is "discharged" from a psychiatric hospital and "terminated" from a community hospital.

21 Schedule 1 psychiatric facilities are subject to the *Mental Health Act* and must offer a program that includes inpatient, outpatient, and a variety of other services. The observation, care, and treatment of patients must be under the direction of a psychiatrist. Schedule 2 psychiatric facilities are required to offer only an inpatient program. Patients cannot be detained involuntarily and are not necessarily under the direction of a psychiatrist.

"normalizing" environment of the larger community came later, in the 1970s, when the use of neuroleptic drugs became widespread.[17] Thus, by the time clinical and therapeutic arguments in favour of deinstitutionalization became the accepted thinking, the population of provincial hospitals had already been reduced by more than half.

Since 1970, the number of institutionalized patients has been reduced by more than half again, from 8,838 in 1970 to 3,957 in 1988, a decrease of 55 percent. These more recent closings of beds have affected a population less able to manage without extensive community supports. Although the provincial budget for community mental-health programs has continually increased, the resources (Table 4) needed to develop adequate and appropriate community-based programs and supports have never been committed by government.

There have been many studies through the years, all of which confirm the lack of coherent and systematic planning for discharged psychiatric patients. Most recently, the Graham Report[18] recommended the development of integrated mental-health services in the community, and advocated the active participation of consumers in the planning and delivery of flexible and adaptable service options. A subcommittee on legislation is developing an operational plan for the report's recommendations; their final report has recently been completed.[19]

This Commission endorses the principles of the Graham Report and believes that the work of the Graham Committee legislation subcommittee should be given prompt consideration by the Ontario government.

Although the movement of patients out of provincial hospitals was straightforward, where the patients went to was less evident. Therefore, the Commission set out to obtain information about the residential places to which inpatient and outpatients are discharged or terminated.[20] In February 1991, a memorandum was sent to the ten provincial psychiatric hospitals and all Schedule 1 facilities[21] in the province (eighty-one hospitals/facilities in all), asking them to collect such data from

Table 3
Psychiatric Inpatient Population (at Year End*) in Ontario

Year	# of Patients in Provincial Psychiatric Hospitals (on the books)	# of Patients in Psychiatric Units in Public Hospitals	# of Patients in Community and Miscellaneous Psychiatric Hospitals **
1961	18,292	—	—
1966	13,753	645	229
1970	8,838	1,118	387
1975	5,416	1,414	433
1980	4,930	1,851	730
1985	4,372	1,833	830
1988	3,957	1,830	823
% change 1961–1988	-78%	+184%	+259%

On-the-books figures include patients in approved homes or on leave of absence.

*The 1961–75 end of year is December 31; 1980–88 end of year is March 31.

**It appears that the Clarke Institute of Psychiatry was considered as a Miscellaneous Psychiatric Hospital for 1975, 1985, 1988, and is captured in those figures.

Table 4
Expenditures on Mental-Health Services in Ontario

	Community Mental Health	OHIP (Mental Health)	Regional Psychiatric Hospital	General Hospital (Inpatient)	Health
79/80	30,307,842	70,320,486	183,609,505	113,273,259	4,271,933,711
80/81	32,419,649	86,460,421	200,425,517	130,223,040	4,895,043,777
81/82	17,753,728	108,535,068	232,094,363	147,777,662	5,812,552,088
82/83	23,456,974	138,392,855	272,638,406	155,022,991	6,770,135,955
83/84	30,068,268	158,146,718	296,215,839	170,960,701	7,583,752,812
84/85	34,735,234	175,205,668	306,501,090	185,557,009	8,342,898,900
85/86	41,379,177	196,188,128	331,388,993	200,561,580	9,254,496,977
86/87	50,766,370	230,575,677	357,959,741	229,221,255	10,158,310,686
87/88	61,449,149	279,214,637	383,483,503	248,615,451	11,532,680,421
88/89	74,636,940	302,257,744	419,431,774	203,560,892	12,566,253,595

The Ministry of Health notes that the data reported in this table were not collected on a consistent basis over the period from 1979 to 1989. Thus, it is not possible to calculate a meaningful rate of growth for the individual columns.

These figures are taken from: Regional allocation of *estimated* expenditures on mental-health services by Ministry of Health—Community Information, User Support Branch.

Data for 1989–90 and 1990–91 not available.

March 15 to April 15, 1991.[22]

With a response rate (total or partial) of 91 percent, we were able to determine the following (see Table 5):

As of February 1991, there were 6,118 psychiatric beds in Ontario. The total number of discharges/terminations in the sample month was 4,698; i.e., more than three-quarters of all beds "turned over" during the month.[23] The vast majority of all discharges (2,922) and terminations (817) were to independent or private living arrangements.[24]

There were 124 inpatients discharged to boarding homes (1,488 on an annual basis);[25] there were a further thirty-one outpatients terminated (372 annualized) to boarding homes. As well, fifty inpatients and twelve outpatients went from institutions to "rooming houses" and "hostels."

From this data we can deduce that more than 2,000 outpatients and 500 inpatients are discharged annually to unregulated housing[26] in Ontario.[27]

PERSONS WITH DEVELOPMENTAL DISABILITIES

Until the 1970s, professionals, government, and families generally favoured institutionalizing persons with developmental disabilities. It was believed that these persons, who often also had physical disabilities, had little potential for personal growth. During the past twenty years, however, services have moved from a custodial and medical model to a developmental approach that recognizes and encourages the potential of persons with developmental disabilities. One aspect of this is the affirmation of their right to live in the community.

From 1975 to 1985, provincial funds invested in community-based services increased from $8 million to $181 million. A "Multi-Year Plan" was announced in June 1987. Included as its long-term goals were the establishment of a comprehensive community service system for all people with developmental

22 The time period was chosen for convenience only. Five facilities collected data for either March or April rather than mid-March to mid-April.

23 The crude mean turnover rate is 0.77, although the range and variance in length of stay are extremely high.

24 The categories of housing presented in Table 5 are those of the Provincial Psychiatric Hospitals Disposition Data Form.

25 The annual figures are simply the totals for the sample month multiplied by twelve. The assumption is that the sample month is representative of annual discharge flows.

26 For purposes of this Report, we do not distinguish among any of the specific categories enumerated in the definition of "boarding home" that appears in Table 5.

27 This does not, however, imply that 2,500 individuals are involved, as the same person may be admitted and discharged several times during the course of a year.

Table 5
Location of Discharge from Psychiatric Hospital Beds in Ontario, March 15–April 15, 1991

	Inpatient Discharges	Outpatient Terminations
Sample Size	61	40
Total Number of Discharges/Terminations	3,710	988
Location of Discharges		
Private/Independent Living	2,922	817
Other Institutions	196	18
Supportive/Regulated Housing	122	16
Unknown	124	48
Extended Care	95	28
Boarding Homes	124	31
Other	45	13
No Fixed Abode	32	5
Hostels	26	4
Rooming Houses	24	8
	3,710	988

Categories of Housing have been defined as follows:
a) Private/Independent Living—includes private homes/ apartments/family, subsidized housing, hotels/motels
b) Boarding Homes—includes boarding homes that are municipally licensed (second-level lodging homes); unlicensed; of unknown status; and supervised and domiciliary boarding homes includes those regulated by Habitat Services in Toronto
c) Rooming Houses
d) Supportive/Regulated Housing—includes group homes, co-ops, HSC (Residential), Approved Homes, MCSS homes, foster homes, correctional halfway houses
e) Extended Care—includes nursing homes, homes for the Aged, HSC (Nursing)
f) Hostels—includes shelters and temporary residences
g) No Fixed Abode—includes discharges to the street
h) Other Institutions—includes hospitals (general and psychiatric), correctional institutions, and other treatment centres
i) Unknown—includes discharges Against Medical Advice (AMA), and Absence without Leave (AWOL)
j) Other—includes deaths and deportations

disabilities, and the planned phase-out of institutional placement of these people.

However laudable those aims, living in the community often means living in unregulated rest homes. Yet adults with developmental disabilities are often the most vulnerable of the vulnerable adults.

Seven-year strategic objectives associated with the Multi-Year Plan set targets for the development of community services and community-living places for people with developmental disabilities. For example, 683 such people living in nursing homes were targeted for placement in the community under the Multi-Year Plan; as of December 1990, 327 had been so placed.[28]

Deinstitutionalization of adults with developmental disabilities has generally proceeded at a slower but more consistent pace than that of the psychiatric population. In 1979, there were 4,957 adult residents with developmental disabilities in Schedule 1 facilities; by 1991 this number had dropped to 3,033, a decrease of 39 percent.[29] (See Table 6.) This population in Schedule 2 facilities first increased substantially, from 475 adult residents in 1979 to 678 in 1986; however, since that time there has been a gradual decline, to 590 residents in 1990.

The total number of residents (adults and children) in Schedule 1 and Schedule 2 facilities has dropped by about half in fifteen years, from 7,766 residents in 1976 to 3,810 in 1991. During a similar period, community-based accommodation (group homes and supported independent living)[30] has nearly tripled, from 2,645 places in 1979 to 7,344 in 1991.

The Ministry of Community and Social Services (MCSS) intends that by the year 2010 there will be no Schedule 1 or 2 facilities in Ontario, but there will be 17,000 community-based accommodation spaces and 44,000 adults using community-based services. This is an ambitious goal, which the Commission endorses and supports. We also urge that the plan be adequately funded, for the current number of community-

28 The Ministry of Community and Social Services estimates there are currently between 28,000 and 35,000 persons with developmental disabilities in Ontario using government-funded services of some kind, including about 12,000 people in Schedule 1 and 2 facilities, nursing homes, and community-based accommodation. MCSS also estimates that at least 50,000 people with developmental disabilities may be living in the community without using government-operated or -funded developmental services.

29 There are eleven Schedule 1 facilities directly operated by the province of Ontario. There are currently nine Schedule 2 facilities that receive government funding but are operated by community-based boards of directors.

30 There are approximately 700 group homes for adults with developmental disabilities in Ontario, ranging in size from two to fifteen beds, with the majority in the four-to-six-bed range.

The Supported Independent Living (SIL) program provides support for adults with developmental disabilities to move from residential facilities, group homes, or parental homes into mainstream accommodation. The program provides appropriate supervisory and training services to promote a more independent and self-sufficient lifestyle. In 1987–88 there were 1,525 people in the SIL program; in 1990–91 there were 2,075.

The Family Home program

Table 6
Statistics on Accommodation Services for People with
Developmental Disabilities in Ontario

Year	Schedule 1 Facilities # of Adult Residents	Schedule 2 Facilities # of Adult Residents	Total # of Residents in Schedule 1 and 2 Facilities (Adults and Children)	Community-based Accommodation (spaces)	# of People Using Community-based Services (estimate)
1974	—	—	—	700	—
1975	—	—	—	888	—
1976	—	—	7,766	1,245	4,600
1979	4,957	475	7,191	2,645	—
1986	4,200	678	5,477	4,884	25,000
1987	3,904	684	5,083	5,305	—
1988	3,769	638	4,800	5,678	—
1989	3,635	634	4,607	6,243	27,000
1990	3,554	627	4,461	6,725	—
1991	3,033	590	3,810	7,344	29,000
2010 (proj)	0	0	0	17,000	44,000
% change 1979–91	-39%	+24%	-55%	+178%	

provides funding for families who are willing to share their home with one or two adults or children with developmental disabilities.

based accommodation spaces must more than double within the twenty-year period if Ontarians with developmental disabilities are to be adequately accommodated when they become adults.

Developmental Disability and Rest Homes

The children's services program of MCSS funds services for

children with developmental disabilities. When children receiving such services turn eighteen (or twenty-one, if Crown wards), Adult Protective Services Workers (APSWs)[31] —advocates and case managers—are usually assigned. At this time, too, the task of finding suitable housing and services begins, just as funding drops severely: services in children's programs, which can cost several hundred dollars a day, depending on need, are replaced by social assistance—$688 per month under the Guaranteed Annual Income System—Disabled [GAINS(D)].

The waiting period for places in group homes or independent living arrangements for this population group is typically three to five years. As a result, interim housing must be found. Two options are available, both involving unregulated housing. The first is remaining past the age of majority in a children's home;[32] the second option is a rest home.

We have some data on adults with developmental disabilities residing in rest homes. A 1988 Task Force on Boarding Homes of the Ontario Association of Community Living (OACL)[33] sent out a survey to APSWs across the province; the response rate was 79 percent. The survey found that there were 217 boarding homes in the province in which people with developmental disabilities lived, and that the total number of APSW clients in these boarding homes was 369.[34]

Several important facts about the residents were derived from the study:

1. almost 40 percent of the residents saw their families once a year or less, but almost 25 percent had weekly visits from families;

2. nearly 40 percent of the residents had been placed in boarding homes by their families; 10 percent came from psychiatric facilities, and nearly 20 percent were placed by a child-welfare agency;

3. 37 percent of the residents were in boarding homes because there was no other option;

31 The APSW system grew out of the 1971 Williston Report, which recommended phasing out large psychiatric institutions. In 1976, MCSS introduced an adult protective services program for persons with developmental disabilities in which the workers would be funded 100 percent by the ministry but would be sponsored by local community agencies. Their mandate was to serve as both case managers and advocates, but a 1983 document eliminated any reference to the advocacy function.

32 This path involves a number of broader issues affecting public policy. Children's homes are regulated for a population of children; they are *not* regulated with respect to the needs of adults. See the discussion in chapter 12.

33 Ontario Association of Community Living, *APSW Survey Report*, draft copy, dated January 18, 1990.

34 These figures are an underestimate because the response rate, though high, is less than 100 percent; in addition, not all adults with developmental disabilities choose to have APSWs.

35 We discuss later the meaning of a finding such as this. Specifically we shall question whether operators *should* be providing the needed services (such as day activities, counselling, etc.). The failure of community agencies to provide these supports, as noted in the text, is a matter of great concern to this Commission.

36 Adult Protective Service Association of Ontario, *Home Is Where the Hurt Is: Strategies for Eliminating the Pain.* A submission to the Commission of Inquiry into Unregulated Residential Accommodation, written by Patricia Spindel, consultant to the executive.

37 The report broke down the findings: 379 persons in boarding homes, sixty in rest homes, and fourteen in retirement homes. We indicate elsewhere that the distinctions among these categories are not always clear and we prefer to treat them as a single residential category.

4. some residents chose boarding homes because of the absence of the rules and supervision one would find, for example, in a group home;

5. 87.5 percent of the residents needed services/supports not being provided by the operators of their home;[35] and about 65 percent of the APSW clients in boarding homes needed services/supports not provided by community agencies.

The Task Force concluded that "too frequently relatively young people are 'warehoused'…"

The Adult Protective Service Association of Ontario, the organization representing APSWs, conducted a survey of its membership in February 1991, in part to present information to this Commission.[36] There was a 66 percent response rate. More than 70 percent of respondents "indicated a serious lack of residential services as the most important issue facing their clients."

The APSWs reported a total of 563 clients currently in unregulated residential settings. Of these, 110 adults with developmental disabilities were residing in children's homes; the remaining 453 lived in unregulated for-profit boarding/rest/retirement homes.[37]

We have identified the three categories of vulnerable adults who are to be the primary focus of this Inquiry and have presented some estimates of their numbers in the population. We have also described, in a preliminary way, the unregulated accommodation in which they often reside. The Commission now turns its attention to proposing a framework within which vulnerable adults can escape from society's indifference to, or neglect of, their housing and care needs. The principles on which we have sought to build this framework are the subject of the next chapter.

3 Residents Must Be Central

Problems—and Commissions of Inquiry—do not form in a contextual vacuum, and solutions are not developed in isolation. We begin our analysis with an awareness of the fiscal crisis in Ontario and Canada, an understanding that resources are no longer available to deal with a vast array of pressing social needs. Decisions made in earlier years to throw money at social problems in the hope that they would somehow resolve themselves are neither feasible nor desirable, particularly in today's economic climate.

We are also aware that the economic crisis has not been caused by vulnerable adults, many of whom exist on marginal incomes. We are fundamentally unwilling to recommend or endorse policies that require these vulnerable adults to pay the price of governments' past economic and social mismanagement. We are committed to protecting vulnerable adults from the consequences not only of inadequate social policies and community neglect, but also of regressive economic policies that have further empowered the powerful and left the rest behind. Our goal is to facilitate the empowerment of disempowered and vulnerable persons in Ontario.

In our March 1991 Discussion Paper, the Commission presented its central principle, that the client/consumer survivor/resident must be the focus of any analysis.

1 The Discussion Paper noted
that the empowerment envisaged by the central principle
is not absolute and unquali-
fied. "The market assumption
of sovereign consumers making informed choices cannot
apply in full to a vulnerable
population." With a vulnerable population, there is a
simultaneous need to protect.

Some submissions have expressed reservations about the Commission's commitment to consumer empowerment. In particular, the Alzheimer Association of Ontario and Ontario Friends of Schizophrenics have argued that the vulnerability of their populations often precludes autonomous action: Alzheimer's is a progressive, irreversible brain disorder that affects cognitive functioning; therefore, individual decision-making is often impossible or inappropriate. People suffering from schizophrenia are on medication to control potentially destructive behaviour; they must not be allowed the option of not taking their medications.

The Commission takes due note of these concerns. Our general position is that vulnerability is not an absolute: we believe that individuals should be permitted, encouraged, and assisted to act autonomously and become empowered *whenever and to the maximum extent possible.*[1]

We must create a community in which vulnerable adults can begin to take control of their lives, including control over where, how, and with whom they live. We cannot give power, but we can facilitate the development of a framework in which empowerment can occur. We must also offer to protect vulnerable persons, on the understanding that protection cannot be imposed. Many vulnerable persons require and desire protection from both the harsh vicissitudes of life and exploitation by unrestrained economic market forces.

These two words—"empowerment" and "protection"—represent the key values that underpin the work of this Commission.

Empowerment and Protection

The early development of Canada's welfare state placed little emphasis on the importance of the consumer of services in the social-service system. Bureaucrats and service providers, often paternalistic and assumed to be benevolent, believed they knew what their clients needed, if not what they wanted. Subsequently, it was discovered that professionals and bureaucrats were not always benevolent and did not inevitably have the best interests of their clients at heart.

The concept of empowerment grew out of a market ethos in which sovereign consumers decide their own preferences and priorities. For some, people's right to control their own lives without undue interference is an end in itself, a normative view of how society ought to be organized. For others, empowerment is a means to other ends, among them redressing the significant inequalities in incomes, rights, and entitlements current in Canada.

Rather than making decisions on behalf of people, surely it is preferable to support individuals in deciding for themselves. Empowerment requires the investment of time and money in the enhancement of vulnerable adults' capacity for autonomous action. It requires that society aid and assist them in making informed choices about how to live their lives; professionals become support staff to consumers[2] rather than controllers of the environment in which clients have to exist.

The battle is: who gets to define my life. I am sitting in a room where virtually everybody believes it is all right for a bunch of service people to define my life, and that in fact the role of the government is to create more damn services … that will define my life.

Only I can figure out how things work for me. I cannot work with a bunch of people trooping through my place, trying to decide for me who I am and what I need. I will spend the rest of my life … trying to keep them organized, trying to keep the teapot full.[3]

For consumers to have real choice, and to exercise that

2 The term "consumer" is often used to describe the person who is to be empowered. Although some people see this label in a positive light, others resent the transformation of what should be a caring and helping relationship with the disadvantaged into a crass marketplace exchange.

3 Judith Snow, oral presentation to symposium on long-term-care reform, held at Canadian Hearing Society, December 1–2, 1990.

choice, three conditions must be satisfied:

> 1. there must be *supply*, i.e., options and alternatives; otherwise, choice is meaningless;
> 2. there must be *information* available, i.e., consumers must know about the options; and
> 3. there must be *access*, i.e., consumers must have the power and the resources, personal and financial, to avail themselves of the alternatives.

Some vulnerable persons have a limited capacity to exercise informed choice. However, an assumption of limited capacity with regard to all choices is simplistic and demeaning. Unless a legal determination of mental incapacity has been made, individuals must be directly and actively involved in all decisions that affect their lives.

In the past, our society and governments simply identified criteria for "capability" and then assumed "clients" met these criteria. We gave them an inadequate welfare cheque and left them to cope in the open market, but did little to make possible even a minimally acceptable lifestyle in that market.

If we are to do it right this time, we must ensure that services and supports are in place, that meaningful choices are available, and that vulnerable adults are offered assistance in developing decision-making skills.

When consumers have real choices and are capable of identifying their own priorities and preferences with adequate supports, there is much less need for society to make decisions on their behalf—even benevolent and protective decisions. Only in those areas in which consumers do not have choices or are deemed incapable of making informed choices is mandatory intervention appropriate. To neither protect nor enhance choices and consumer competence is to abandon our collective responsibilities to the most vulnerable members of our society.

The Supports Needed for Empowerment

For people to become empowered, they must first and fore- most have adequate incomes. Therefore, Ontario's major social-assistance review is of critical importance to vulnerable persons in this province. This Commission endorses the major initiatives on social-assistance reform in Ontario (*Transitions* and *Back on Track*). We urge the Ontario government to implement social-assistance reform as quickly as possible.

Empowerment also requires a range of human supports to assist vulnerable persons in exercising their rights as con- sumers. Vulnerable adults may require substantial amounts of support to survive in a market economy.

Three aspects of empowerment are most relevant to this Inquiry: advocacy, the delinking of accommodation from care, and the direct funding of individuals.

ADVOCACY

Advocacy, both formal and informal, is an essential support to help disempowered people identify and articulate their wishes and needs, and, ultimately, begin to assume control over their lives by pursuing their rights and entitlements.

In April 1991, the government introduced Bill 74, the *Advocacy Act, 1991,* a basic framework for a province-wide advocacy system, administered by an independent Advocacy Commission.[4] Advocacy services—rights advocacy, case advo- cacy, and systemic advocacy[5]—will be provided to vulnerable adults who live in facilities or in the community.

Advocates are to act on the wishes and instructions of their clients.

Advocacy alone is not sufficient to empower residents in rest homes; however, it is an essential form of investment in people, which should generate a long-term social return as

4 Many of tPhe operating details will be worked out by the Commission itself, and the amount of funding and size of the program are not yet known.

5 The three types are defined as follows:
1. rights advocacy: informa- tion and assistance will be provided about the vulnera- ble person's rights in special circumstances, particularly cases of proposed guardian- ship, in medical consent situ- ations, and when giving power of attorney;
2. case advocacy: the advo- cate will act as an "articulate intermediary," assisting vul- nerable persons "to express and act on their wishes, ascertain and exercise their rights, speak on their own behalf";
3. systemic advocacy: this focuses on wider concerns, specifically "to help vulnera- ble persons to bring about structural changes at the political, legal, social, eco- nomic, and institutional lev- els."

6 The present legislation, the *Mental Incompetency Act*, contains procedures that are expensive and time-consuming. As a result, family members and service providers often act on their own perceptions of allegedly incapable persons' best interests to make personal-care decisions for those persons. At present there is no public official with authority to act in personal-care matters for incapable persons who lack family or friends to make decisions for them.

the competencies of vulnerable persons are enhanced and strengthened.

We believe that following the passage of the *Advocacy Act, 1991*, adequate funding and staffing should become a priority of the government so that the program might become operational as soon as possible.

Substitute Decision-Making

As persons living in rest homes may become mentally incapable at some point, it is important to have clear standards for deciding when this occurs and simple procedures (including emergency procedures) for providing a decision-maker in such circumstances.

Bill 108, the *Substitute Decisions Act, 1991*, introduced in May 1991,[6] includes a streamlined process to appoint private guardians (such as family or friends) for mentally incapable persons; assured access to a substitute decision-maker for all mentally incapable persons through a new Office of the Public Guardian and Trustee; partial guardianship; and an emergency procedure including temporary powers.

DELINKING ACCOMMODATION FROM CARE

Separating accommodation from support services is a direct corollary of individual empowerment. If people are to make decisions about their lives, they must be able to choose where they wish to live, rather than being required to live in a particular setting because care is delivered there. To tie housing to the use of health or social services is to infringe inappropriately on individuals' right of self-directed action. (Whether such infringements are ever justifiable is discussed in Part III.)

"Aging in place" describes a service model in which portable, community-based services come to individuals, who can then remain living in their own homes as long as such services can meet their needs. The approach avoids the high costs of excessive institutionalization; more important, however, it recognizes that consumers of services should not be required to move from place to place in order to receive needed services.[7]

One consequence of this thinking is that the group home is being de-emphasized as a model of service delivery. In the group home, accommodation and support services (usually counselling) are delivered by the same agency: when consumers receive housing, they also accept the entire service package. However, the roles and responsibilities of landlords and service providers are quite distinct. Logically, housing should be provided by housing agencies, services by care providers.

An important (and underrecognized) 1987 document[8] strongly advocated as much delinking of housing and support services as possible:

the special needs [of a person] should not be the primary factor defining the choice of residence.... People with special needs should be able to choose from as wide a range of [housing] options as the general public, bearing in mind normal constraints such as affordability.

The report concluded that a supportive housing policy has three key goals—independence, integration, and stability—and that linking housing to support services undermines all three.[9]

The Commission endorses the trend to delink accommodation from care and urges that initiatives continue to be developed.

DIRECT FUNDING

Direct funding as a means of empowerment presupposes the

7 A series of regional consultations on (public) housing and support services for the elderly were held in 1989. A summary of these consultations reported:
Tenants do not want to leave their apartments if and/or when their needs for support services increase. If they become unable to take care of themselves, they would prefer to receive support services in their apartment for as long as possible....Very few tenants said they would be willing to go to Nursing Homes or Homes for the Aged.
(Memorandum to Housing Authority Managers from Tenant Support Services Branch Re: Housing for the Elderly, Ministry of Housing, January 13, 1989).

8 *More Than Shelter*, Interim Report of the working Committee on Supportive Community Living, (Ministry of Housing, January 1987).

9 A 1990 discussion paper on supportive housing observed that all affected ministries— primarily Health, Housing, and Community and Social Services— "are now committed to the intent and principles" of supportive housing, which may entail delinking of services. *Discussion Paper on Supportive Housing*, prepared by Burt Perrin Associates for the Ministry of Housing and the Ministry of Community and Social Services, August 14, 1990, p.31.

10 Individuals are deemed to be the best judge of their own priorities, best able to decide their own priorities among housing and all other needs (including food and services). In theory, there would be no checks or controls on how the money is spent, though this might not be practicable.

11 The program operates on the assumption that the family will be primary care-givers. Families have an option to administer the SSAH funds themselves. They can either hire the service worker on a contract or they can assume a formal employer/employee relationship that entails benefits, withholding taxes, etc. Family members cannot be hired.

12 *Strategies for Change: Comprehensive Reform of Ontario's Long-Term Care Services* (1990) and *Redirection of Long-Term Care and Support services in Ontario: A Public Consultation Paper* (1991). With direct funding, persons would receive an amount of money equal to the cost of the services they would receive if these services were purchased on their behalf by the long-term-care system.

availability of community-based services. Individuals receive an assessment of need by some community agency or government; they then decide how these needs are to be met. They may choose to purchase a package of services or one or more separate services. Payment might be made directly by individuals or by an agency on individuals' behalf.

In the pure case, individuals are given a lump sum of money, which can then be spent as desired: the proportion spent on housing, support services, and other things is up to the individuals themselves.[10]

There is little direct funding in Ontario, although the Special Services at Home program (SSAH) of MCSS does fund directly. The program was designed (in 1982) for families who are primary care-givers for children with developmental disabilities; it has since been extended to include adults with developmental disabilities who are living at home with their families as well as to children with physical disabilities. SSAH provides funds to purchase supports and services not available from agencies in the community, such as family relief or respite care and special services assistance with particular tasks.[11]

The long-term-care proposals of the previous and current governments contain another initiative for direct funding of physically disabled adults.[12]

The Commission endorses the direct funding of social benefits and urges that more such initiatives be developed.

The Rest Home: Accommodation or Care?

In our Discussion Paper of March 1991, the Commission posed a dichotomy as a "fundamental question that faces the

Commission": is accommodation with care to be conceptualized primarily as housing or as care?

Some responses have convincingly argued that the rest home is *both* housing and a setting in which care is provided. The major industry association formally views the rest home as holding a unique place between traditional housing and a full-care facility such as a nursing home: rather than retain this dichotomy, they suggest a continuum of care, on which the rest home occupies a distinct place.

Personal visits by and submissions to the Commission have confirmed that, indeed, there is no simple dichotomy: some retirement homes are targeted at the "well elderly"; they offer a particular style of living in which care services receive scarcely a mention. Other rest homes are nursing homes in every way save provincial regulation, licensing, and per diem funding under the *Nursing Homes Act*. One of the great strengths of the rest-home industry has been its flexibility, its ability to respond to a range of needs identified in the market.

The question posed by the Commission remains an important one, however, for it is our purpose to suggest future direction, rather than to describe current practice. In part because of the legal and definitional void, rest homes have come to fill an array of service needs, without any governing coherence or compatibility with other social priorities. Our task is to recommend a measure of coherence and direction for the industry that will blend with other government and private-sector initiatives, while not unnecessarily infringing upon market activity.

Governmental priorities in long-term care and elsewhere have moved towards funding community-based services and agencies and, to some extent, people directly. New care-giving institutions on the nursing-home model are not being contemplated by government. Any private-sector initiatives to create new institutional care facilities will stand or fall on their ability to read the market, independent of government policy, involvement, or support.

13 This would constitute another route to expanding nursing-home places. If community-based in-home services are not expanded, these places will be sorely needed as the population continues to age.

Most important, however, is the consumers' view of rest homes. "Residents," as the term makes clear, see rest homes as their home, not a place of temporary sojourn. It is their sole permanent accommodation. Indeed, those going into retirement homes usually sell their homes or give up their apartments and take furniture and other personal belongings with them.

The rest home is also seen as permanent accommodation by operators and government. It is also seen as a site where variable amounts and types of care are given; however, the accommodation function is the central, ongoing characteristic.

RECOMMENDATION 2: That the rest home's primary function be viewed as the provision of residential accommodation in which some element of care is also provided.

COMMUNITY RESIDENCE OR INSTITUTION?

The relationship of rest homes to licensed nursing homes and, by extension, to the proposed long-term-care system has been raised in many submissions to the Commission. Some have argued that rest homes should be formally considered to be low-level or first-stage nursing homes, funded by the province at a suitable per diem rate, and regulated comprehensively. Some have advocated the absorption of rest homes into the nursing-home sector, without restricting them to low levels of care.[13] Either approach would incorporate rest homes into the institutional sector of the long-term-care system and expand the number of nursing-home beds.

Others argue that new "institutions" in any form are fundamentally at odds with the thrust of long-term-care reform. Rest homes, they argue, should be a form of residence, part of the community rather than part of the institutional world.

The rest-home industry, as we have noted, holds a middle

view, that their premises are a point on the continuum of long-term care between community care in one's own home and a full-care facility.

However, the concept of "continuum of care" has been supplanted in public policy-making by the even more powerful idea of "aging in place." Rather than being moved around as they age, people should stay in their homes as long as possible, with services coming to them. It is this view that has led to governmental decisions, over many years, not to develop new institutions, but rather to focus on portable and flexible services delivered to people in their homes.[14]

RECOMMENDATION 3: That the government of Ontario expand, as a matter of priority, community services that enable people to remain in their own homes.

14 The Commission does not deny the need for institutions, and accepts that there is probably some limit for institutionalization rates below which the cost of community services would be prohibitive. We merely argue, as others have done, that many more people could be better served in the community and that Ontario has been overly preoccupied with an "institutionalization" model in relating to persons with long-term- care needs.

Figure 1
Viewing the Rest Home

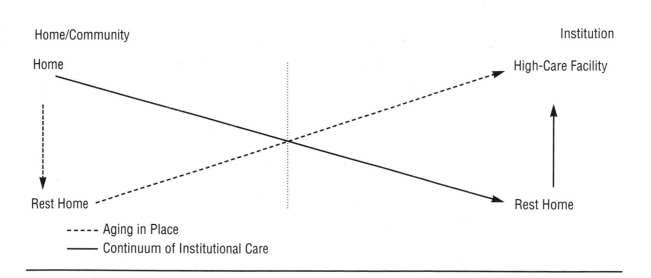

Figure 1 presents two views of the rest home. The solid line presents the continuum-of-institutional-care model, in which the rest home occupies an intermediate stage; the dotted line presents the rest home as an alternative to a private residence in the community, rather than part of the world of the institution.

In both cases, the rest home lies between the private home and the high-care facility. However, the first alternative views the rest home as a low-level care institution, a modified nursing home. This implies per diem provincial funding and comprehensive regulation. In the second alternative, the rest home is treated as a private residence rather than an institution. This involves no ongoing per diem funding to operators; rather, residents would be eligible for any and all in-home services available or developed in future as part of the long-term-care reform.

It is the strong view of this Commission that the second alternative represents the preferable description of the rest home. We cannot recommend new low-level care institutions knowing that during the next few years they might well be dismantled or de-emphasized in favour of portable services.

RECOMMENDATION 4: That the rest home be viewed as an alternative form of accommodation in the community, and not as the first stage in a continuum of institutional care.

We see the future rest home as one of several community residential options within a fully mature system of long-term care. Many care services now delivered in nursing homes will be delivered to people in their own homes, which may include rest homes. Some persons now placed in nursing homes so their needs can be met would be able to remain in the community.

A dichotomy of accommodation will emerge: one's own residence as long as possible, followed by a high-care, government-regulated facility when and if necessary. Government-funded low-care institutional beds will be phased out, as services are able to be delivered in individuals' homes.[15]

In short, the Commission views the rest home as a form of residence, freely chosen by people who prefer such a setting to other housing options, including their former homes.[16]

LONG-TERM CARE

A substantial number of submissions and presentations have urgently advocated that rest homes be incorporated in the Ontario government's long-term-care reform initiative. They consider it absurd to undertake so fundamental a reform, while ignoring a major component such as rest homes. Indeed, rest homes have been omitted from the long-term-care initiative to date[17] and it is certainly appropriate that this Commission consider them within this context.

The Commission holds that rest homes should be viewed as part of the community and should not become new low-level care institutions. Rest homes, if they are to find a market niche, will do so as an alternative form of private accommodation for persons who want and are willing and able to pay for care services offered by the homes. The rest home will, in some ways, compete as provider of care services with the in-home services that will emerge from long-term-care reform.

Take one example: assistance with bathing is a common service offered in retirement homes, and residents often purchase this service from operators. There is no eligibility criterion other than that residents have the money to buy the service and wish to do so.

Government-funded programs also offer assistance with bathing. For those who qualify, Home Care operates as a medicare service funded under the *Health Insurance Act* with no user fee.[18] However, because total resources in the Home Care program are limited, service may not be available to all who meet the program's criteria. Therefore, administrative discretion is often used to ration service. Local Home Care

15 We may note the intent of the British Columbia government to withdraw from the funding of low-care institutions, to be replaced by enhanced community care.

16 Consistent with the principle of empowerment adopted by the Commission, the decision of where to live and where to receive care must always be made, to the maximum extent possible, by the persons concerned.

17 Rest homes were originally omitted from the long-term-care initiative because it was necessary to put closure of some sort on what was a massive undertaking; moreover, there was no legal definition of "rest home" with which the policy-makers could work.

18 As part of long-term-care reform, there are plans to de-insure Home Care services from the *Health Insurance Act*. It is important that the government identify explicit rationing criteria to determine eligibility for Home Care once it is no longer an entitlement.

19 In either case, they can also privately purchase the care from other suppliers in the community. Some consumers, ineligible for Home Care, will choose to purchase care services in rest homes.

20 Section 3 of the *Nursing Homes Act* prohibits any person from establishing, operating, or maintaining a nursing home unless the facility is licensed by the Ministry of Health. The legal definition of a "nursing home" then becomes critical.

Under the Act, a nursing home "means any premises maintained and operated for persons requiring nursing care or in which such care is provided to two or more unrelated persons." "Nursing care," in turn, is defined to include both "intermediate nursing care" and "extended care." The former means "nursing and personal care given by or under the supervision of a registered nurse or registered nursing assistant under the direction of a physician to a resident for less than one and one-half hours per day." "Extended care" has the same definition, with the added specification of "a minimum of one and one-half hours a day."

This was the basis of the observation in the Commission's Discussion Paper (p. 6, footnote 3) that "delivery of nursing care to two or more unrelated persons in a premises requires licensing under the *Nursing Homes Act*."

administrators may refuse or limit such services to rest-home residents on the assumption that they are receiving care in the rest home. Thus residents of a retirement home may be compelled to pay privately for this service even though they qualify for Home Care.

As in-home social and health services become more readily available in the community, residents with adequate income who qualify for these services will have several options. If they choose to live in retirement homes, they may purchase care services from the operators; or, if eligible, they may receive these services from Home Care. They may prefer to remain in their own homes and, if eligible, receive assistance in that setting.[19] The success of the retirement-home industry will depend on its ability to persuade consumers that it is the preferable option.

Further discussion of this approach, and our recommendations, are included in chapter 6, "Life at the Top."

"BOOTLEG" NURSING HOMES

Much reference has been made to "bootleg" nursing homes, a phrase widely used to describe rest homes that deliver high levels of care, including nursing care, to residents on a commercial basis. They serve, in effect, as nursing homes, although they are not licensed, regulated, inspected, or funded by the province under the *Nursing Homes Act*.

The *Nursing Homes Act* requires the licensing of all premises that meet the Act's definition of a "nursing home." Premises that come within the definition but are not licensed may be closed; at the same time, the province limits the number of nursing-home licences it issues.

Strictly speaking, under the *Nursing Homes Act*, any premises providing any nursing care by or under the supervision of an RN or RNA to two or more unrelated persons may require a licence to operate legally.[20] In practice, however, the Act is not interpreted so strictly. The Ontario government provides per diem funding to licensed nursing-home operators only for "extended care" (more than ninety minutes of nursing care for a resident each day).

A bootleg nursing home is therefore a rest home that provides more than ninety minutes of nursing care a day for two or more unrelated residents and does not have a nursing-home licence under the *Nursing Homes Act.*

The bootleg nursing home effectively creates a two-tier system of nursing-home care—those regulated and funded by the Ontario government, and those unregulated and funded on a private commercial basis.

Bootleg nursing homes operate with the acquiescence of operators, residents, and government. Residents may need high-level personal and nursing care; however, both licensed nursing-home beds and acceptable community-based home services may be unavailable. Families with the resources to pay privately may be desperate to find placements for relatives whose needs have grown; rest-home operators are happy to oblige, as payment is set without government involvement, sometimes in excess of the nursing-home per diem.

Ministry of Health (MoH) inspectors seem unwilling to close down unlicensed bootleg nursing-home beds while there are no alternatives available. It is also difficult to determine when particular individuals receive more than the ninety-minute nursing-care minimum, as rest homes are not required to record such data. The Residential Services Branch of the Community Health and Support Services Division (CHSSD) (a part of MCSS and MoH), who are responsible for enforcing the *Nursing Homes Act*, assert that the Act was not intended to prevent the private purchase or sale of unlimited amounts of nursing care; however, the Commission's reading of the *Nursing Homes Act* suggests the contrary.[21] Indeed, we feel that steps must be taken by the CHSSD to ensure its Residential Services Branch has clear criteria for enforcing the *Nursing Homes Act.*

21 Section 17(2) of the *Nursing Homes Act* states: "Where an inspector has reasonable and probable grounds to believe that any premises are being used as a nursing home without being licensed under this Act, the inspector without a warrant ... may enter upon such ... premises for the purpose of determining whether or not the person is in contravention of section 3 [the requirement to have a licence to operate a nursing home]."

RECOMMENDATION 5: That the Community Health and Support Services Division develop a precise legal definition of a "nursing home" so that it is clear which premises offering "nursing care" require a licence.

This definition may retain the current ninety-minute minimum for nursing care or any other cutoff point that is deemed appropriate. Such a determination would then imply that a legal rest-home operator can provide no more than this threshold of nursing care.

This two-tiered system of nursing-home care is, of course, institutional care. Persons with adequate financial resources have always had the option to privately purchase care and services to be provided in their personal residence. As the Commission recommends that a rest home be considered to be a "personal residence," rest-home residents must have the same right to privately purchase care in their private homes.

We recommend that rest-home operators be prohibited from selling more than a specified amount of nursing care. Historically, the state has decided that once health-care needs reach a certain point, these needs should be provided only by persons who are licensed and regulated. The complexity of the service required and the vulnerability of a potential purchaser dictate that only "approved" sellers may deliver institutional health care. The point beyond which unlicensed sellers will be excluded will be that distinguishing nursing care from rest-home care.

The net effect is that residents of rest homes will be free to privately purchase whatever amounts of nursing care they desire. They may also receive, from the reformed long-term-care system, any amount of nursing and personal care for which they qualify. However, operators of rest homes will be able to sell nursing care only up to the threshold for licensing as a nursing home.

This means that rest homes operating as bootleg nursing homes, i.e., providing more than threshold levels of care on an unregulated basis, cannot be permitted to continue to do so. Residents requiring nursing care beyond the threshold amount should be eligible for in-home care from the long-term-care system, or be accommodated in a facility licensed to meet their needs. Those not eligible for services through long-term care or who desire more than the amount of nursing care operators may sell may purchase such care from another private provider. Those persons who choose to purchase up to the specified amount of nursing care from operators as part of a mandatory package of accommodation and care may, of course, do so.

We assume that operators and outside suppliers will be required to function at arm's length, and we recommend that operators have no financial interest in any outside supplier delivering nursing-home-level care to residents of their rest homes.

RECOMMENDATION 6: That no rest-home operator be permitted to sell more than the threshold amount of nursing care to any resident of that rest home.

Bootleg nursing homes are an inevitable consequence of an aging population, slow growth in licensed nursing-home beds, and a failure to develop adequate community services. Many residents of bootleg facilities are severely at risk, as the case material received by this Commission has documented again and again. Needed community-based services are not yet in place, and many residents of the bootleg facilities have high-care needs that cannot be met outside institutions.

"Regularizing" the Bootleg Homes
For those rest homes currently delivering more than the threshold amount of care, there are two policy options: the premises may either become licensed and receive per diem funding, subject to regular inspection; or operators may cease

selling high amounts of care. The first option would increase the number of licensed nursing-home beds, which runs counter to the thrust of long-term-care reform. It would also be costly to the Treasury and reinforce a system that appears to generate little consumer or public satisfaction.

The second approach, restricting the services provided by operators or closing these premises, is practical only if the care services are available from other sources, i.e., expanded community-based services delivered to people in their own homes. This option, too, will require public expenditure.

The question is not whether to spend, but on what to spend. For all the reasons outlined in this Report and other governmental initiatives, the Commission believes that a major expansion of community-based services is the only viable alternative. However, if the government of Ontario does not fund major initiatives in this area, it must consider licensing and regulating these high-care rest homes or creating more legal nursing homes. The status quo is simply too dangerous for too many people.

"Regularizing" these rest homes or creating new licensed nursing homes is the option of last resort. It will be expensive and will not, in our view, deliver the best quality of care. But it should, at the very least, protect some residents who are now at risk.

Pending resolution of this problem, we stress that bootleg nursing homes are rest homes within our definition of the term; as such, all recommendations in this Report apply to them. These premises cannot be immune from both the *Nursing Homes Act* and the Commission's proposals.

Combined Rest Homes and Nursing Homes

There is also a closely related concern. The Residential Services Branch informed us that as of April 1991, seventy-one licensed nursing homes (nearly one in five of the 335 such homes in the province) have an unregulated rest-home component. Approximately 3,000 unregulated rest-home beds are attached to or on the same site as licensed nursing homes that have 30,489 licensed beds. As these rest-home beds are not regulated under the *Nursing Homes Act*, they are outside the mandate of the Residential Services Branch.

Many retirement homes actively market their affiliation with a licensed nursing home on the premises. It is implied that nursing-home-level care will be provided in the rest home, or that rest-home residents will have preferential access to nursing-home beds. One retirement-home operator told this Commission that he had little problem with residents whose care needs grew beyond his ability to meet them, for he had an "arrangement" with a local nursing-home operator. Entry to his retirement home was a means to "jump the queue" to the nursing home. Thus, there is two-tier institutional nursing care: those with sufficient incomes may buy accelerated entry via the retirement home; those lacking such resources must wait in line.

The rest-home-cum-nursing-home operators can control admission to scarce nursing-home beds. Certificates of eligibility for "extended care" are issued by individual medical doctors, who serve as the gatekeepers to the insured system of nursing-home care; such certificates have proven to be fairly easy to obtain. The queue for nursing-home beds then occurs at the point of entry to the nursing home, as the supply of beds is smaller than the number of certificates of eligibility. Nursing-home operators can then decide which persons with extended-care certificates will be accepted in their premises.

The Service Co-ordination Agencies (SCAs) planned by long-term-care reform will remove much of the nursing-home operators' control over access to nursing-home beds. However, we must stress that admission to nursing-home beds should be determined solely by level of need.[22]

RECOMMENDATION 7: That the reform of long-term care ensure that admission to a nursing home is not influenced by a person's prior residence in a rest home.

22 The fact of residence in a rest home should be irrelevant. However, any amounts of care received in the rest home may, like care received in a private home, reduce the level of "need" and therefore the priority ranking to secure a nursing-home bed ahead of a person who receives no care. Operationally, rest homes cannot be *assumed* to provide any particular amount of care; need should be determined on the facts of each case.

23 This is most likely to occur when the nursing- and rest-home beds share a common reception area and are built to a single, i.e., nursing-home, standard: one door may lead to the rest home, another to the nursing home. Perhaps such nursing homes are built to this design in the expectation of future growth in nursing-home places.

24 Some of the dual (rest/nursing) home operations are currently in financial difficulty. As of November 14, 1991, fourteen nursing homes with a licensed bed capacity of 1,493 were in receivership in Ontario; two of these, with a licensed nursing-home bed capacity of 376 (or 25 percent of the total licensed capacity of the fourteen homes) were dual nursing/rest homes. A further thirty-three nursing homes (capacity 4,516 nursing-home beds) were identified by the Residential Services Branch as "experiencing financial difficulties"; of these, fourteen homes (capacity 1,785 nursing-home beds, or 40 percent of the total) were dual operations. As the number of rest-home beds in dual operations is about 10 percent of the number of licensed nursing-home beds in Ontario, dual operations experience financial difficulty at a rate greater than the operations with only nursing-home beds. It is not known how many rest-home beds are affected in the dual operations.

There is one further concern about the combined rest home/nursing home. Presumably, occupants of rest-home beds in nursing homes receive less care than occupants of nursing-home beds in the same premises. However, as the care needs of occupants of the rest-home beds increase, more than ninety minutes of nursing care may be necessary. If there is no nursing-home bed available, the operator may provide such care on a private basis, presumably at higher cost to the resident: the rest-home bed thereby becomes a bootleg nursing-home bed.

Cross-subsidization from the unregulated charges in retirement homes to the regulated per diems in associated nursing homes may also occur. Any implied promise that nursing-home-level care will be offered in a rest-home bed is likely to have one of two consequences: if the beds exist in close proximity, there may be an averaging of care across all beds.[23] The private-pay rest-home residents may receive higher or lower levels of nursing care than they are paying for. Indeed, publicly funded nursing-home per diems may be diverted to uses other than those intended and mandated.[24]

If care levels are not blended, rest-home residents receive precisely the care they contracted for. In these cases, residents may have been influenced by misleading, though not inaccurate, advertising of the nursing-home component.

This Commission believes that there is substantial risk of averaging out levels of care in dual facilities to the probable detriment of the nursing-home residents, in contravention of the *Nursing Homes Act*. If care is not blended, there is little need for the two residences to be on the same site. Quite the contrary, for it creates new large institutions rather than home-like settings.

RECOMMENDATION 8: That the *Nursing Homes Act* or its successor prevent licensed nursing homes from having a rest home on the same premises.

The Branch will need to develop an empirical indicator of "the same premises" that produces an effective physical and operational separation between nursing home and rest home. We assume all current blended sites might be grandfathered, and further development of this form prohibited.

4
The Regulatory Dilemma

1 Office for Senior Citizens' Affairs, *Findings of the Survey of Rest and Retirement Homes* (April 1989). The survey defined a rest home (p.3) as "a home ... which provides for a fee accommodation and residential care to two or more unrelated adult persons but would not include a hospital ... or any other facility if its services are licensed, approved or regulated by provincial legislation." "Residential care" was defined as "supervision and assistance with activities of daily living." Data for this survey were reported by owners/operators.

2 Of the 550 homes to whom the survey was sent, 535 provided information on their size, reporting 23,620 beds in total.

Recent Ontario government concern with rest-home regulation began with *A New Agenda: Health and Social Service Strategies for Ontario's Seniors* (June 1986): "The government will explore all appropriate options ... and take the necessary steps to ensure that rest homes are subject to appropriate regulation." The Office for Senior Citizens' Affairs (OSCA) then launched an initiative to generate a data base on rest and retirement homes, for not even the most basic information on the industry and its residents existed.[1] The Office contracted with the Ontario Social Development Council to develop a comprehensive inventory identifying all rest and retirement homes in the province and to survey these homes. Information was solicited on the characteristics of the homes, residents' profile, and the care and services being provided.

The data were collected as of September 1987 and provide the only detailed information to date on rest homes in Ontario. There was a 79 percent response rate, identifying 550 homes comprising more than 22,000 beds.[2] This is the source of the commonly cited 1991 estimate of about 25,000–30,000 rest-home beds in Ontario.

Among the interesting findings of the OSCA survey were the following:

1. The homes range in size from two beds to more than 500 beds, with a mean of forty-four beds and a median of twenty-seven. Nearly 80 percent of the homes have sixty beds or fewer, and 56 percent have thirty beds or fewer; however, 56 percent of the total beds are in homes with more than sixty beds.

2. Sixty-six percent of the homes (14,551 beds) serve primarily elderly clients—at least 75 percent of residents are sixty-five years of age or older. Residents older than sixty-five represent 84 percent of all residents of rest homes;[3] of those residents younger than sixty-five, persons with psychiatric histories represented the largest group.

3. All but ten of the 433 homes responding to the question item dealing with auspice were privately owned and run for profit.

4. Two thousand five hundred and ninety-four residents (18 percent of residents in the homes responding to the questionnaire) are supported through the domiciliary-hostel provision of the General Welfare Assistance (GWA) Regulations. In those homes serving primarily residents younger than sixty-five, approximately 65 percent of all residents are funded in this way. Such residents are found in 45 percent of rest homes in Ontario.

Former Toronto alderman Anne Johnston was contracted to meet with elected representatives of local governments to discuss the municipal view on regulation. Interviews were conducted with representatives of forty-five municipalities across the province.

In her report of September 1987, Ms Johnston noted that in general, municipalities favoured province-wide standards that could be administered and enforced locally. There was also an expectation of 100 percent provincial funding for any future additional local responsibilities.

An extensive consultation process was begun in March 1987 to identify issues and make recommendations to the

3 The OSCA survey would appear to significantly under-report the numbers of persons under sixty-five years of age in rest homes, compared to the census estimates of the Roeher Institute study, discussed above. Thus, the total population might well have been in excess of 550 homes and 22,000 residents.

4 *Rest and Retirement: A Report on the Regulation of Residential Care Facilities* from the Advisory Committee on Rest Homes to the minister for Senior Citizens' Affairs (April 1989).

minister for Senior Citizens' Affairs. Seventy-eight submissions were received, most expressing support for the regulation of standards of care in rest homes. An Advisory Committee, chaired by Alderman Jacqueline Holzman of Ottawa, submitted its report in April 1989.[4]

The present Commission of Inquiry has some difficulty with the orientation of the Advisory Committee. The Committee held that "All Ontarians have the right to an adequate system of care in rest homes." It is our view that all Ontarians have the right to an adequate system of care. Whether this care is delivered in rest homes or elsewhere should not be prejudged.

The Committee also held that the rest home should be viewed as the resident's home "from a philosophical perspective" but "not … when legal matters are under consideration." No rationale is given for drawing a distinction between philosophical and legal entitlements, though the effect is to preclude, a priori, coverage of rest homes under the *Landlord and Tenant Act(LTA)*.

The Committee's commitment to the "protection of operators" and their "desire to ensure a viable industry" rather surprised us. In the resident-centred approach we prefer, the primary concern would be to protect vulnerable residents. Nor do we consider the assurance of a viable industry to be a goal in itself: the industry exists to serve residents; if and when this need no longer exists, government is not obliged to support a non-viable industry.

The Advisory Committee recommended that standards of care in rest homes be regulated as part of a comprehensive rationalization of the extended- and residential-care systems in nursing homes and homes for the aged, i.e., a single piece of legislation should govern residential care, whether provided in nursing homes, homes for the aged, or rest homes. It also recommended that enforcement be carried out at the municipal level. Until such a law is in force, the Committee recommended provincial enabling legislation that would permit municipalities to regulate standards of care, and drafting by the province of a model by-law.

A Long-Term-Care Task Force was established by the provincial government in 1989. Rest and retirement homes were not within its mandate, as the focus was to be on programs and services already regulated by government.

In sum, there have been several initiatives over the years, reflecting the increasing severity of the problem. There has, however, been no tangible outcome to date.

CANADIAN COMPARISONS

The Commission wished to learn how accommodation corresponding to a rest home is regulated in other jurisdictions across Canada. We therefore created brief descriptions of a "typical" boarding home for an individual with low income and a "typical" luxury retirement home. We asked each province to describe its relevant forms of inspection or regulation.

Ontario is the only province with an unregulated rest-home sector.[5] All other provinces mandate standards. Some deal only with matters of physical plant; others attempt to regulate care, as well. (At the end of this chapter is a brief discussion of the experience of three provinces—British Columbia, Manitoba, and Nova Scotia—that is particularly informative.)

Generally, provinces that regulate standards of physical accommodation and care in rest-home-type accommodation also set the per diem rates that operators may charge low-income persons. Residents who require financial assistance to pay the per diem are means tested. This government "funding" also depends on an individualized assessment of the care needs of prospective residents and may include control over who is admitted to which facility. It is significant that British Columbia is phasing out government fund-

5 The *Fire Marshals Act* and the *Public Health Act* are universally applicable across Ontario.

6 The "objectives," as we have seen, are the protection and empowerment of vulnerable adults.

ing of facilities that provide low levels of care in favour of delivering more care services in the community.

A Range of Views

Two central questions were posed in this Commission's call for submissions:

> 1. Is regulation/licensing the most appropriate response for the provincial government?
> 2. Are there alternatives or complements to regulation that will better accomplish the objectives?[6]

Briefs and presentations to the Commission advocated widely varying approaches. A few argued for no intervention, on the ideological grounds that government should not interfere in the workings of the private market (particularly when, as in the case of rest homes, the market was functioning reasonably well). Most participants favoured regulation of some sort, typically arguing that there is a recognized problem in the rest-home sector; that it is a governmental responsibility to protect vulnerable adults; and that regulation is the best way to achieve this end. Few briefs explored the definition or implications of regulation; most assumed that the term merely described government doing what was necessary to achieve the desired ends.

There is a continuum of possible governmental interventions, which differ in purpose, impact, and cost—from the minimal to the comprehensive.

The least of these is registration: operators register with the public authorities, merely to inform them of the existence and operation of their rest homes. Numerous concerns have been conveyed to the Commission that local authorities do not know of the existence and location of all rest homes and that such data would be useful to public authorities and consumer groups. Clearly, the cost would be minimal, and the implementation uncomplicated.

The next step along the continuum of intervention would be voluntary accreditation or certification. This involves meeting certain professional standards or conditions, usually specified by an industry association. Accreditation may provide useful information for consumers about what operators choose to do or sell. It also implies that setting and meeting accreditation conditions or standards is likely to result in higher-quality care. The costs of this approach, which depend on the conditions or standards set, are usually borne by the operators or accrediting body.

Farther along the continuum is licensing. To hold a licence, one must meet standards that can be checked prior to issuance and/or by regular inspection to ensure the standards continue to be met. Licensing implies certain decisions: are licences issued in limited or unlimited numbers; if limited, are they transferable; i.e., can they be sold. Taxi or nursing-home licences are limited in numbers and are transferable; as such, they are an asset and carry property rights. Removing them amounts to expropriation and can be done only for cause. The process is difficult, time-consuming, costly, and fraught with legal complexity.

At the end of the continuum is regulation: standards are set by government, and authority is provided to monitor and secure compliance. The term "comprehensive regulation" (on the nursing-home model), as used in this Report, means regulation with the following three characteristics:

1. mandatory standards apply in all covered accommodation and include both care and physical standards;[7]
2. government inspectors (either provincial or municipal) enforce the standards; and
3. in some cases, government will fund private operators directly so that the standards can be met.[8]

7 In nursing homes, the standards are contained in the *Nursing Homes Act* and its regulations. Some municipalities enact by-laws that set such standards for all local rest homes.

8 In nursing homes, there is a per diem paid to operators; in some communities, rest-home residents on social assistance may be eligible for per diem funding under the hostel provisions of GWA.

The Commission has considered each point on the continuum of intervention. Our views are set out below.

VOLUNTARY ACCREDITATION

The Commission rejects voluntary accreditation or certification as being insufficient to safeguard the public interest. Voluntary measures, by definition, imply that some operators will not participate and compliance cannot be enforced. However, a voluntary accreditation system might provide useful information. A "star-rating" scheme, similar to that used for hotels, might provide consumers with information about potential residences and thereby lessen the likelihood of poor choices. The onus for the system's implementation must lie primarily with the industry, and would be supplementary to other measures considered in this Report.

> **RECOMMENDATION 9:** That the rest-home industry consider a system of voluntary accreditation similar to the star rating used in the hotel industry.

THE CASE FOR REGULATION

Regulation is often necessary because private-market decisions do not or cannot produce socially acceptable outcomes. For example, if the competence and/or bargaining power of vulnerable consumers cannot be enhanced sufficiently to produce choices that adequately reflect their priorities and preferences (and those of the wider community), the imbalance of power between a vulnerable buyer and a seller will not be rectified by the free market.

Some argue that this imbalance might be offset through the involvement of advocates and other outside supports, but the cost is likely to be prohibitive. If resources adequate to approximately equalize bargaining power are unlikely to be provided, regulation is considered the next best means of protecting vulnerable persons.

More specifically, there are three broad objectives of regulation:

Protecting Vulnerable Persons

Many presentations to the Commission favour regulation as the only way to protect vulnerable adults and to ensure they receive acceptable care. Some vulnerable adults are unable to articulate their preferences, or are unable to act upon them for reasons of disability, powerlessness, socialization into dependence and passivity, overmedication, inappropriate medication, or inadequate resources. These submissions argue that it is the responsibility of the community to ensure through collective intervention that vulnerable adults are not subject to neglect, abuse, or exploitation.

This possibly paternalistic but inevitably benevolent argument holds that given the obvious need for support and a clear governmental responsibility to protect, regulation is the best/obvious/only way to proceed. The costs of the approach and the practical difficulties in effecting successful regulation are usually downplayed.

Protecting Operators

Regulation is also a means to protect the interests of operators. Regulation assumes standards, rules, and conditions that must be met. Those who will not or cannot meet these conditions will leave the industry; those who remain will be seen as more credible.

For many years, the rest-home industry opposed regulation: it considered itself a private-sector initiative that should be free of governmental interference. More recently, the dominant (if not universal) view among owners and operators has changed: regulation and its associated standards are now seen as a way to eliminate less-reputable operators who discredit

9 Regulation would also likely
imply consistent compensation for particular services.

the majority, and to gain recognition and acceptance of the industry in the long-term-care sector and in the business community. However, government-imposed standards must come with funding for residents on social assistance that is adequate for the industry to meet these standards.

Regulation would set parameters for the industry and define precisely what qualifies as a rest home. Thus, operators would be protected from consumers' unrealistic or unreasonable expectations.

Consistency

Lack of uniform treatment has been a recurring theme before the Commission. Families, operators, residents, and interest groups have stressed the inequity of current inconsistent treatment, and the practical difficulties of negotiating one's way through a system wherein conditions and rules are nowhere clearly and comprehensively set out. Regulation requires that the industry comply with specific standards and, in some cases, that everyone do the same thing in the same way. Regulation of the industry would thus likely create consistent province-wide or municipal standards.[9]

The interests of municipalities could be protected by provincial regulation, which could identify the rights and responsibilities of municipalities. Regulations would also clearly define the roles and authority of various professionals, such as public-health nurses and fire inspectors.

THE CASE AGAINST REGULATION

The Commission has heard presentations arguing that regulation, particularly comprehensive regulation on the nursing-home model, is not appropriate to the rest-home sector.

Housing groups have generally opposed rigorous standards because higher costs to rest-home operators will inevitably decrease the availability of low-income accommodation. Some advocacy groups have opposed comprehensive regulation because they oppose the creation of new private-sector, government-funded or -subsidized institutions: they particularly do not want to emulate the nursing-home model and advocate instead the urgent development of community-based in-home services.

There are six main arguments put forward:

Disempowerment

Perhaps the most compelling argument against extensive regulation is that residents can be excluded from important decisions affecting their accommodation. Rules and standards are determined politically or bureaucratically, and enforced by the regulator. The residents have little involvement in deciding what is acceptable, and little power over ensuring its attainment.[10]

Decreased Supply

Regulated standards increase costs to operators. Some operations will no longer be economically viable and will close down. The result will be a reduced supply of accommodation.

It is assumed the luxury retirement-home industry operates at a relatively high standard and would be little affected, in dollar terms, by new regulatory requirements. Thus it is unlikely that any accommodation in this sector would leave the market as a direct result of new regulated standards.

The issue is critical, however, at the low end of the market. Given that many residents live on fixed incomes, operators would be unable to pass on increased costs. Thus, profits would be reduced, and some housing would be converted to other uses, thereby decreasing the supply of rest-home places. And, of course, some operators would simply ignore the regulations.

Advocacy groups for the most marginally housed have

10 There is also little incentive for residents to become more independent in rest homes; by their very nature, regulations impose a constant and uniform standard that may have little relevance to individual needs and capabilities.

11 Elasticity of market demand—the sensitivity of response patterns among consumers to changes in price—would influence the sharing of these higher costs between buyer and seller.

12 Old Age Security/Guaranteed Income Supplement/Guaranteed Annual Income System

13 By way of illustration, we note a proposal from the Regional Municipality of Hamilton-Wentworth submitted to the provincial government in 1989. (City of Hamilton and Regional Municipality of Hamilton-Wentworth, *A Pilot Project to Implement a New Second-Level Lodging House By-Law* [May 1989]). In this document, the sum of $1.2 million was sought to upgrade the inspection of lodging homes and to plug some perceived gaps in the coverage of the by-law. Though the funds were originally sought as a pilot project, ongoing support was anticipated.

In the Commission's view, the more one regulates, the more those regulated attempt to find loopholes, and the loopholes are identified and plugged with more regulation. A regulatory system, almost by definition, can never be "complete" as long as those regulated are free to alter their actions.

repeatedly stressed opposition to regulation, because it inevitably results in dehousing, particularly in communities in which the supply of low-quality housing is severely limited.

This issue is among the most straightforward—and the most troubling—to come before the Commission. The intent of regulations and standards is to protect vulnerable persons; however, if the effect of regulation is to eliminate scarce housing, is this protection? Is substandard housing that may place residents at immediate physical risk better than no housing?

Higher Cost

The increased costs of meeting higher standards would be passed on to consumers whenever and to the maximum extent possible.[11] Many rest-home residents cannot absorb higher costs without commensurate increases in social assistance. The Commission set out the need to offset these higher costs in the Discussion Paper (p.17):

> If government mandates a certain level (and cost) of service, and if government determines what consumers can pay through social assistance or OAS/GIS/GAINS,[12] then government must bridge the gap between what it expects from owners and operators and what it is prepared to provide to consumers. This is a statement of both ethical propriety and operational necessity.

Without such increases, standards would be ignored, often with the tacit acquiescence of the regulatory authorities.

The typically substantial administrative costs associated with regulation are considered necessary to ensure compliance, which involves detailed technical and legal procedures. In addition, the more comprehensive the regulation and the more extensive the inspection, the greater the staffing costs.[13]

We must ask if scarce public funds are best spent in building up an endless regulatory system, given that every dollar spent on a regulatory system cannot simultaneously be devoted to community-based programs and service delivery.

Technical Problems

Regulation is most effective as objective measurement of processes and structures. In practice, however, not everything can be so measured. Some important indicators of quality of care tend to be very subjective; and that which is not quantifiable will often be ignored in a regulatory system: if it can't be measured, it can't be enforced.

If some elements of a system are regulated and controlled, operators will tend to cut corners on the unregulated aspects, where there is less or no scrutiny. For example, one can regulate nutrition relating to a minimum daily caloric intake, but not whether food is tasty or even palatable. Moreover, regulation depends on extensive record-keeping to document compliance, reinforced by a combination of good will and occasional inspections. Yet the Commission has been repeatedly told by residents of boarding homes that food standards—to continue the example—are met when inspectors are present, but ignored at other times.[14] One can attempt through regulation to ensure food meets nutritional standards, is safe and free of dangerous ingredients, though even this is operationally difficult. Beyond that, however, meaningful consumer satisfaction is likely to be measurable only on a subjective basis.[15]

As a result, standards for quality often tend to have the effect of guidelines rather than legal requirements.

Staffing/Bureaucratic Problems

Professional inspectors make informed judgments based on their training and knowledge. Those exercising professional discretion also understand that strict enforcement through a legal process tends to be slow, while an informal approach can often clear up matters quickly. Thus they tend to favour conciliation and reject an adversarial stance in an attempt to

[14] See Donna M. Woolcott, *Nutritional Value and Quality of Food Served in Contracted Second-Level Lodging Homes in the Regional Municipality of Hamilton-Wentworth*, University of Guelph, January 1992, p.29.

None of this information is particularly new: the Commission has examined experiences in other areas—from child care to consumer purchases of funerals and travel—subject to the operational dilemmas of regulation. The travel industry is perhaps the closest analogy, as purchasers obtain a package of accommodation, meals, and certain services. Experience in the travel industry supports the view that in certain areas (for example, quality assurance), there is little that can be done from a regulatory perspective.

[15] The Commission is aware of a study done in 1988 by a dietetic intern involving a two-week assessment of the nutritional value and quality of foods served in a non-representative sample of second-level lodging homes in Hamilton. The student found that five of six homes offered milk with every meal, but four of these used skim milk powder "which was not accepted by most of the residents" and one home "was observed to over-dilute the skim milk." (Memo from Medical Officer of Health to Chairman and Members, Health and Social Services Committee, Regional Municipality of Hamilton-Wentworth, June 2, 1988.) See also Woolcott, op.cit.

16 Another aspect of the problem is the reliance on a quasi-criminal prosecutorial model of enforcement. This depends on the ability to collect suitable evidence and the will to prosecute, and requires a high standard of proof.

build good working relationships with operators. The hope is that self-regulation and ethical behaviour will exist even when no inspector is present. Many inspectors consider themselves educational and training consultants and resource persons for operators, who are well disposed but may be ill equipped. They do not want to be policemen.

Inspectors may also identify with operators more than with the residents for reasons of economic class, social background, or professional status. Operators and inspectors develop a permanent working relationship; residents come and go. Moreover, the supports and protection promised to residents through a regulatory system may not materialize because of enforcement problems, lack of political will, or local political priorities.

The public interest may also be sacrificed, not necessarily by conscious collusion but through the gradual development of a community of interest among the permanent players. The professionals—the suppliers of accommodation and care and the inspectors—are more disposed to maintain congenial relationships with one another than to satisfy the consumer. The problem is exacerbated when the consumers tend to be particularly vulnerable, as is the case with rest-home populations.

Collegial relationships among the permanent players lead to a reluctance to impose legal sanctions. Informal persuasion, while strongly commended as a first approach, can be effective only when backed up by the threat of more stringent measures if necessary.

Sanctions and Penalties

In many regulatory systems, sanctions are not imposed, even when standards are not met, at least in part because of the difficulties of satisfying legal due-process requirements.[16] Political ambivalence regarding the needs of vulnerable persons is widespread, as is the fear of imposing inordinate cost burdens on operators and/or dehousing vulnerable residents.

An additional problem is the lack of a range of sanctions.

For example, licensing often permits only extreme penalties—suspension or revocation. A by-law prosecution may result in the imposition of a fine. A small fine is merely a nuisance; a large fine will be passed on to residents in the form of fewer or lower-quality services and/or higher prices, or the operator will close down.

With a shortage of housing and a lack of alternative accommodation for vulnerable residents, the threat of penalties—even of closing a residence—is unlikely to have teeth. The regulators need the housing as much as or more than those being regulated need the residents. In some cases, like that of Cedar Glen, it is not the inspectors but the operators who hold the real power.

The nursing-home experience in Ontario provides corroboration. The 1990 Annual Report of the provincial auditor concluded that "the procedures used … to monitor the quality of care in nursing homes required significant improvement."[17]

The Commission has considered the two-stage compliance management program used in nursing homes:[18] at the first stage, compliance advisers attempt to "focus on the resolution of deficiencies by consultation rather than on prosecution."[19] When consultation, education, and collaboration are not effective, enforcement officers are called in for further monitoring, and investigation if necessary.

The number of charges laid under the *Nursing Homes Act* has dropped from 497 in 1984, to twelve in 1988, to zero in 1989. In 1989, there were no homes charged, no charges laid, and no convictions under the *Nursing Homes Act*.[20] In addition, the provincial auditor has observed that over 40 percent of homes did not receive any visits during the year other than the annual licence-renewal visit. The report notes that these changes "can, in part, be explained by the new Compliance Management approach…. Additionally, homes have not been properly transferred into the Enforcement section. Moreover, the results of judicial decisions have shown that violations of many provisions … cannot be successfully prosecuted."[21]

17 Office of the Provincial Auditor, 1990 Annual Report, p.39. The Commission cannot comment on the efficacy of any improved compliance mechanisms introduced recently or proposed for introduction.

18 This was implemented in early 1988 and officially began in April 1990.

19 Auditor's *Report*, p.145.

20 Auditor's *Report*, p.144–45.

21 Auditor's *Report*, p.143, 145.

22 The hostel system is discussed at length in chapter 7.

23 The City of Toronto has recently passed a personal-care by-law, but Habitat utilizes contracts with participating operators. The Region of Ottawa-Carleton developed a by-law, but has held off enacting it in the absence of provincial enabling legislation.

24 Based on the most recent figures provided to us by the Ministry of Municipal Affairs. (Municipal Analysis and Retrieval System, data base, July 6, 1990.)

Current Practice in Ontario

There is no specific Ontario legislation regulating rest homes, only laws of general application, such as public-health and fire-safety legislation. Some local governments have assumed responsibility for local rest homes in an attempt to ensure minimum standards. (These primarily affect rest homes at the lower end of the market.)

Some municipalities enact local by-laws, often reluctantly, because the province "is not doing its proper job." Another approach is more limited in scope: standards are set by contract between a municipality and individual operators receiving domiciliary-hostel funding under the *General Welfare Assistance Act* (*GWAA*);[22] and per diem payments are dependent on compliance with those standards. In most communities, however, enforcement is difficult, under either the by-law or contract approach. There are limited local resources, particularly as social-assistance costs consume an increasing share of local attention and monies.

We shall briefly look at the approaches of four communities to the regulation of rest-home accommodation: two (Hamilton and Windsor) have comprehensive rest-home by-laws and negotiate hostel contracts. The other two (Ottawa-Carleton and Metro Toronto, through Habitat Services) utilize contracts.[23] Other municipalities follow the general approach used by one of these four or rely only on general provincial and municipal powers.

THE BY-LAW APPROACH

The number of municipalities with local by-laws has roughly doubled from a year ago, to approximately sixty.[24] Some acted after particularly intolerable events in unregulated accommodation gained public and media attention; others acted to prevent such situations from occurring. Some by-laws have been developed with substantial operator input; all focus on meeting needs, delivering quality care, and protecting vulnerable persons.

Coverage, content, and enforcement vary widely. Some by-laws regulate physical standards—such as lighting levels in rooms, bedroom space, dining-room size, and resident/toilet ratios. Others also regulate care—such as nutritional sufficiency of meals, procedures for the administration of medications, and minimum resident/staff ratios.

All municipal by-laws are passed pursuant to section 208(61) of the Ontario *Municipal Act.* It is generally agreed that the *Municipal Act* permits licensing and regulation of physical standards and sanitary conditions; however, municipal by-laws that regulate care standards would likely not be upheld by the courts.[25]

Hamilton and Windsor have systems of comprehensive regulation by municipal by-laws covering all rest-home accommodation.[26] The two by-laws are broadly the same; however, Hamilton sets an upper limit of twenty-four beds in any residence eligible for a hostel contract. This "cottage-industry" model has been criticized by operators as inefficient and precluding economies of scale. Windsor, at the other extreme, has several massive rest homes. The largest has approximately 450 beds, and six homes have more than 100 beds; there are few small operations in the for-profit sector.

The cities of Etobicoke and of Toronto also have municipal personal-care by-laws. Toronto's by-law (passed in July 1991) is more modest than Hamilton's or Windsor's.

It is evident to this Commission that if regulation by comprehensive municipal by-law is to continue, local communities must be given an explicit legal basis for such by-laws. Current approaches, largely based on compliance by acquiescence, lack a foundation sufficient for municipal action.

25 The one exception, which is clearly legal, is the local Windsor by-law, passed after 1982 provincial enabling legislation. Operators in Windsor have observed, however, that the standards specified in the by-law are vague and subjective (because of the difficulties assessing non-measurable standards discussed earlier). As a result, they question whether the content of the by-law would be upheld, though the legal authority for the by-law itself would remain unchallenged.

26 Windsor's by-law, dating from 1978 (and formalizing a by-law from 1970), generally covered personal-care matters; however, it allowed considerable flexibility for the inspecting officials, such as the Medical Officer of Health. Windsor's by-law currently covers twenty rest homes with approximately 1,550 residents, of whom 560 are subsidized under the hostel provisions of GWA.

Hamilton's municipal by-law, passed in 1980, regulates in detail not only physical structures but also standards of personal care. The by-law was developed after a strong recommendation from the chief coroner of Ontario, who had conducted an inquest into one of three deaths in the city's lodging homes in 1977. When the Hamilton by-law was passed, the city was regulating forty-two houses, accommodating approximately 600 persons. Today the city licenses and regulates seventy-three facilities with a total capacity of 1,576.

27 Hamilton and Windsor require compliance with the by-law as a condition of receiving a hostel contract, i.e., compliance is, in effect, a condition of the contract.

28 Mental Health Program Services of Metropolitan Toronto (MHPS) is the legal name of the non-profit agency that administers Habitat Services. MHPS has a dual mandate, the operation of Habitat Services in Metro Toronto and the development of a co-ordinated system for mental-health services in the City of Toronto. We deal primarily with the former role.

29 Habitat arose out of the shared concerns of Toronto and Metro, three provincial ministries (MoH, MCSS, and Housing), and the Supportive Housing Coalition. Habitat is the first involvement of Metro Toronto in subsidizing operating costs for housing former psychiatric patients. All the participants were involved in housing people having psychiatric histories, although the particular focus was on the Parkdale area of Toronto. Those discharged from Queen Street Mental Health Centre and, earlier, from Lakeshore Psychiatric Hospital have been drawn to Parkdale because of its proximity to the former institution and its traditional availability of low-cost, low-standard accommodation.

THE CONTRACT APPROACH

Some municipalities regulate through contract rather than attempting to enforce a by-law without provincial enabling legislation. Ottawa currently relies on contracts under the hostel provisions of the GWA Regulations. The standards required are roughly comparable to those in the Hamilton and Windsor by-laws; however, rest-home operator participation in the hostel system—and, hence, compliance with the conditions in its contract—is voluntary. Those rest homes that do not hold hostel contracts are not subject to the contract standards.[27]

Habitat Services

Habitat Services,[28] founded in 1986, is a community-based non-profit agency in Metropolitan Toronto that negotiates and enforces contracts with individual operators. Funds are provided in part under the hostel provisions of GWA.[29] The contract specifies physical standards, which must be met for an entire house if even only one resident is funded by Habitat, and personal-care requirements for Habitat-covered residents.

A life-skills or social/recreational program in homes under contract is contracted to Community Occupational Therapy Associates (COTA), a non-profit agency. It is central to the Habitat program that the housing provider (Habitat) be distinct from the service provider (COTA).

As of January 1991, Habitat had contracts covering 610 beds in thirty-two boarding homes, all but three operating for profit. (Habitat projected that 950 beds would be covered in 1993–94.) For a resident to be subsidized, Habitat must do the placement; as of January 1991, there were sixty-one identified agencies from whom referrals were accepted. Residents express concerns about the quality of Habitat housing but acknowledge that physical and personal-care standards are substantially better than in non-Habitat housing.

Because it is funded through the Ministry of Health (MoH),

Habitat is restricted to people with psychiatric histories. Those vulnerable adults excluded from the program, such as those with developmental disabilities, inevitably obtain only poor-quality rest-home accommodation.[30] They have only the modest protection of the local personal-care by-laws in the cities of Toronto and Etobicoke, and no local protection in the rest of Metro.[31]

Not all Ontario municipalities participate in the domiciliary-hostel program under GWA. One municipality has withdrawn recently, thereby forgoing its power to regulate through contract; others are contemplating such moves and have threatened withdrawal.

Towards a New Approach

The arguments regarding regulation are wide ranging, yet the Commission found only a relatively narrow band of feasible options.

The option of retaining the status quo was rejected in the Discussion Paper, for it was the failure of a non-regulatory approach that led to the original need for this Commission. Nothing in the interim has emerged to change our minds. The case for government activity is based not on ideology but on empirical evidence: neglect and inadequate protection lead, in some cases, to abuse, exploitation, and death. The Commission has seen enough evidence, both hard and anecdotal, to be satisfied that there is a significant problem. Government has a responsibility—and an opportunity—to offer protection to vulnerable adults.

We are also reluctant to recommend comprehensive regulation because of the many disadvantages we have identified as inherent in the approach.

Comprehensive regulation would create a system of low-level or first-stage nursing homes. Some have argued that this is desirable or necessary, given the population demographics

30 Housing outside the Habitat program is a source of low-quality accommodation in Metropolitan Toronto to an extremely vulnerable population, some of whom might be homeless were higher standards imposed across the board. The potential loss of housing for this most disadvantaged group is a very real operational problem, particularly in the centre of Toronto.

31 If applicants are diagnosed as having both a psychiatric disability and a developmental disability, they are then eligible for Habitat.

32 Without provincial enabling legislation such by-laws may be *ultra vires*.

33 Contracts can be signed between residents and operators, or between municipalities and operators.

34 At the same time we note the potential dehousing effect of higher standards set in by-laws. Those who remain housed will live in better conditions, but others (in particular those on social assistance) will lose accommodation, as some operators cannot or will not meet higher standards.

35 The standards obtained through contracts depend on the bargaining power of the parties: this power varies with the supply of housing in the community and the financial resources at the disposal of the consumer (or the municipality on behalf of residents funded through the domiciliary-hostel system). The standards set through by-laws also depend on relative bargaining power, mediated by the judgments of local councils about the resources of potential consumers (in particular those on social assistance), the ability of operators to provide a particular level of accommodation and care in exchange for those resources, and other political considerations.

and the shortage of licensed nursing-home beds. Others argue against the creation of more inflexible institutions, with all the problems associated with such inflexibility, and stress instead the need for portable and in-home services. We have already indicated our support for the latter position.

Data from the provincial auditor provides a powerful argument against comprehensive regulation of rest homes in Ontario. As well, the many reservations about this approach to protecting vulnerable adults seem to be validated by the experience of the nursing-home industry.

The Commission cannot endorse comprehensive regulation of rest homes on the nursing-home model.

CONTRACTS OR BY-LAWS

Some municipalities have enacted by-laws that set standards for the physical environment of rest homes that may be above that permitted by provincial legislation. Some by-laws also cover care in rest homes, an area in which there are no provincial standards.[32] Some presentations before the Commission have argued that municipalities should have the authority to set standards of care in local rest homes; others have maintained that a contractual approach would be more effective.[33]

In the Commission's view, there are three crucial factors in comparing contracts and by-laws: coverage, empowerment, and flexibility.

One of the major strengths of by-laws is that no rest home is exempt from the higher standards;[34] as such, the approach may be particularly effective in raising standards for those on OAS or social assistance who have neither the resources nor bargaining power to obtain higher standards on their own. (The standards obtained through contracts, as we have noted, apply only to those holding contracts.)[35]

The by-law approach is more likely to exclude residents

from the decision-making process; by-laws give municipal authorities the right and responsibility to determine what is acceptable. Enforcement is also the responsibility of municipal officials. Contracts (and leases) between residents and operators have a greater ability to achieve our central goal of resident empowerment. They provide residents with direct involvement in determining standards and the right to seek operators' compliance.

Municipal rest-home by-laws are usually combined with municipal licensing.[36] Failure to meet standards may lead to prosecutions under the by-law; a persistent failure to meet standards (often evidenced by by-law convictions) may lead to the ultimate sanction, removal of the licence, i.e., the legal permission to operate a rest home. By-laws are generally enforced by prosecutions in courts; these may result in convictions, which in themselves may be a deterrent, and the imposition of fines.

Prosecutions, convictions, and impositions of fines may not be the most appropriate response to a failure to meet standards. Moreover, they may not be a deterrent: penalties may be minimal if the offence is considered to be not serious; and multiple offences may be needed before substantial fines are levied. The response time may be long due to scheduling and backlogs in the courts.

Contracts permit considerable creativity. Parties can agree in advance on their rights and obligations. The terms of the contract and the common law dictate the effect of the actions of the parties, the consequences, and the remedies. A substantial breach or default in performance may result in termination.

Thus we believe that contracts can provide for more appropriate consequences and penalties in the context of the rest home. This is particularly so in domiciliary-hostel agreements, which can provide for temporary or permanent loss of funding in response to a failure to meet standards and can be more responsive to a history of poor compliance. Other con-

36 These licences, when given, may create a property right.

37 This approach is not possible with a lease, in which case the relevant provisions of the *LTA* would apply.

38 Again, these conditions do not apply in case of a lease. When a government, in this case a municipality, is party to a contract, there may be greater due-process requirements than in contracts between private parties. For this reason, some have suggested that a community agency may be in a better position to make the domiciliary-hostel agreements. It could then more easily be specified that contracts, unlike licences, need no hearing to cancel or suspend them, and that they can be cancelled without cause.

ditions and outcomes can be specified, as well, including intervention for the welfare of residents: a reduction in the number of domiciliary-hostel residents permitted in a rest home; emergency care or supervision, or the provision of necessities with the costs chargeable to the operators.

Standards in by-laws must be precisely worded to sustain a conviction and the standard of proof required is the highest possible: beyond a reasonable doubt. Discretionary standards are more easily provided for in contracts for services. Objective measurements or assessments of quality of care required in a by-law approach can be replaced by more subjective assessments of consumer satisfaction.[37]

Determinations can be made by individual consumers, or by an agency (including the municipality) on behalf of and after consultation with residents. The residents or municipalities can refuse to pay for services below the quality contracted for or can refuse to continue purchasing such services. For example the Habitat contract specifies that "the parties specifically agree that the determination of [Habitat Services], in its absolute discretion, as to whether or not any of the Standards are met shall be final and binding on the parties" (section 16).

The authority to terminate a rest-home licence is one way to attempt to ensure compliance with standards. However, licences can be difficult to cancel; and generally, they are not cancelled for minor infractions. The process can be slow, requiring municipal hearings and substantial due process.

Contracts can avoid due-process requirements that are as onerous as those that must be contained in by-laws; these requirements may be negotiated by the parties to the contract.[38]

It is the Commission's view that consumers should determine what standards are acceptable (above minimum safety and health levels) through contractual negotiations with rest-home operators. (These minima will be discussed in detail in Part III.)

RECOMMENDATION 10: That standards (physical and care) above the minima recommended by the Commission be achieved through contracts with operators.

Part I of this Report has set out the framework within which we approach our task. We have presented a formal definition of a rest home, distinguishing it from other settings, such as nursing homes. We have also drawn three conclusions that will be of considerable importance throughout this Report:

1. The rest home should be viewed as residents' permanent accommodation. It is not a new type of institution or a place of temporary sojourn.
2. Comprehensive regulation on the nursing-home model is not the best way to achieve our twin goals of facilitating empowerment and offering protection to vulnerable adults.
3. Above specified minimum safety and health levels, quality for physical and care standards can best be attained through voluntary contracts, not through comprehensive by-laws.

Part II of the Report examines the implications of these findings, focusing particularly on the key issues of coverage under the *Landlord and Tenant Act* and rent control. Part III presents our preferred approach, which includes regulation for the attainment of certain minimum standards. As well, we shall present a variety of measures that, we believe, will not only promote empowerment and protection of vulnerable adults, but will do so at lower public cost than comprehensive regulation, with greater accountability for public spending, and less interference in individual decision-making and private commerce.

1 A personal-care facility may have all beds funded, all beds on a private-pay basis, or a mix.

2 Where a residence has some funded and some unfunded accommodation, there may be a problem with cross-subsidization. For example, the higher standards in a funded bed may be met by using funds received for the private-pay bed.

APPENDIX:
Experience in Three Provinces

In order to provide a working context for our discussion, we summarize here the way three other provinces treat rest-home-type accommodation, i.e., residences in which room, board, and minimal levels of care and/or supervision are provided by owner/operators. All three provinces have chosen regulation as the means by which standards are set and enforced.

BRITISH COLUMBIA

Known as "personal-care facilities" in B.C., rest homes are, by and large, operated on a for-profit basis. Enforcement of rest-home standards of physical accommodation and care is a provincial responsibility.

The province funds some accommodation in personal-care facilities through a per diem set by the government (currently 85 percent of OAS/GIS payments). Residents not in receipt of OAS/GIS may undergo a means test to qualify for subsidy. For other personal-care accommodation, no provincial funding is available; residents may pay privately.[1]

Provincially funded accommodation is subject to higher program and quality-assurance standards.[2] As well, the province decides who is eligible for funded personal-care accommodation on the basis of individual assessments of care needs; then the province controls admission to such beds as they become available. Operators set the charge for private-pay beds and decide who is admitted.

Personal-care accommodation has been part of a continuum of provincially funded residential care in British Columbia. Recently, however, the government has started to phase out funded personal-care beds. Facilities must either upgrade to intermediate-care accommodation or become private-pay. Eventually, all rest-home-type accommodation will be available only on a private-pay basis.

This plan may have several possible consequences: persons with low incomes and minimal care needs may be unable to find accommodation in a care facility, irrespective of the availability of care provided in their own homes; private-pay residences for low-income persons may be withdrawn from the housing market or may continue to operate at standards commensurate with low-income residents' ability to pay.

MANITOBA

Manitoba also regulates all rest-home-type residences. Called "residential-care facilities," most are operated on a for-profit basis. The resident population consists primarily of persons with developmental disabilities (68 percent); other residents are frail elderly persons (15 percent) and persons with psychiatric histories (16 percent).[3]

Each facility is licensed to provide one or more of five levels of care. Regulated standards cover physical conditions, levels of supervision, administration of medications, nutrition, and personal rights, but do not address personal-care or medical services. The province is responsible for enforcement of standards.

To be admitted to residential-care facilities, individuals must have their care needs assessed by the provincially mandated Regional Supervising Agency. Admission is restricted to persons who are ambulatory and capable of self-sufficient action in case of emergency.

The per diem rate for elderly persons is not provincially regulated. Rates vary from $600 to $900 a month. Seventy-five percent of the residents depend entirely on OAS/GIS and a provincial income supplement of up to $33 a month.

3 Most frail elderly persons in facilities reside in the next level of regulated facilities, known as "personal-care homes," equivalent to Ontario's nursing homes.

4 There is one rate for each of the five levels of care.

For persons with developmental disabilities or psychiatric histories, the province determines per diem payments on an assessment of individual care needs.4 Rates range from $479 to $703 a month. For residents on Income Security (social assistance), the province pays the rates and personal and clothing allowances.

Both funded and private-pay admissions are controlled by the province, which attempts to ensure that only persons whose needs can be met in the rest homes are admitted.

NOVA SCOTIA

The Nova Scotia government regulates and inspects rest-home-type accommodation. Known as "residential-care facilities," these are almost all operated on a for-profit basis and primarily serve elderly persons and persons with psychiatric histories.

Residents who require assistance are needs-tested for income and assets. Municipalities provide the subsidies for per diem payments to operators.

The province sets the per diem rate for subsidized residents (at cost plus 10 percent), currently $25–$30. Rates are determined by regional negotiation among the province, municipalities in the region, and local operators. The province assesses the care needs of applicants requiring financial assistance and controls admissions of such applicants to the facilities.

Approximately 50 percent of residents are private-pay. These residents may pay a higher per diem than subsidized residents, but there is an expectation that the extra charges relate to extra services.

The residential-care facilities precede nursing homes and homes for the aged on the residential-care continuum. All are governed by the same legislation; however, the standards for some types of care differ.

PART II

The Rest Home As Home

One of the important conclusions in Part I of this Report was that rest homes should be viewed as residents' permanent accommodation rather than as institutions or places of temporary sojourn. We also observed that the rest home differs from conventional private housing in that it provides accommodation with care.

Residents of rest homes are, in general, vulnerable or potentially so. Social intervention has therefore been deemed the appropriate means to meet the policy goals of protection and empowerment for this population. We have rejected comprehensive regulation on the nursing-home model, because such an approach is unlikely to meet these twin goals. In Part III we shall consider more modest regulation, which attempts only to ensure minimum safety standards are satisfied.

First, however, we approach the crucial questions of coverage of rest homes under the *Landlord and Tenant Act* (*LTA*) and Bill 121, the proposed *Rent Control Act, 1991* (*RCA*). We devote a chapter to each of the major types of accommodation setting of interest to this Inquiry. "Life at the Top" examines issues of particular relevance to retirement homes for persons with high incomes. "Life Near the Bottom" focuses on boarding (lodging/rest) homes for those with low incomes, with particular attention to the domiciliary-hostel system, funded under the *General Welfare Assistance Act* (*GWAA*).

We describe the quality of life experienced by those at the top and at the bottom, and highlight the problems that have been presented before us. We assess both the advantages and the limitations of coverage under these Acts. If coverage is to be recommended, we must indicate how the legislation should be amended to provide for the unique environment of the rest home, in which care services are provided along with accommodation and meals.

5
The *Landlord and Tenant Act* and Rent Control

At present, unless specifically exempted, all residential premises in Ontario are covered by the *Landlord and Tenant Act* (*LTA*); and in addition, all rental units in residential accommodation will be covered by Bill 121, the *Rent Control Act, 1991* (*RCA*).[1] The status of rest-home accommodation under these Acts is uncertain: operators maintain that rest homes are currently exempted from the *LTA* and rent regulation; some residents and their advocates have held the opposite. Attempts to resolve this debate have generated a tremendous amount of argument before the Commission and in other fora. Thus, confronting this central issue will directly influence much that follows in this Report.

As the *LTA* does not protect tenants against eviction for economic reasons and rent control does not protect tenants against arbitrary eviction, they can be effective only in tandem. Therefore, we will consider them together.

Owners and operators are opposed to coverage under the *LTA* and rent control; community and advocacy groups are generally in favour, although opinions differ on whether to include group and treatment homes. Residents of retirement homes have mixed views; residents of boarding homes almost unanimously support coverage.

Operators argue that coverage would impair their ability to

1 This Act will replace the current rent regulation legislation, the *Residential Rent Regulation Act* (*RRRA*).

2 *Reference Re Residential Tenancies Act*, [1981] 1 S.C.R. 717, at p.718 *per* Dickson, J.; *Re Baker et. al. and Hayward* (1977), 16 O.R. (2nd) 695 (Ont. C.A.), at p.699 *per* Wilson, J. A.; *Interim Report on Landlord and Tenant Law Applicable to Residential Tenancies*, Ontario Law Reform Commission, 1968, pp. 10–11, 43–44.

3 *Rent Control: Issues and Options*, A Consultation Paper from the Ministry of Housing, February 1991, p.8.

4 The *LTA* also specifies the procedure for eviction. The landlord must serve the tenant with a notice of termination with the amount of advance notice varying according to the grounds for eviction. If the tenant does not move out in accordance with the notice, the landlord must apply to the Ontario Court (General Division) for an order to terminate the tenancy. There are two court appearances, the second before a judge, if the tenant disputes the application for termination. A hearing is held and both parties are given an opportunity to present their cases.

operate efficient businesses, and would prevent them from "discharging" residents they consider inappropriate. (The need for speedy discharge is particularly important in settings where residents share rooms.) Operators consider that coverage under *LTA* violates their concept of the rest home as a point on the continuum of residential-care facilities. Moreover, rent control limits the operators' ability to set prices in response to market forces.

Residents respond that without the *LTA* and rent control they might be subject to arbitrary eviction and excessive rent increases that might force them to leave their homes. They also note that Part IV of the *LTA* was enacted to redress the imbalance of bargaining power between landlords and tenants, which historically favoured the former.[2]

The Ministry of Housing's Green Paper, February 1991, stated that the "preferred approach" was for rent control to cover the accommodation component of "facilities such as unlicensed rest and retirement homes."[3]

CONTENT OF THE ACTS

Part IV of the *LTA* provides protection to residential tenants, specifies the rights and responsibilities of landlords and tenants, and contains procedures for resolving disputes.[4]

The *LTA* provides "security of tenure" for residential tenants: tenants may remain indefinitely in their rented premises subject only to specified grounds for eviction. The "fault" grounds for eviction include the following:

1. the tenant fails to pay or is persistently late in paying the rent;
2. the tenant or guest has damaged the rental unit or its environs; carried on an illegal act or business in the rental unit or building; substantially interfered with the reason-

able enjoyment of the premises by the landlord or other tenants; and/or seriously impaired the safety or lawful rights of another tenant.[5]

The *LTA* also stipulates that:

1. tenants have the right to sublet or assign their apartments; landlords may reserve the right to consent, but such consent must not be unreasonably withheld;
2. landlords must give twenty-four hours' notice before entering tenants' premises (except in an emergency);[6]
3. neither party may change the locks giving entry to the rented premises without the consent of the other;
4. landlords must keep the premises in good repair, fit for habitation, and in compliance with health, safety, and housing standards;
5. landlords cannot withhold or interfere with the supply of vital services; and
6. landlords may not substantially interfere with tenants' reasonable enjoyment of the premises as a way to force tenants to leave or prevent them from asserting their rights as tenants.

The proposed *RCA* strengthens the existing rent-regulation provisions and controls the timing, procedures for, and amounts of, rent increases.

CURRENT STATUS

The *LTA* and the proposed *RCA* exempt from coverage "accommodation occupied by a person for penal, correctional, rehabilitative or therapeutic purposes or for the purpose of receiving care."[7]

Most rest homes claim exemption from the *LTA* and rent regulation on the grounds that they are "accommodation

5 There are also "no-fault" grounds for eviction: for example, landlords may require the premises for their own occupation or that of their immediate families, or landlords may wish to demolish the premises.

6 Entry without notice is also permitted if the landlord has reserved the right in the tenancy agreement to show the unit at reasonable hours to prospective tenants after notice of termination of the tenancy has been given.

7 Clause 1(c)(ix) of the *LTA* and paragraph 3(1)(e) in the proposed *RCA*. The *RCA* continues an exemption of such premises from rent regulation under the *RRRA* [paragraph 4 (1)(e)].

8 Accommodation occupied "for rehabilitative or therapeutic purposes" is also not defined in the legislation or in relevant case law.

9 Rent Review Hearings Board Decision in *Tenants of the Grenadier v. We-Care Retirement Homes of Canada Limited and 582958 Ontario Limited*, dated November 25, 1991. The decision is being appealed to Divisional Court.

10 The purchase of care services was not required as a condition of residing in the rental unit. Paragraphs 200, 213, 220.

11 Paragraphs 199 and 213. Meals were found to be subject to rent regulation as separate charges for meals were like separate charges for parking on a per space basis (paragraph 216).

12 Paragraphs 200 and 204.

13 Rent Review Hearings Board Decision in *Diversicare VI Limited Partnership v. All Tenants of 312–314 Oxford Street, London, Ontario*, dated July 27, 1988. This decision was upheld by Divisional Court of the Ontario Courts of Justice, in an unreported decision released October 27, 1989.

occupied by a person for the purpose of receiving care." Much of the ambiguity about coverage of rest homes arises because "care" is not defined, and the meaning of "for the purpose of receiving care" is unclear.[8]

Two recent cases before the Rent Review Hearings Board have decided that the particular retirement homes are subject to rent regulation; however, as the decisions are based on the facts of each case, it may not follow that all rest homes in Ontario are covered. One Board found that the accommodation portion of a Toronto retirement home's charges was subject to rent regulation, but the charges for care services provided by the operator were not.[9] The Board noted that in this retirement home, the care services were contracted for on an optional basis.[10] Thus, there was a "separation of care costs from the [cost of] services normally included in the unit rent definition."[11] Another significant aspect of this case was the "independence" of the residents and "their freedom of access and privacy (their own key and a locked-door situation)."[12] In London, a Rent Review Hearing Board ordered that a retirement home be covered, apparently because most residents did not use the care services offered.[13]

The *LTA* and the proposed *RCA* also exempt from coverage all accommodation "subject to" fourteen enumerated statutes dealing with health and social services. This exemption is widely claimed by premises—such as licensed nursing homes and municipal homes for the aged—that receive government funding. Some group homes and non-profit housing providers funded by provincial government ministries also claim this exemption, but it is unclear what the criteria are for deciding that particular premises are "subject to" the listed statutes.

In the only case in this area known to the Commission, a court found that a non-profit housing provider that contracted with and received funding from the Ministry of Community and Social Services (MCSS) to provide accommodation, meals, and counselling to socially disadvantaged persons was "subject to" the *Ministry of Community and Social Services Act*, and thus exempt from the *LTA*. The court stated that the exemption is intended to cover accommodation that is "under the auspices" of provincial government agencies.[14]

The Commission holds as a fundamental principle that when the law deals with a person's non-transient housing there must be certainty whether that housing is subject to the *LTA* and rent control. We recommend that both the *LTA* and the proposed *RCA* be amended to ensure such certainty:

RECOMMENDATION 11: That the government of Ontario accept as a principle the desirability of certainty concerning coverage of all residential accommodation for vulnerable adults under the *Landlord and Tenant Act* and the proposed *Rent Control Act, 1991* and that these statutes be amended to this effect.

COVERAGE OF REST HOMES UNDER THE *LTA* AND THE PROPOSED *RCA*

Many vulnerable persons require care and support in order to live in the community. This need should not, however, deny them the rights of other persons in the community. Indeed, their very vulnerability argues in favour of *LTA* and *RCA* protection. The receipt of care does not diminish the fact of residence. Care, as we have observed, complements accommodation, but should not supersede the rights and responsibilities that come with residential accommodation.

As rest homes are permanent residences, the Commission sees no reason to treat rest-home residents differently from residential tenants in the context of landlord-tenant relations.

14 *R. v. File*, an unreported decision of His Honour Judge Babe, in Provincial Court (Criminal Division) at Toronto on May 24, 1987.

15 The type and intensity of services provided to the residents in such housing varies—from assistance with some of the instrumental activities of living, such as shopping and banking, to assistance with the basic activities of daily living, such as eating, to various forms of intensive rehabilitation and treatment.

Rest Homes and the *Landlord and Tenant Act*

The substantive rights that *LTA* conveys are of great importance to vulnerable residents, as the power imbalance in favour of operators may be substantial. In fact, many of the most unacceptable operator behaviours repeatedly identified by residents—denying access to the premises to visitors, service providers, and family members; locking residents out of the home for periods of time as a punishment or because their presence was inconvenient to the operators; and disregarding the residents' privacy—will be immediately and clearly resolved with *LTA* coverage.

Residents of rest homes *must* have all the rights given to residential tenants; the importance of ensuring that this goal is achieved can scarcely be overstated. *LTA* is the most effective and normalizing way to accomplish this.

RECOMMENDATION 12: That rest homes be subject to Part IV of the *Landlord and Tenant Act.*

We recommend the "care" grounds for exemption be eliminated from the *LTA*, as the residents' receipt of care from owners/operators is irrelevant to a landlord-tenant relationship.

RECOMMENDATION 13: That the *Landlord and Tenant Act* be amended to delete the phrase "or for the purposes of receiving care" from clause 1(c)(ix).

There is a wide array of non-profit supportive housing and group homes available to vulnerable persons,[15] much of which will fall within the Commission's definition of a rest home. If not otherwise exempt, such accommodation would be subject to the *LTA* if the "for the purposes of receiving care" exemption is deleted from the *LTA*. (We discuss grounds for exemption later in this chapter.)

EXEMPTION FOR "REHABILITATIVE OR THERAPEUTIC PURPOSES"

The *LTA* [clause 1(c)(ix)] contains an exemption for accommodation occupied "for ... rehabilitative or therapeutic purposes." Non-profit agencies that consider their group homes to be therapeutic environments focused on this exemption in raising the issue of *LTA* coverage.[16] Some of these group homes choose to assume they are covered by the *LTA*;[17] others prefer to assign certain tenants' rights to their residents but maintain they are not covered by the *LTA*. In all cases, they argue that they must have the ability to discharge residents rapidly for treatment-related reasons. For example, in one alcohol/drug treatment centre that chose to operate under *LTA*, a resident refused to take the medication that was a condition of acceptance into the program. The resident became argumentative, disruptive, and physically threatening to residents and staff. The entire program was severely harmed by the resident's behaviour. The operators informed the Commission that had they known they would not be able to remove the person rapidly from the premises, they would never have agreed to operate under the *LTA*.

A failure to take medications, counselling, or treatment, or even to abstain from alcohol is not grounds for eviction under *LTA*; however, without such conditions, treatment programs are merely housing programs. Church, community, and other agencies point out that they entered the housing arena as a means of providing treatment or rehabilitation; they do not wish to be landlords.

The Commission has been shown signed contracts and agreements between agencies and client/residents. These purport to offer *LTA* protections while requiring compliance with

16 It is also possible for private, for-profit treatment residences to claim this exemption.

17 They generally do so for reasons of philosophy in that they wish their clients to assume the status of residents in as normalizing an environment as is possible.

18 Treatment residences that are government funded and/or regulated could continue to operate outside the *LTA* by claiming an exemption under clause 1(c)(viii) of the *LTA*. This clause exempts residential premises that are subject to fourteen enumerated health and social-services statutes.

treatment-related provisos in order to remain in the program —and, therefore, the housing. Such agreements are intended to endow the rights of *LTA* as far as is possible without threatening the essence of the program.

However, housing-advocacy groups and legal aid clinics argue that capricious eviction, rights abuses, and due-process denial are not unknown in the non-profit sector, and that the guarantees in "agreements" are largely voluntary and without explicit legal foundation. As well, a range of housing providers might claim the exemption even if their therapeutic or rehabilitative function is secondary to the provision of housing. A housing provider exempt on this basis might threaten eviction of a resident resisting "unreasonable" treatment or rehabilitation, or "house" rules.

We are concerned about the potentially wide interpretation of the exemption "for rehabilitative or therapeutic purposes." To provide a blanket exemption for any self-labelled residential "treatment" program while leaving "rehabilitation" and "therapy" undefined might simply re-open, under a different label, the broad exemption currently available to accommodation occupied "for the purpose of receiving care."

However, eliminating the "rehabilitative or therapeutic" exemption proved unacceptable to the Commission because this would threaten the viability of many legitimate charitable and commercial treatment residences. There are many creative and successful treatment programs operated without government funding and regulation. If this exemption were deleted, government alone would determine which treatment and rehabilitative residences would be exempt from *LTA* through its power to fund or regulate.[18] Such power might further entrench narrow medical interests and processes at the expense of holistic approaches. The Commission does not recommend giving government the right to distinguish "legitimate" from "non-legitimate" treatment in this way.

We do, however, recommend that an adequate legal distinction be made between a rest home, which offers care, and a group home that offers treatment or rehabilitation[19] so that criteria for the exemption for the latter can be specified clearly. The Ministry of the Attorney General in conjunction with the Ministry of Health (MoH) and MCSS should identify such criteria.

RECOMMENDATION 14: That the Ministry of the Attorney General and other affected ministries define specific criteria for qualifying under the "rehabilitative or therapeutic purpose" exemption from the *Landlord and Tenant Act* [clause 1(c)(ix)]. These criteria should then be given legal effect through an appropriate amendment to the *Landlord and Tenant Act* or its regulations.

It is beyond our mandate to define the meaning of "rehabilitation" or "therapy," but certain differences between these concepts and "care" are evident: residents typically enter a rest home for an indefinite, open-ended period, i.e., it is their home. Most treatment programs are of finite duration, with specific goals and targets. The goals usually relate to acquiring new skills or habits or altering behaviour. When these goals are achieved or failure is acknowledged, the resident is expected and required to "go home."

For exemption from the *LTA*, the primary purpose for occupying the accommodation must be to receive rehabilitation or therapy; accommodation with care that includes an element of rehabilitation or therapy should not qualify for exemption.

At present, residents must challenge housing providers' assertions that accommodation is exempt from the *LTA* on the basis that it is occupied for rehabilitative or therapeutic purposes. This "self-exemption" by operators is not acceptable.

Once criteria for exemption have been established, the exemption of specific residences on rehabilitative or therapeutic grounds should be determined by the landlord-tenant court. It will thus be necessary to amend the *LTA* to provide

19 The issue has been raised before us with specific reference to alcohol- and drug-dependency treatment programs. At present there are many such treatment programs in Ontario, some funded as hostels under General Welfare Assistance. Those programs that do not meet the new criteria to be developed under Recommendation 14 would not qualify for exemption from the *LTA* although they could nevertheless remain as hostel accommodation under GWA.

20 A notice of an application for a declaration of exemption on this basis should be given to all residents of the premises, to the Ministry of the Attorney General and to the appropriate service-providing ministry, for example, the MCSS and the MoH. Consideration should also be given to providing advocacy groups with notice of the application and providing appropriate intervenor status for such groups.

Prior to the effective date of such a provision, all residences that wish to seek such an exemption must have time to do so. Thereafter, all persons occupying such accommodation without such a court declaration should be covered under the LTA. Operators who wish to alter their status when persons are already living in a residence may do so only for new residents. Once such an exemption is given by the courts, all persons who enter the treatment residence must be notified that such a declaration has been obtained. Failing such notification, persons entering residence should have all the protections of the LTA.

21 Clause 1(c)(viii) of the LTA and clause 3(1)(f) of the proposed RCA. The identified statutes are as follows: the *Public Hospitals Act*; the *Private Hospitals Act*; the *Community Psychiatric Hospitals Act*; the *Mental Hospitals* Act; the *Homes for Special Care Act*; the *Homes for Retarded Persons Act*; the *Homes for the Aged and Rest Homes Act*; the *Nursing Homes Act*; the *Ministry of Correctional Services Act*; the *Charitable*

for such court declarations. In the absence of such a declaration, no residence may claim exemption from the LTA on the basis that it is occupied for "rehabilitative or therapeutic purposes."[20]

EXEMPTION BY BEING "SUBJECT TO" FOURTEEN PROVINCIAL STATUES

Residential accommodation that is "subject to" one or more of fourteen listed provincial health and social-services statutes is also exempt from the LTA.[21] This exemption can be claimed by group homes and supportive-housing providers only if they have some formal link to government.

The Commission has heard that some housing providers claim an exemption from the LTA solely on the basis of providing services funded under one of the listed statutes; other such providers do not claim such an exemption. Because it is not clear what "subject to" the listed statutes means, residents and owner/operators are often uncertain whether the LTA applies.

It appears that any supportive-housing provider or group home providing services and/or accommodation funded by a ministry under the identified statutes may be exempt from the LTA.

However, it is not clear to this Commission why residences subject to these acts are exempt and on what basis the listed statutes were chosen. (It might be that the listed statutes were seen as regulatory, i.e., that they protected residents or made the housing providers accountable in some way.)

The Commission does not accept that mere funding under a listed statute, or minimal "regulation" by or financial accountability to a government ministry is sufficient for exemption from the LTA. For purposes of LTA coverage, the source of funding—be it the residents or the government under a listed statute should be irrelevant.[22]

In our view, programs under government auspices should meet certain criteria in order to obtain exemption from the *LTA*, irrespective of whether they are "subject to" particular legislation. We believe that exemption from *LTA* can be justified only if there is some formal accountability mechanism from the housing provider to the government; as well, there must be protections for residents analogous to those forgone by virtue of the residence being exempt from coverage under *LTA*.

The Commission recommends that the Ministry of the Attorney General, in conjunction with the affected ministries, identify clear criteria for exempting accommodation under government auspices from coverage under *LTA*. These criteria should replace clause 1(c)(viii), under which exemptions are based on being "subject to" enumerated statutes.

It should be made clear that government-funded and -regulated accommodation intended as a temporary accommodation—hospitals, for example—should not be covered by *LTA*. The Commission also believes permanent accommodation funded or regulated by government should be exempt from the *LTA* only if the following protections are provided to residents:

1. security of tenure or protection from arbitrary eviction, i.e., the right to remain housed unless there are legitimate causes for termination of the tenancy;
2. due process, i.e., protection from arbitrary decision-making with respect to residents' security of tenure;
3. protection against economic eviction, i.e., the price of accommodation set or regulated by the government; and
4. protection of the basic rights of residents, as provided in a bill of rights.[23]

Special grounds for eviction, related to participation in a residential program, may be needed in some types of residences—for example, when residents complete a program, no longer

Institutions Act; the *Child and Family Services Act;* the *Developmental Services Act;* the *Ministry of Health Act* and/or the *Ministry of Community and Social Services Act.* The present *RRRA* does not contain this exemption.

22 As discussed in chapter 1, both the *Ministry of Health Act* and the *Ministry of Community and Social Services Act* (statutes listed under the *LTA* exemption) do not provide for program accountability, protection from arbitrary eviction and other due-process rights for residents in accommodation where the housing provider receives funds under those acts. The two acts are primarily funding mechanisms.

23 Such a bill of rights and its enforcement are discussed in Part III.

need a specially designed living unit, refuse to abide by essential program rules, or are no longer able to benefit from the program. Such grounds for termination could be developed by the concerned ministry or ministries.

Moreover, applicable substantive and due-process protections must be contained in the appropriate statute or regulations. Voluntary or contractual protections agreed to by ministries, operators, and residents are not sufficient.

> **RECOMMENDATION 15:** That the Ministry of the Attorney General delete from the *Landlord and Tenant Act* the exemption for accommodation subject to fourteen listed statutes [clause 1(c)(viii)]; and that the Ministry of the Attorney General, in conjunction with affected ministries, identify in the *Landlord and Tenant Act* or its regulations clear criteria for exempting premises accountable to the government. These criteria are to include the following:
>
> 1. the accommodation is not intended to be permanent accommodation; or
> 2. protection against arbitrary and/or economic eviction, due process for evictions, and protection of basic rights through an enforceable bill of rights are provided for residents in the relevant legislation.

The Ministry of the Attorney General could then exempt classes of premises, such as homes for the aged, if it is satisfied that all premises in the class meet the criteria. The regulation should also allow application to the Ministry of the Attorney General to exempt individual premises from the *LTA*.

EXEMPTIONS FROM THE DEFINITION OF "REST HOME"

Any accommodation that qualifies for exemption from the *LTA* on the grounds of rehabilitation or therapy, i.e., that its primary purpose is treatment rather than permanent accommodation, should be excluded from the Commission's definition of a rest home (and therefore from many of the recommendations in this Report).

We also recommend that any accommodation exempted from *LTA* coverage based on criteria developed to replace the listed statutes should also be excluded from our definition of a rest home.[24] In addition, short-term emergency shelter should be exempt from the definition of a rest home.

> **RECOMMENDATION 16:** That any accommodation exempt from the *Landlord and Tenant Act* on the grounds that it meets the criteria for "accommodation occupied ... for rehabilitative or therapeutic purposes" [clause 1(c)(ix)] or based on the criteria to replace the exemption for accommodation subject to fourteen listed statutes [clause 1(c)(viii)], or provided as short-term emergency shelter, be excluded from the definition of "rest home" as set out in this Report.

A "Rest-Home" Clause Under *LTA*?

Operators and some resident groups have urged the Commission that if rest homes are to be covered under the *LTA*, there must be new provision in that Act to recognize the unique problems that can arise in this setting.

Of particular concern to operators are residents whose care needs have increased so that they can no longer be met by services provided by the operator or delivered to the home from the community. Under the *LTA*, they argue, eviction of such residents would not be possible.[25] Nor could they evict persons who are prone, for example, to setting fires.[26] Operators argue that they cannot be expected to wait until a fire has been set or other destructive behaviour has occurred before evicting; they must have the right to discharge on short notice.

24 The criteria for exemption will include a range of protections for residents and thus it would be superfluous to define such accommodation as rest homes for purposes of the recommendations in this Report.

25 A legislated ground for termination of a residential lease based on the inability to meet the care needs of a tenant would almost surely violate both the Charter of Rights and Freedoms and the Ontario Human Rights Code, both of which prohibit discrimination on the basis of disability.

26 This is often given as one example of persons with difficulties who typically reside in some rest homes. The argument is made that community housing for such persons would not be available without an exemption from the *LTA*.

27 Provided that there has been no court order to the contrary, residents are assumed to be capable of making decisions about their own lives. These include decisions that are potentially harmful to themselves or decisions that others may disapprove of. An operator, or others, may seek a court order appointing a guardian on the basis that the resident was incapable of decision-making with respect to some or all personal matters. Such guardian could decide where the resident should live. In the absence of such an order, individuals can do as they wish in the privacy of their homes provided they do not contravene the rights of others as set out in *LTA*.

28 Eviction should be an option even when the conduct arises from the operators' and the communities' inability to meet the care needs of residents.

29 These grounds could permit the eviction of a senior who has become unduly aggressive and disruptive within the rest home. People with Alzheimer's disease, for example, experience a deterioration that can become acutely troublesome both to other residents and to operators and staff.

It is the Commission's view that such problems are fundamentally a matter of supervision. Only a few seconds are required to start a fire or create other dangers; with or without *LTA*, it may be impossible to apprehend people before the harm is done. Persons with pyromaniac tendencies, like other vulnerable persons, require supervision appropriate to their need level. Certain people require intensive supervision when discharged from a hospital into the community. Exemption of their accommodation from the *LTA* will not solve the problem; the remedy lies in better discharge planning and practice of community care and deinstitutionalization.

At the same time, the Commission recognizes the legitimacy of the more general concerns about the conduct of some residents whose needs can no longer be met.

In considering grounds appropriate for eviction, we must distinguish between behaviours that negatively affect operators or other residents and those that have no such effect. For example, individuals' care needs may increase beyond the capacity of the home and they are unwilling to depart voluntarily; however, there is no negative impact on others. The Commission sees no need for a new ground for eviction under these circumstances. Indeed, we would oppose eviction of residents who make decisions that may harm themselves but no one else.[27]

However, when residents' conduct has a negative impact on others, a response becomes necessary and eviction should be an available option.[28] Under subsection 109(1) of the *LTA*, there are grounds other than non-payment of rent on which a landlord may seek early termination of a tenancy:[29]

1. when the tenant "causes or permits undue damage" to the premises by "wilful or negligent acts" (paragraph a);
2. when the tenant's conduct "substantially interferes with the reasonable enjoyment of the premises for all usual purposes by the landlord or the other tenants" (paragraph c); and
3. when "the safety or other bona fide and lawful right,

privilege or interest of any other tenant is ... seriously impaired ..." by an act of the tenant (paragraph d).

The Commission is satisfied that one or more of these clauses provides adequate grounds for termination of rest-home tenancies when the residents' conduct has an adverse impact on others. A new and distinct "rest-home" ground for termination of a tenancy under the *LTA* is unnecessary.

However, a clear problem remains: eviction under the *LTA* can take several weeks, during which irreparable damage may be done to the property or rights of the landlords or other residents. Residents sharing rooms with those whose behaviour would warrant eviction were, understandably, most adamant that speedy departures be facilitated. In the most urgent situations, operators or other residents can contact the police, mental-health professionals, or an emergency response team. The Commission, however, does not wish to emphasize either a medical or criminal law response to such behaviour. The preferred response would be under the *LTA* whenever possible.

The Commission therefore recommends a "fast-track" rest-home amendment to the *LTA*. This would allow court orders for the rapid but *temporary* departure of residents if the time required for an application for eviction were likely to result in serious harm to other tenants or the landlord. The "fast track" would not result in eviction, but would simply prohibit tenants from occupying the premises until the landlords' application had been processed or until there were an alternative resolution of the matter, such as additional services provided to troublesome residents.[30]

Such situations can occur in any residential premises; however, this fast-track procedure should be available only to operators of registered rest homes (see chapter 10). This departure from the current landlord-tenant law would be justified, in the Commission's opinion, by the particularly vulnerable status of many residents and by the communal nature of much rest-home living, particularly in boarding homes where

30 Care or supervisory services from a community agency, either on an emergency or continuing basis, might persuade operators or the court that an order to temporarily vacate the premises is not necessary.

31 We recognize this response is at times inadequate, but the issue before the Commission is parity of treatment between the rest home and residences elsewhere in the community.

several strangers often share a bedroom.

In many cases, a temporary forced departure from a rest home may constitute a permanent departure: once alternative accommodation is secured, a person may no longer wish to return to the original setting. Thus, before orders to temporarily vacate are made, residents should receive notice and be given the opportunity to argue their case. Fast-track orders should not be permitted on an ex parte basis. It is our intention to speed the process in specific circumstances and not to alter the content of the *LTA*.

> **RECOMMENDATION 17:** That the *Landlord and Tenant Act* be amended to provide that landlords of registered rest homes may apply for an order requiring a resident to temporarily vacate a rest home until a pending application to terminate the tenancy is heard in situations in which paragraphs (a), (c), or (d) of subsection 109(1) of the *Landlord and Tenant Act* applies and in which the time required to proceed with the application for termination would likely result in serious harm to the person or property of other tenants or the landlord.

Once the temporary removal of the resident or an eviction has been secured, the landlord's obligation is at an end. The MCSS, the MoH and/or the long-term-care program must assist the resident just as they must assist any individuals in private homes who become unable to cope independently: either supports must be provided so that the individuals can remain in the community, or a suitable institutional placement, such as a nursing home or home for the aged, must be secured.[31] The problem is not the landlord's to resolve.

OTHER *LTA* CONCERNS

Two further objections to the *LTA* have been raised by the

rest-home industry:[32] twenty-four-hour advance notice for entry to rented premises, except in emergency situations; and the right to assign or sublet premises.

It is our view that the twenty-four-hour advance notice requirement is reasonable for one's home. Supervision, assisting with medications, and general housekeeping all require the consent of residents.[33] It is every person's right to refuse such services, and it is not our intention to interfere with this right.

Assigning or subletting premises may be necessary if a long-term lease has been signed or when adequate notice cannot be given. If a resident on a monthly tenancy dies, for example, it might then be nearly three months before the estate is free of its legal obligations. In the case of a long-term lease, the estate would be responsible until the end of its term. Operators might not wish to demand the charges from an estate for reasons of public relations or compassion, but it would be their right to do so. As well, if residents on long term leases leave because of general dissatisfaction, their financial obligations continue for the full term of those leases.[34]

Operators argue that tenants might sublet to people with excessively high care needs, thereby circumventing the operators' criteria for entry to the rest home. However, while landlords cannot "unreasonably withhold" consent to a sublease, it may be reasonable to refuse consent on the grounds that the sublessee's needs cannot be met by the operator or by community service providers on the premises.[35]

Rest Homes and Rent Control

The Ministry of Housing's "preferred approach for discussion" was that the accommodation component of rest homes be

32 Ontario Long-Term Residential Care Association, *Position Paper on Rent Control* (April 13, 1991).

33 The law respecting persons incapable of consenting is undergoing change. Simplified procedures for obtaining a legal consent on behalf of such persons is the goal of new legislation.

34 Under the *LTA,* the landlord has an obligation to mitigate damages. This is discussed further in chapter 6, "Life at the Top."

35 Note that tenants have the right to sublet, but landlords may provide *in the tenancy agreement* that this right is subject to their consent. Someone with care needs below those sold in a mandatory package might choose to acquire the sublease. Since such new residents are paying for services they neither need nor use, we see no problem for the operator. An additional concern is tenants' subletting to someone young, given that retirement homes have been built around the interests and needs of seniors. If the home is unable to care for the non-senior, the response is as indicated above; if the issue is social mix and resident heterogeneity, we need note only that all accommodation is subject to the Ontario Human Rights Code, which prohibits discrimination on the basis of disability or age, unless an age of sixty-five or over is a "requirement, qualification, or consideration for preferential treatment" (section 14).

36 See note 3.

37 Ontario Long-Term Residential Care Association, *Position Paper on Rent Control* (April 3, 1991). Of particular concern was the fear that the Ministry of Housing and its rent review officials lack understanding of the issues relating to residential care: if regulation was to occur, it ought to be done by a ministry with experience in human service-delivery issues. The Ministry of Housing readily acknowledged its inexperience in dealing with care-related matters.

38 The formula used in Florida limits increases in the price of care services to the price index plus specified percentage. Accommodation costs in Florida operate through a complex system of initial endowments and guaranteed partial repayment. The net effect is that the price of accommodation is not controlled, but the price of care services is controlled. This is the precise opposite of the Ministry of Housing's "preferred approach" for Ontario.

39 CMHC staff in several branch offices around the province collected data on retirement homes through telephone interviews with residence administrators or owners. This data must be interpreted with care, as the survey in some communities was informal.

40 The question asked was, "What is included in your per diem?" It thus presumably refers to the mandatory package and not optional services.

covered by rent control.[36] The prices of care services would not be controlled, but "it would be prohibited to tie the provision of such services to the provision of accommodation to a particular tenant ... unless required to do so under government funding programs." Thus accommodation would be "debundled" from care services on a mandatory basis. ("Care" was not defined in the Green Paper; this was to be resolved in the legislation or regulations.)

The rest-home industry vehemently opposed the proposal, arguing adverse cost implications; the practical impossibility of separating accommodation and care; and the fact that individual residents' needs could fluctuate, sometimes day to day. They cited the responsible behaviour of the industry, noting that rent increases during the previous two years had averaged 4.8 percent annually.[37]

Operators also claimed that the interests of residents could be protected better through means other than rent control: in Florida, for example, allowable rate increases for services in retirement homes are tied by contract to an accepted price index.[38]

When introducing the *RCA*, Bill 121, in the Legislature on June 6, 1991, the minister of Housing stated that the rest-home issue would be deferred pending the recommendations of this Commission.

We have examined the empirical evidence on price behaviour in the industry using surveys conducted by Canada Mortgage and Housing Corporation (CMHC).[39] There is no province-wide figure with which to compare the industry's estimate of 4.8 percent annual rent increase over two years, but localized results are informative.

A structured questionnaire was used to collect data in the Toronto Census Metropolitan Area (CMA), which includes Metro Toronto and the regions of York, Peel, and Halton.[40] Based on those retirement homes for which CMHC had data, rents in the Toronto CMA increased by 11.2 percent in 1989 and by 13.3 percent during a twenty-one-month period ending in December 1990 (an annualized rate increase of 7.6 percent).[41] In the city of Toronto, rents increased by 11 percent in 1989 and by 27.8 percent during the same twenty-one-month term (annualized at 15.9 percent). In Scarborough, rents increased by 40.8 percent during the twenty-one months. CMHC notes that new projects with higher rents coming onstream during the time period studied increased the overall average rent levels. Vacancy rates in Metro Toronto, excluding recently completed projects, rose from 16 percent in February 1989 to 18 percent in March 1991.[42]

Ottawa had a 23.3 percent vacancy rate in December 1989 —reflecting massive overbuilding—and a 16.4 percent vacancy rate a year later. The rent increase during that period was 3.1 percent, with the smallest increases at the luxury end of the market (2.2 percent in premises with per diem rates of $65 and up). The projected rent increase for 1991 was 6 percent.[43]

The industry has argued that high vacancy rates, particularly in the luxury market, check excess price increases.[44] However, the corollary to such a tradeoff is that when the vacancy rate declines, rent increases become larger. The CMHC Ottawa survey supports this assumption: in the year beginning December 1989, when the vacancy rate was 23 percent, there was a 3.1 percent increase; a year later, when the vacancy rate had dropped to 16 percent, the projected rent increases doubled, to 6 percent.

The vacancy rate does not create stability in the industry: when it is high, some operators will undoubtedly leave the industry, reducing the surplus; those remaining will attempt to adjust their rents in response to the shortfall in revenues resulting from low occupancy.

In any case, public policy cannot be based on the assumption that this excess capacity will continue as a check ensuring low rates of rent increase. Many potential investors have access to good market information, and it is widely acknowledged today that many rest-home markets are substantially oversupplied. As well, the vulnerability of residents and the

41 The increase rises from 13.3 percent to 14.3 percent if the rest of the Toronto branch of CMHC is added. The addition mainly consists of Durham Region, where rents increased by 48.8 percent over the twenty-one-month period, and Simcoe. Annualized rates are calculated by the Commission and are simply pro-rated to twelve months; they do not include compounding.

42 The vacancy rate rose from 10 percent to 24 percent in the City of Toronto and from 7 percent to 14 percent in Etobicoke, while it dropped from 23 percent to 12 percent in North York. The vacancy rate rose in Peel and Halton regions, but dropped in York and Durham regions, and also in Simcoe.

43 Information from other communities is more limited: a Hamilton CMHC branch survey in December 1990 found a 17.4 percent vacancy rate (ranging from 32.2 percent to 5.2 percent), with a projected 1991 rent increase of 5 percent. A London branch informal survey of a few homes in the region reported projected rent increases for 1991 of 0 percent to 4 percent; 1991 vacancy rates were about 10 percent in the low-to-medium price range and 20 percent in the high bracket. The Thunder Bay office had no information of any sort, and the Sudbury office had individual data on four private retirement homes.

44 They suggest there is a tradeoff involving an inverse relation between the vacancy

rate and the rate of price (rent) inflation, and furthermore that a vacancy rate in the 15 to 20 percent range seems to be compatible with stable or relatively low rent increases. There is an analogy with conditions in the labour market with its inverse relation between unemployment and the rate of wage inflation.

45 Were we to recommend comprehensive regulation for the rest-home industry, to create a new system of nursing homes in Ontario, then prices to the consumer (rent for housing) would be set through the relevant regulatory process: rent control would be superfluous.

reluctance of frail seniors to move from place to place limits their ability to exploit high vacancy rates to receive lower rents.

The power imbalance between residents and operators increases once individuals have moved into a home: high vacancy rates may result in reduced prices at first; thereafter, residents are increasingly vulnerable, and price rises may be resisted less or not at all. Such market segmentation, in which a seller can charge different prices to different consumers, may result in low overall price increases, yet very high price increases for individual vulnerable residents.

Under the present law, much energy is expended on deciding whether a particular rest home provides accommodation "for the purposes of care," and is thus exempt from rent control. For this Commission's purposes, this is a useless exercise: we are charged not with interpreting existing or proposed legislation but with recommending future policy.

We see no reason why rents for one type of residential accommodation should be left uncontrolled when those for all other rental housing are subject to control. Those residences in which prices of accommodation are set through some other provincial legislation should, indeed, be exempted,[45] but we cannot accept a regulatory void.

Provincial law mandates a maximum allowable rate of rent increase for residential premises; it is unacceptable that residents who happen to reside in rest homes should be subject to price increases in excess of this ceiling. As long as rent control is the law of Ontario, residents of rest homes are entitled to its protections, because the rest home is their accommodation.

RECOMMENDATION 18: That rest homes be subject to rent control. That paragraph 3(1)(e) of the proposed *Rent Control Act, 1991* (Bill 121) be amended to remove the phrase "or for the purpose of receiving care."

As we have indicated, coverage under rent control should be consistent with that under *LTA*, and the two statutes should proceed in tandem. The *LTA* exemptions recommended by the Commission should therefore be contained in the proposed *RCA*.

> **RECOMMENDATION 19:** That any accommodation exempted from *Landlord and Tenant Act* coverage on the basis of a court determination that it is occupied for "rehabilitative or therapeutic purposes" [clause 1(c)(ix)] or on the basis of the criteria that will replace clause 1(c)(viii) also be exempt from rent control.

RENT CONTROL AND CARE SERVICES

The Ministry of Housing's Green Paper favoured rent control for only the accommodation element of rest home charges; care services would be offered only on an optional basis and their prices would not be controlled. It was assumed that the freedom of residents to purchase services from outside suppliers would constrain excess price rises for such services.

We acknowledge that competition yields restraint, but we are unable to support mandatory delinking of accommodation and care services.[46] Such formal separation means little if alternative suppliers are not available; in rural areas, for example, there may be little choice but to buy from residence operators.

More important, the retirement home is a private entrepreneurial activity, and we are unwilling to dictate to operators what they may or may not sell.[47] In addition, operators note that a forced separation would negate the very essence of the industry: rest homes would become accommodation-only premises if residents chose not to buy optional services; yet the essence of the industry is the sale of both housing and care services.

46 The discussion does not apply to non-care services, such as parking, that cannot be debundled from the accommodation portion except as permitted by the *RCA*.

47 There are restrictions on the sale of certain "health-care" services. See the discussion of bootleg nursing homes in chapter 3.

We recognize that permitting the sale of a mandatory package in which only the price of accommodation is controlled may lead to inordinate inflation in the prices of mandatory care services. The intent of rent control would be easy to evade by combining low rents for accommodation and expensive, mandatory care packages exempt from control.

Moreover, some argue for controlling the price of optional care services (those not included in the mandatory package) on the basis that these services may be necessary for the resident's daily functioning. For example, assistance with bathing may be essential to some residents, even if this service is offered only on an optional basis.

Calls to control the prices of both the mandatory care package and the optional care services grow out of the substantial imbalance in bargaining power between residents and operators. It is argued that this imbalance can be redressed only through direct control of pricing.

The Commission is aware of no widespread general demand for price controls in Ontario, and we see no need to recommend a major change in public policy in this area. Control of all care prices would necessitate unwanted and expensive new bureaucracy. If owners/operators require the purchase of care services as a condition of renting the premises (i.e., as part of the mandatory package), then such care services must be subject to rent control.

RECOMMENDATION 20: That any care service sold on a mandatory basis in a rest home be subject to rent control in the same manner as the basic accommodation.

Under the proposed *RCA*, an annual guideline for rent increases would be set, based on identified operating costs. These would not make provision for the costs associated with "care"; as a result, the annual increase for a rest home with mandatory care services would be calculated on incomplete information.

We do not deem it feasible or desirable to calculate a distinct guideline for rest homes with mandatory care services: we cannot envisage a single index that could apply to the different types, quantities, and qualities of mandatory care services offered by all homes. On a practical level, rest-home accommodation represents only a very small part of the total accommodation covered by rent control in Ontario: there is no cost-efficient way to develop a distinct guideline for one minor element of the total system. Therefore:

RECOMMENDATION 21: That charges for accommodation and mandatory care services in rest homes be subject to the same annual guideline increase as charges for other accommodation subject to the *Rent Control Act, 1991.*

Thus, the cost of both accommodation and mandatory care services will rise annually by the percentage set by the rent-control guideline. Should costs of the mandatory care services rise faster than the guideline, operators will be disadvantaged; if mandatory care costs rise more slowly than the guideline, they will benefit. There is no a priori reason to assume one or the other will occur consistently.

REST HOMES AND MEALS

Room-and-board settings that offer only accommodation and meals, i.e., no care services, are currently subject to rent control; their entire package, including meals, is covered.

Some rest homes require the purchase of some or all meals as part of a mandatory package; others offer meals as optional extras, on a fee-for-service basis. As operators should be able to choose what they wish to sell, both approaches are acceptable.

However, any *required* purchase must be subject to rent control. It would be unacceptable for the government to con-

48 The Act would also permit applications for rent increases due to capital expenditures if tenants consent to the capital expenditures.

49 Wages restrained from increasing due to rent control or other reasons mean, in effect, that those earning the wages are subsidizing those receiving the service.

trol the price of accommodation but leave the costs of mandatory meals unrestrained; clearly, food prices would rise to evade the intent of the price control. On the other hand, optional purchase of meals should be treated like care services for rent-control purposes.

RECOMMENDATION 22: That the costs of any meals provided as part of the mandatory package in rest homes be subject to rent control in the same manner as the basic accommodation.

Since most or perhaps all homes require that at least some meals be bought as part of the basic accommodation package, in practice this would often mean rent control on both accommodation and food. (The choice would be that of individual operators.) The same option, with the same implications for rent control purposes, should be available to operators in room-and-board-only settings.

STAFF WAGES AND *RCA*

Under the proposed *RCA*, landlords could apply for a maximum increase above the guideline of 3 percent in a year for municipal taxes, utilities, and capital expenditures. In some cases, rent increases (up to 3 percent each year) for capital expenditures could be carried forward for two years.[48]

The Commission believes that wage increases to low-paid staff in rest homes should also be grounds for increases above the annual guideline.[49] Rest-home employees, many of whom are women and minorities earning at or near minimum wage, are effectively subsidizing residents, who may, in many cases, have higher incomes. The redistribution of income that results is regressive. There is a tradeoff between the goal of rent-control protection to residents and equity for poorly paid employees. It is our view that a strong case can be made in favour of the latter goal, even at the expense of the former.

RECOMMENDATION 23: That wages of low-paid staff in registered rest homes be treated as an extraordinary operating cost under the *Rent Control Act, 1991* and as such may constitute the basis of an application for rent increases above the annual guideline.

6
Life at the Top

Agreements to enter a retirement home are private transactions between buyers (tenants) and sellers (operators). There is no public financial interest involved or any formal needs assessment. Admission is based on individuals' expressed wishes to live in a particular setting and their ability to pay monthly rents, about $2,000 and up. Retirement homes are a form of housing with limited care services sold to those with the means and desire to purchase them. In short, moving to a retirement home involves a decision on how to spend one's own money.

Residents' motivations differ. Some wish to live among their peers and friends, and to participate in organized social activities in a protected environment; others want to be free of the responsibilities of home ownership. For most, however, there is a common element: *insurance*, the belief that should assistance be needed it is readily available. This may mean having an emergency-call system in each room and twenty-four-hour monitoring on-site, or a more general sense of assistance being available to deal with needs that may arise as one declines with age.

To meet such broad expectations, this type of accommodation ranges from luxury retirement and "lifestyle" housing to high-care facilities that are, in effect, bootleg nursing homes.

In the former, a person typically purchases accommodation in a self-contained unit; some, all, or no meals; and an emergency-response system. Personal-care services, which may include health services, are available, either as part of a mandatory package purchased by all residents or as fee-for-service options. As well, there will usually be some form of social programming. Marketing is often targeted towards the "well elderly," stressing an "independent lifestyle." Some homes specify that should physical or mental decline reach a specific stage, residents must leave.

The high-care rest homes do not formally offer more than ninety minutes of "nursing" care a day. In practice, however, care is dictated by needs and financial resources. Some retirement homes have a "high-care" unit available to new entrants and to current residents whose needs increase.

What all this accommodation has in common is that it is a commodity purchased on the open market with individuals' own money. As no public funds are involved, the state's primary interest is to ensure that the market works as it should.

Many, perhaps most, seniors who enter luxury retirement homes do not consider themselves "vulnerable" as we have used the term, and they often resent any government incursion into their right to make a market purchase.[1] However, entry into a rest home is not a one-time purchase, like a package holiday or a restaurant meal: it is an ongoing purchase by today's competent purchaser and tomorrow's vulnerable senior. Many seniors sell their own homes in order to move into retirement residences, and are unlikely to move again, particularly as they become more frail and vulnerable with increased age.

Often conditions of entry into a rest home are not those of fully informed buyers and sellers voluntarily entering into exchange relationships. Rather, there is a significant power imbalance in favour of operators, who unilaterally decide the timing and conditions of entry to and departure from the home.[2]

1 Landlord-tenant and rent-control legislation presume a generalized need for protection of renters, to redress the imbalance of power between landlords and tenants. To this extent, the Ontario government directly controls the process and outcome of private transactions.

2 Analogies have been drawn to supplier-determined medical care. Individuals may initially decide to enter the retirement home (or doctor's office); thereafter, the seller of the service decides how much will be bought by the purchaser. "Need" is determined not by the buyer, as in most market purchases, but by the seller, who may have a financial incentive to sell more service. Retirement-home operators may exercise this power by threatening to discharge residents who fail to buy enough of what the operators want to sell.

A second analogy has been drawn to monopsony with inelastic demand, a situation in which there is a single (or few) sellers of a commodity or service, so purchasers cannot readily switch to alternative suppliers. (Local telephone, gas, and hydro services are typical examples.) Frail seniors are often reluctant to resist price increases by moving elsewhere.

Thus operators primarily determine consumers' needs; consumers often have little practical choice but to purchase what the operators want to sell them.

Entering the Retirement Home

The purchase of rest-home residence involves a free market transaction; therefore, operators should be at liberty to sell whatever they want, subject to the constraints of the market and the need to equalize bargaining power between buyers and sellers. At the same time, consumers should have comprehensive and detailed information about what they are buying, now and in the future.

Operators may sell a mandatory package of accommodation and specified care services that must be purchased by all residents. In addition, they may offer optional care services, to be purchased on terms negotiated between individual buyers and sellers.

Care services may be totally debundled, i.e., only accommodation is obligatory and all care services are offered on an optional basis. The package may be all-inclusive, i.e., all accommodation, food, and care services are provided for a fixed monthly payment. As well, there can be any arrangement in between.

REST-HOME "RENT"

Nothing this Commission recommends will intrude on operators' rights to offer whatever mandatory package they wish. In order to preserve this right, the proposed *Rent Control Act, 1991* (*RCA*) will need to be amended. The broad definition of "rent" in subsection 1(1) of the proposed Act must state that charges for optional care services in a registered rest home are not "rent" within the meaning of the Act. Section 31 of the proposed Act prohibits certain "additional charges," including key money. This section will have to be amended to clarify that requirements by operators of registered rest homes that residents purchase mandatory care services do not contravene the Act. Section 31 would continue to protect residents and prospective residents from attempts by operators to require the purchase of optional care services.

> **RECOMMENDATION 24:** That subsection 1(1) and section 31 of the proposed *Rent Control Act, 1991* be amended to indicate, respectively, that in a registered rest home, charges for optional care services are not "rent" and that the purchase of care services as part of a mandatory package of accommodation and care services does not constitute an illegal "additional charge."

The same mandatory package must be offered to all purchasers,[3] not as an end in itself but to ensure effective rent control. Otherwise, operators might sell different mandatory packages, requiring one resident to buy a certain package at a given price and another resident to buy a different package at a higher price. It would be impossible, short of total price control of care services provided by operators, to determine how much of the higher cost of the second package is due to enriched care and how much is accommodation costs that may exceed the legal maximum rent.

> **RECOMMENDATION 25:** That registered rest homes be permitted to sell any mandatory package of accommodation and services they wish, provided that the same mandatory package be sold to all residents.

Section 18 of the proposed *RCA* permits operators to base an application for a rent increase (3 percent above guideline) on the cost of new or additional services to a rental unit, if the tenant consents. This provision is not intended to apply to personal-care services or to common services that affect all residents, such as security services or elevators. If this section were to apply to care services, different rental units might have different mandatory care packages. Therefore, section 18 must be amended to

3 That is, all mandatory packages must include some (not the same) accommodation and the same care services.

4 Changes to the mandatory package for all residents are discussed below.

indicate that care services are not included.[4]

RECOMMENDATION 26: That section 18 of the proposed *Rent Control Act, 1991* be amended to exclude personal-care services, in order to ensure that the same mandatory package is available to all residents.

CREATING INFORMED CONSUMERS

Rest homes may accept residents whose care needs are greater than the homes are capable of meeting. In addition, residents decline with age and their need for care increases: persons entering a rest home at a high level of functioning may over time develop needs that cannot be met in the residence.

Operators may wish such residents to move to higher-care facilities. The residents may agree, but there may be no suitable spaces available. Or, the residents may be unwilling to move in the belief that their care needs can be met in their "home." In response, operators may wish the residents to purchase optional extra care, but the residents may feel their individual requirements are covered by the mandatory package.

Residents should know in advance that many rest homes can effectively offer only relatively low levels of care, and that such homes are primarily housing, not nursing homes. Some residents sell their homes and run down their capital purchasing optional care services in a rest home, only to discover that, eventually, even the mandatory package is no longer affordable, and they must leave the home.

The problem is to reconcile what operators are willing and able to provide with what residents want, need, or expect. Part of the solution lies in better market information. Certainly, entry policies, the types of care included in the mandatory package, and available optional services must be made clear in writing in advance of entry.

Operators may define their entry policies in terms of the types of care offered, and are under no obligation to accept someone whose care needs cannot be met within the home. (The Ontario Human Rights Code does not permit discrimination on the basis of disability, but entry could probably be denied on the grounds that the care needs of a particular person could not be met in the home.)[5]

Full market information must be available to prospective residents before they decide to move into a rest home. (The information must be exhaustive, precisely because the consumer may be or is likely to become vulnerable.) Consumers should know what housing and care situations await them. They can then make informed choices about where they wish to live and under what conditions. In effect, we wish to produce a "no-surprises" scenario, in which intervention is minimally intrusive but maximally informative to all involved parties.

Some operators have argued that "if it ain't broke, don't fix it," pointing to the generally good reputation of their industry and the lack of widespread complaints or dissatisfaction.[6] We hold, however, that public policy should not focus on behaviours per se, for behaviours are unpredictable (and expensive to monitor). Rather, we prefer to develop structural conditions that will lead to socially acceptable outcomes. The primary purpose of our proposed intervention is to influence the bargaining process, not to determine the outcome. This intervention must be sufficient to create a system in which residents are not dependent on the good will of suppliers.

The Information Package

We now consider the information that should be provided to all residents and prospective residents, and how that information should be provided.

5 Rest homes are currently subject to the Ontario Human Rights Code, and we recommend they remain so. The Human Rights Code requires "reasonable accommodation" by landlords, and this may include physical alterations to the building. The boundaries of "reasonable accommodation" are yet to be determined. Whether care needs can be met would be argued before the Human Rights Commission following a complaint of discrimination on the basis of disability.

6 Consumer satisfaction is a difficult concept to measure empirically and the Commission does not have data in this regard.

7 The standardized list of services might build upon the services that operators indicated they commonly provided in the 1989 rest-home study done by the Office of Seniors' Issues.

RECOMMENDATION 27: That comprehensive information be provided in writing to each prospective resident of a rest home, covering the following:

1. services available as part of the mandatory package, identifying any limitations on their use, and the price of the mandatory package;
2. optional services available from the operators, identifying any limitations on their availability, and the price of each such service;
3. minimum staffing levels, and qualifications, if any, of staff;
4. details of the emergency-response system, if any, or an indication that none is available; and
5. internal procedures, if any, for dealing with complaints.

THE MANDATORY PACKAGE

To ensure that full information about the mandatory package is available, the Commission recommends that an enumerated master list of services appear in every rest-home lease, annotated as to whether each service is included in the mandatory package. Any restrictions on the use of services in the mandatory package must be indicated.

A standardized list of the most common services, preferably drawn up with the assistance of the industry association, should be used by all rest homes in the province, for ease of comparison.[7]

RECOMMENDATION 28: That the lease include a prescribed standard list on which information is provided as to whether each enumerated care service is included in the mandatory package, identifying any limitations on its use.

Information about the qualifications of the staff and the amount of supervision available to residents is important. Details of any emergency call system—how it is activated, the nature and extent of monitoring, and emergency responses—must be identified in the lease. If, for example, an RN is on duty on the premises twenty-four hours each day, one can assume the care offered is fundamentally different than if an RNA is available during the day shift, and the maintenance worker may be wakened in case of an emergency at night.

The response to the emergency system is also important to know: will the staff simply phone 911, or is there a more comprehensive response? If assistance with medications is provided, the minimum qualifications and/or training of the staff responsible should be clearly stated. Likewise, the number of staff on each shift is important information for prospective residents.[8]

> **RECOMMENDATION 29:** That detailed information on the emergency-response/call system, if any; minimum staffing level on each shift; and qualifications of staff be provided as part of the lease, or a statement be provided that no commitment beyond any legal requirement is made with respect to standards for these services.

Staff qualifications, the extent of supervision, and the emergency response are particularly important, as these are often the primary reasons residents enter a retirement home. Numerous complaints in this area have been received by the Commission: residents expected higher levels of supervision than they received; and staffing on weekends, at nights, and on holidays was unacceptably low. Once again we stress that provided minimum legal requirements are satisfied,[9] operators are free to sell any form and amount of staffing and supervision that the market will bear. They should indicate, however, if no commitment is made to employ staff with particular qualifications.

8 We recommend in Part III mandatory minimum staffing ratios on all shifts. If the home has higher ratios, this information should be provided.

9 See note 8.

10 Printed prices represent the maximum allowable for each optional service, like published hotel rates. Operators may, of course, sell optional services for less.

OPTIONAL SERVICES

Information about the availability of optional services is just as important as information about mandatory services. We therefore recommend that operators also complete a standard form listing optional services. This form should indicate that each service is available as an option on a fee-for-service basis at a specified price, or that it is not offered by the home and other arrangements with outside suppliers must be made by the residents. Any service offered but not on the standard list may be added, with relevant pricing information. Completion of these forms should be required in all rest homes, including those receiving domiciliary-hostel funding.

Residents and operators may contract for optional services for any period of time, separately from the lease. (For example, they may agree to the provision of a particular care-service option at its listed price for one year.) In the absence of a specific contract for optional services, the standard list would constitute an offer by operators to sell services to residents at a certain price. The list may offer various pricing alternatives and may impose limits (minimum or maximum) on the amount that may be purchased.

The standard list or rate sheet for optional services must be posted prominently within the home or provided on a printed form, available to anyone on request.[10] This requirement will not only give complete information to potential residents but also protect current residents who wish to buy additional services: publicly posted prices will establish a ceiling for a given service, and should lessen the tailoring of prices to take advantage of the vulnerability or dependence of individual residents.

RECOMMENDATION 30: That information about and prices for optional services provided by operators be readily available on a prescribed standard form list. This list, completed by the operator, must be posted publicly in the rest home or available on request.

Operators cannot withhold posted pricing options from particular persons as their use patterns change. Operators may remove any option entirely when a new list is prepared; however, as long as an option is presented as available every resident must be free to purchase it.[11]

RECOMMENDATION 31: That operators not be permitted to withhold any optional service or its posted price or charging method from individual residents.

Although we do not recommend direct control of prices for optional care services purchased on a fee-for-service basis, purchasers must be aware of pricing trends so they can make informed choices. Some homes have a history of stable and modest price increases; others tend towards dramatic price rises. Consumers should be informed of these histories. The Commission is therefore recommending that the posted price list for optional services also indicate, for each service, the average annual increase in per unit price during the previous two years (or since inception if it is a newer operation).

RECOMMENDATION 32: That the price list include details of price increases for each optional service during the previous two years.

Residents must also have up-to-date information on their current account with the retirement home. They may, for example, be aware that a particular optional service is provided only at additional cost, while not fully appreciating the cumulative cost of regular usage. Residents should sign a receipt for each optional service.

RECOMMENDATION 33: That each resident shall sign a receipt for each optional service and shall receive on a weekly basis an enumerated statement of optional or additional charges incurred during the preceding seven days.

11 That is, the operator cannot sell an unlimited-use option as long as actual use is low, but require a resident to purchase on a fee-for-unit-of-service basis when usage increases. This recommendation should respond to a frequently heard complaint that services such as a meal tray in bed are provided gratis on an occasional basis, but when particular residents' needs become greater, a charge is levied on those persons.

12 If a resident is unable to sign, some other arrangement acceptable to both operator and resident (or guardian) may be specified in writing and in advance.

13 Services sold on a debundled basis will be subject to the Goods and Services Tax; the mandatory package is apparently exempt. However, we cannot alter our recommendations to facilitate exemption from the GST, although operators may wish to consider tax liability when deciding what and how to sell.

Copies of the receipts should be attached to a weekly statement.[12] Frequency of collection of these charges can be negotiated privately between the parties, but the information must be provided weekly.

PRICE INCREASES

Many homes currently specify that all prices will be fixed for a period of one year from the date of entry. This is highly commendable and helps ensure a "no-surprises" scenario for the settling-in period.

The Commission has previously recommended that any care service that is part of the mandatory package be subject to the same protections as accommodation; otherwise, there will be a strong incentive to evade the intent of rent control through excess increases in the charges for mandatory care services. However, we do not recommend that optional care services be subject to rent or price control.

There are obvious implications to this approach: if the price of the optional care package is uncontrolled, operators who wish to be outside the rent-control system will debundle as many care services from the mandatory package as is possible. Services sold on a user-pay basis will be exempt from rent control; the same services, sold as part of the mandatory package, will be covered.[13]

Some operators might choose to offer a low-priced mandatory package, including few or no services, and high-priced optional care services for which prices will be free to rise. Residents would then be likely to expect high quality in the optional services provided, and to express displeasure if they did not get their money's worth. As the services are optional, residents would be free to seek alternative suppliers. Moreover, if homes offered vastly different cost breakdowns, such information would be a useful guide to potential consumers (and advocates) to what might be expected in different settings. Any data greatly out of line may also alert potential residents to business practices in that particular setting.

Timing

Although price increases for the optional services would not be controlled, some measure of stability would be needed. Although formally designated as optional, certain services may be vital to residents' daily living. The freedom to refuse services when prices increase may be severely limited, particularly in the absence of community-based alternatives. In addition, the Commission recognizes that vulnerable persons typically change their place of residence only with great reluctance.

As well, residents have expressed frustration at being "nickel-and-dimed to death" by small but frequent increases in individual care-service prices. None of these increases may be excessive, but the cumulative effect may be a substantial overall rise, in excess of what residents wish or are able to pay.

In recommending an approach to the timing of price increases for optional services, we face a tradeoff between flexibility for individual operators and the need for vulnerable residents to anticipate future costs and to avoid the need to repeatedly change their place of accommodation. We are also influenced by the lack of practical choices for residents purchasing certain optional care services. Residents may face annual increases for the allowable rent growth, plus 3 percent for capital or extraordinary operating costs, as well as cost increases for optional services; thus, the total annual increase for residents reliant on many optional services may be high.

RECOMMENDATION 34: That price changes to the list of optional services be permitted only at six-month intervals. In addition, optional services may be withdrawn from all residents only at six-month intervals. Tenants must be notified in writing ninety days in advance of any increase in optional service prices or of termination of any optional service.

As prices may increase or the services terminate while a fixed term lease is in effect, residents may face significant increases in the prices of optional, but vital services, while tied to an annual lease. Therefore, we recommend that the *Landlord and Tenant Act* (*LTA*) contain a provision permitting residents to terminate a fixed-term lease if the prices of optional care services that they use are increased, or if the service is terminated during the term of their lease. Proper advance notice of the resident's intent to depart would be required, in accordance with the *LTA*. If operators did not increase the price of optional care services used by a particular resident or withdraw them during the term of the lease, the escape provision would not be applicable.

Under the *LTA,* residents on a month-to-month lease may terminate a lease on the last day of any month of the tenancy provided that they give sixty days' notice. Therefore, month-to-month tenants would not need the escape clause: they would have at least thirty days to decide whether to pay the higher prices or seek a new home.

RECOMMENDATION 35: That the *Landlord and Tenant Act* contain an "escape clause" for residents of rest homes permitting them to terminate fixed-term leases with notice if an optional service that they use is withdrawn or the price of an optional service they use is increased during the term of the lease.

CHANGING THE MANDATORY PACKAGE

We have already indicated that operators may not change the composition of the care-services part of the mandatory package for individual residents. However, operators may wish to make such alterations for all residents; for example, they may wish to save money by replacing twenty-four-hour RN availability with that of an RNA; or they may wish to respond to increased need or competition in the marketplace by instituting a new twenty-four-hour RN service for all residents. They may want to change a mandatory-package service into an optional extra, payable on a fee-for-service basis; or they may want to incorporate an optional extra into the mandatory package.

In a landlord-and-tenant relationship governed by the *LTA* and the proposed *RCA*, neither party may unilaterally alter the tenancy agreement, i.e., the composition or cost of the mandatory package. Thus, operators would be permitted to make such changes only in accordance with the applicable law.

Should operators wish to enrich the mandatory package without charge or consent, the addition is unlikely to be resisted by residents. However, should operators wish to increase the cost of the mandatory package to reflect this upgrading, such increases in cost must be fully subject to rent-control guidelines. Operators may wish to absorb these higher costs within the annual guideline, which applies to both the accommodation and care-services portion of the mandatory package.

We recommend that operators be permitted to base an application for a rent increase (3 percent above guideline) for all units based on the cost of new or upgraded mandatory care services. This will require an amendment to the proposed *RCA*.

RECOMMENDATION 36: That costs incurred in providing new or enriched care services in the mandatory package of registered rest homes be allowable expenses in calculating the "3 percent above-guideline" increase under the proposed *Rent Control Act, 1991*.

14 For example, if the operator wishes to make an entire building wheelchair accessible, such costs may be applied for under the proposed *RCA* within the 3 percent above-guideline ceiling for eligible capital expenditures.

15 A downgrading of the mandatory package while keeping the price constant would, of course, be equivalent to a price increase.

16 Unilateral alterations to the tenancy agreements are not permitted under rent control and the *LTA*.

17 In addition, residents who choose to remain despite the reduction in services could oppose any eviction application brought by the operators thereafter. Paragraph 121(3)(a) of the Act prohibits the court from terminating a tenancy if the landlord is in breach of a material covenant in the tenancy agreement (a term of the contract important in the circumstances).

Such an enrichment of the mandatory package may result in higher costs to the residents, even if the "improvement" was not wanted. The situation is analogous to that in which the landlord of a conventional apartment wishes to upgrade the common facilities.[14]

Downgrading of the mandatory package is more troublesome, for lower "rent" may seem inadequate compensation. Individual residents may enter a specific rest home precisely because of the security offered by a certain service. This perceived security would not readily be offset by a monthly charge reduced by a few dollars.[15]

Operators should be able to alter the composition of the mandatory package in response to competitive or fiscal pressures, provided that the interests of tenants are appropriately protected. However, when operators reduce services provided in the mandatory package, they breach their leases with the residents.[16] Such breach of contract gives residents three options for remedy.

First, residents can seek a reduction of rent because services have been discontinued or reduced (*RCA*, section 26). The rent officer may permanently reduce the maximum rent chargeable, temporarily reduce the rent being charged, or order that the rent not be increased for a designated period of time.

Second, under section 113 of the *LTA*, residents can request that the lease be terminated or the rent lowered to compensate for the reduction in services. The court can order a temporary or indefinite rent rollback. Termination of the lease would likely be granted only if the service reduction were a significant breach of the tenancy agreement.[17]

Third, residents can seek common-law remedies for breach of contract, i.e., damages or an order for the operators to do what they contracted to do (specific performance). The latter remedy is rarely granted; courts have proven unwilling to monitor private relations to the extent of ensuring that a party performs and continues to perform particular contractual duties. Therefore, a court is unlikely to order operators to restore the discontinued service; however, it would likely order the payment of ascertainable damages.

All the above remedies depend on the initiative of residents, and asserting them requires time and money. The expense, complexities, and inconveniences inherent in all legal proceedings would ensure that disputes about reductions would be limited to services important to residents.

This Commission therefore does not feel it necessary to make recommendations with respect to reduction of mandatory services. When the reduction is trivial in nature, no legal consequences are likely to follow. Where the reduction is significant, residents have remedies available under present law.

Related Matters

ACCESS TO SERVICES

One of the most efficient checks on potential abuses of pricing power is the competition of the marketplace. If residents are aware that alternative suppliers of services exist and that they can access them, marketplace competition is likely to operate in the residents' interest.

Residents can also decline any or all outside suppliers in favour of purchasing services from the operators or the operators' "preferred" supplier, even if comparable government or community services are available without fee. The only requirement is that residents know the options and make informed choices.

It would be useful to have printed information setting out community-delivered services available to the public at large. Residents would then be able to make informed choices according to their preferences and priorities. By using community-based services now available (and those that will, in the future, be provided through the long-term-care system), residents could delay or prevent running down their financial assets and, eventually, being forced to move from the residence.

> **RECOMMENDATION 37:** That appropriate community information services be funded by the government to collect and distribute information on the availability of community-based services for vulnerable adults.

Some operators now sell optional services that a resident could receive without charge through an agency such as Home Care. It is not the operators' responsibility to inform residents of their eligibility for Home Care or other community services; this task should properly fall to an advocate, case manager, or the residents' doctors. However, operators may be required to distribute information about available alternative services that come to residents, just as they must distribute residents' mail unopened.

As well, operators of rest homes cannot deny or impede access to community-based or other outside services (including Home Care). Nor can operators charge fees to permit the delivery of portable services, unless a direct outlay is required of them.

Coverage of the premises under *LTA* will give outside suppliers a right of entry, when invited by a tenant. The setting provided to an outside supplier must be comparable to that available for an in-house service.

> **RECOMMENDATION 38:** That operators not be permitted to deny or impede access to the rest home by any outside service providers requested by the resident, that use of the premises must be given on terms no less advantageous than those under which the operators deliver the same or similar services, and that no fee be charged to outside sup-

pliers for entry, except to defray or offset direct costs to the operators.

"An outside provider" encompasses both private and non-profit suppliers, including traditional care-providing professions and any alternatives (such as homeopathy, naturopathy, acupuncture, etc.) that a resident may choose.[18] Residents have a clear right to maintain their own medical doctor or other service provider; operators may not pressure residents to use the services of the house doctor.

It is the residents' right to choose any service available from Home Care, other community agency, or private market source over any optional service offered by operators.[19]

> **RECOMMENDATION 39:** That no residents be required or coerced to purchase optional services from any named service provider (including the operators or the house doctor) over suppliers of their own choice.

Because a rest home is the residents' home, residents are eligible for all community services delivered by agencies such as Home Care. Just as these services can enable people to stay in their own homes longer—perhaps indefinitely—so, too, can they offer stability to residents of a rest home.

At present, some agency services for people in their own homes are effectively denied to residents of rest homes. Because the demand for these services exceeds the supply, administrative rationing occurs. Many service providers presuppose that residents of rest homes automatically receive care at the home; therefore, they are not a priority for limited community-based services.

Such a view is unacceptable. It is the Commission's position that residents of rest homes must have all the rights of community residents. They must therefore qualify for community-delivered services on exactly the same basis as persons living in their own homes.[20]

As the long-term-care project develops, the shortage of

18 Provided only that there are no externalities—interference with the rights of other residents—no restrictions may be placed on whom residents wish to have visit them.

19 Once rest homes are under the *LTA* and the proposed *RCA*, operators will be unable to require residents to purchase any optional service from any particular provider (including themselves) as a condition of continued residence.

20 See discussion on long-term care, chapter 3 and Recommendation 3.

21 A senior with OAS/GIS/GAINS has a minimum monthly income of $900, with which to find alternative accommodation.

community services for individuals in their own homes should ease somewhat. In the interim, rationing is inevitable, but not the systematic exclusion of residents of rest homes.

RECOMMENDATION 40: That Home Care and other community-based agencies consider residents of rest homes to be equally eligible for their services as anyone else in the community, i.e., they may not discriminate against individuals on the basis of their residence in a rest home.

DEPARTURE

One retirement home visited by the Commission had, until very recently, a policy prohibiting wheelchairs and/or walkers, and was promoted and advertised as a community for the well elderly. At a certain stage of decline, residents were expected to leave the community. (It is our sense that policies requiring departure solely on the basis of physical decline contravene the Human Rights Code. In any case, competitive pressures to fill spaces in rest homes appear to be ending such practices.)

Usually residents live at their rest home until they require more care than can be obtained in the home. They could not be required to leave except as provided in the *LTA*, e.g., if they have used up their capital and can no longer pay the rent, they must move out. Even should this happen, they cannot be immediately evicted to the street. The *LTA* provisions for eviction for non-payment of rent would have to be followed.

Operators have no ongoing obligation to residents once the rent cannot be paid, nor does the state have any obligation to maintain them at the same level of accommodation, as it was their free decision to spend their money on this type of housing. Regrettably, such persons have to leave the rest home, probably for a lower overall standard of living.[21]

It is in everyone's interest to anticipate these outcomes as early as possible. Landlords have a right to investigate the creditworthiness of potential residents, and under the *LTA* they can ask for the last month's rent in advance. If it appears that an individual resident will have to leave the home, departure should be planned.[22]

The unanticipated early departure of residents creates problems for both residents and operators. Operators have the right to notice under the *LTA*.[23] (For reasons of good will, they may not insist on enforcing this advance notice provision, although they have a right to do so.) Under the *LTA*, operators must make a reasonable attempt to re-let the premises, thereby mitigating the damages. Departing tenants (or their estates) have the right to sublet or assign; once the premises are re-let, the tenants' financial obligations are at an end.

At present, operators may have no incentive to rent vacated premises if there are other vacancies in the building, as the rent is guaranteed for the vacated unit. To offset this possibility, we recommend that the rental of the first available unit of the type and price vacated be deemed equivalent to a sublet, thus freeing the departing tenants (or their estates) from further financial obligation.

RECOMMENDATION 41: That rental of the first unit of the type vacated by a departing resident ends the financial liability of the departing tenant or estate.

TIED SELLING AND CONFLICT OF INTEREST

Overlapping ownership can have adverse effects on the interests of residents and the broader public. Physicians, psychologists, or lawyers who own rest homes to which they may refer clients have a financial interest in ensuring that all beds are filled, irrespective of the needs of individual patients.[24] The

22 In some cases, departure can be delayed or made unnecessary by the provision of portable community-based services to the resident within the home.

23 The Act requires sixty days' advance notice by a tenant plus any unexpired portion of a third month, if the tenancy is monthly. If the tenancy is annual, the financial obligation continues until the end of the year. As with any other residential accommodation, this continuing financial obligation would also apply in case of the death of the resident, with the ongoing responsibility borne by the estate.

24 The situation is perhaps analogous to referrals to a medical laboratory. Doctors are prevented from owning such facilities to avoid the possibility of conflict of interest.

Commission is not suggesting that inappropriate referrals are made, but rather that the potential exists; and the public interest is best served by minimizing the possibility of conflict of interest.

The Commission received a submission from a person concerned about overlapping ownership in his community and the possibility of inappropriate referrals by the local doctor. Another submission raised the difficulties of bringing action against a rest home when the local physician, who might have provided expert information on his patient's condition, was the defendant by virtue of his ownership of the premises.

A few days later, we received a letter from a medical doctor in a different part of the province, describing how he had tried for some time to persuade anybody to establish a needed care facility in his community. Eventually, out of frustration, the doctor had begun such an operation himself. Although his motives are clearly exemplary, the outcome is unacceptable in public-policy terms: once a facility is established, there is a strong financial incentive to ensure full occupancy. There is also a potential conflict of interest in serving the residents as physician and owning the home.

> **RECOMMENDATION 42:** That no lawyers, social workers, or persons regulated under the *Regulated Health Professions Act, 1991* be permitted to have any professional relationship with residents in a rest home in which they have or their immediate family has a financial interest.

Any persons in contravention of this recommendation, at the time it is enacted, should be exempted for a specified period of years.

A further problem arises when operators serve as trustees for residents. The potential for financial abuse is great because trustees may sell or rent residents' previous homes, and substantial sums of money may be involved.

Under the proposed *Substitute Decisions Act, 1991*, certain persons, including rest-home operators, would be precluded from being appointed guardians of either the persons or the property of incapable residents of a rest home. Operators would also be excluded from witnessing the signatures of rest-home residents on a continuing power of attorney for property or person. The Commission believes that these exclusions should be extended to include the spouses and children of rest-home operators.

RECOMMENDATION 43: That subsection 10(2), section 24, and subsection 54(1) of the proposed *Substitute Decisions Act, 1991* be amended to exclude the immediate family of rest-home operators from being witness to a continuing power of attorney by a rest-home resident, and from being appointed by a court as the guardian of the person or property of an incapable person who resides in the rest home.

COMPLAINTS AND UNDELIVERED SERVICES

Consumer dissatisfaction with services and their delivery in rest homes is broadly based and wide ranging—from the poor quality of the food, to being left too long in a bath (which is also too hot), to programs and services promised but not delivered.

When basic safety is at risk, a public response must be mandatory and fast. (Some ways to ensure such responses are discussed in Part III). Beyond basic safety, however, the issues become more fraught.

There are informal mediative mechanisms as well as more formal remedies. Mediation is often a preferred option (although mediators must always be sensitive to systemic power imbalances).[25] A request, formal or informal, that a

25 The power imbalance between operators and residents may lead to fear of recriminations if residents' unhappiness is expressed too vocally or frequently. A number of submissions to the Commission have indicated that this is a major concern to seniors, and a major inhibition of their theoretical rights to satisfaction as consumers.

problem be redressed will often resolve matters satisfactorily. Because the residents may feel vulnerable, a third party may raise the issue on the residents' behalf. A residents' council, if one is in place, may resolve matters, or operators may wish to establish an impartial adjudicative mechanism. This might take the form of a home ombudsman, who is outside the system but acceptable to all parties, or informal third-party arbitration, in which each side appoints one member, who together choose a chair. The Ontario Long-Term Residential Care Association (OLTRCA) has an informal grievance-resolution mechanism that may also be appropriate in some cases.

> **RECOMMENDATION 44:** That informal mediation be pursued as a "first-line" response to disputes within a rest home whenever possible.

Informal dispute resolution takes many forms, and it would be inappropriate for the Commission to mandate a specific approach. By its very nature, mediation requires good will and a readiness to compromise, and such an attitude cannot be legislated.

We also urge that the industry consider a fast, informal, and effective ombudsman system. The costs of such an approach should not be extensive and could be shared by a small levy on each participating bed, or from the registration fees levied by the industry associations.

> **RECOMMENDATION 45:** That the rest-home industry consider adoption of an ombudsman system for fast and informal resolution of disputes.

We also recommend that each home identify in writing what dispute-resolution mechanism it adopts, if any, or that none is in place. This information should be part of the information package if there is one, and should be available in advance on request. If a home chooses not to commit itself in advance to a particular mechanism, potential residents will understand, before moving in, that grievances will have to be redressed on an informal ad hoc basis or through formal procedures.

RECOMMENDATION 46: That operators indicate in writing in advance any voluntary adjudicative procedures they are prepared to adopt.

Mediation may not be attractive to some residents; they may prefer recourse to the courts or other formal procedures. This right must be protected. The formal remedies available to a resident obviously include all avenues offered to the general public. If a mandatory service is promised but not delivered, residents may seek the remedies available in the *LTA*, the *RCA*, and the common law. In the case of optional services, residents may wish to pursue contractual remedies, perhaps in small-claims court.

To the extent that grievances reflect a vague, ill-defined dissatisfaction rather than a specific, concrete issue, there may be little operators can do to satisfy residents. Ultimately the residents' responses are subjective. The real issue may be that the residents are simply unhappy in that particular setting. The only solution may be for residents/consumers to take their money elsewhere. The Commission understands that moving is not a pleasant prospect for frail and elderly persons; however, when all other options are exhausted, it is appropriate and necessary for consumers to exercise their financial power, however difficult moving may be.

7
Life Near the Bottom

1 Paragraph 1(1)(j) of the Regulations defines a "hostel" as "any place of board or lodging maintained and operated by a municipality or the council of an approved band or by a person or organization under an agreement with a municipality, the council of an approved band, or the Province of Ontario, for needy persons ..."

2 All social-assistance rates in this chapter are those in effect in October 1991.

Many rest homes—those that we describe as boarding or lodging homes—primarily accommodate people with low incomes. Some residents receive social assistance under paragraph 12(3)(b) of the *General Welfare Assistance Act* (*GWAA*) Regulations. Under these "hostel provisions,"[1] a municipality may contract with private (for-profit or non-profit) operators to deliver accommodation, meals, and, usually, limited care services to individuals "in need," as determined by the *GWAA* needs test. Operators receive a per diem payment from the municipalities up to a provincially determined maximum (currently $33.40 per day or approximately $1,015 per month).[2]

Participation by municipalities in the hostel program is optional: if they choose to participate, they are required to enter into a contractual agreement with each operator, but there are no provincial guidelines governing the content of such agreements.

Some rest-home residents may be on social assistance, but not funded through the hostel provisions. Those considered to have "disabilities," which includes many persons discharged from psychiatric hospitals as well as persons with psychiatric and/or developmental disabilities, are supported under GAINS(D) [Guaranteed Annual Income System—Dis-

Table 7
Housing and Income Options for Single Adults on Social Assistance, October 1991

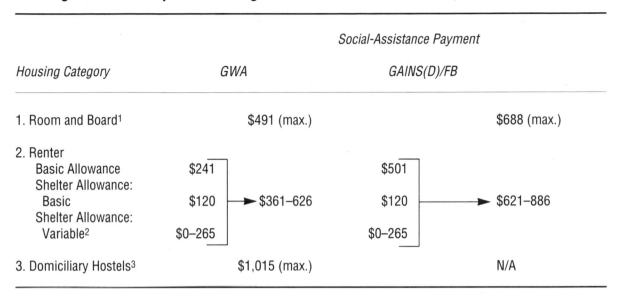

	Social-Assistance Payment	
Housing Category	GWA	GAINS(D)/FB
1. Room and Board[1]	$491 (max.)	$688 (max.)
2. Renter		
Basic Allowance	$241	$501
Shelter Allowance: Basic	$120 → $361–626	$120 → $621–886
Shelter Allowance: Variable[2]	$0–265	$0–265
3. Domiciliary Hostels[3]	$1,015 (max.)	N/A

1. These rates include a mandatory Special Boarders' Allowance of $50 (effective August 1991) to meet personal requirements.

2. The variable shelter allowance is paid to all renters with shelter costs in excess of the basic amount ($120), to a ceiling of $265, regardless of actual shelter costs. The Ministry of Community and Social Services estimates that about one-third of all recipients who receive the renter rate pay rents above the ceiling.

3. Participation in the hostel program is optional for municipalities. Payment is made directly to operators. In addition, residents receive a personal-needs allowance of $112, which is paid to the operators.

abled]. (This is referred to as Family Benefits (FB) or simply "disability pension.") Their current income is a maximum of $688 per month (under the room-and-board rate). Others receive assistance under the municipally delivered *GWAA*, with a maximum monthly payment of $491 (room-and-board rate).[3]

Some seniors also live in rest homes: often their only income is the basic Old Age Security (OAS) plus federal and provincial supplements.[4] The total with maximum supplements is $899.97 per month; none of this depends directly on

3 General Welfare Assistance (GWA or GW) is intended as short-term assistance and is delivered by municipalities who exercise discretion over many of its terms and conditions (within provincial guidelines). Family Benefits is intended to support persons with longer-term need, and is delivered by the province; rates and conditions are constant across Ontario. Many vulnerable persons first receive GWA:

those without disabilities may remain on GWA unless they become "permanently unemployable" or reach sixty years of age. They then may qualify for GAINS(D), which operates within Family Benefits. The three categories of benefits under GAINS(D) are: permanently unemployable (PUE); disabled; or sixty to sixty-four years of age.

The Canada Assistance Plan (CAP), passed in 1966, is the major piece of federal legislation in the field of social assistance. Eligible costs are shared fifty-fifty with the provinces, and in Ontario, GWA spending is shared fifty-thirty-twenty by the federal/provincial/municipal governments. Provinces (or municipalities) initially decide to make CAP-eligible expenditures, and until recently, there was no overall ceiling on federal matching payments.

In the 1990 federal budget, the government announced it was imposing a 5 percent ceiling on the growth of CAP payments to Ontario, Alberta, and British Columbia for two years: this is the "cap on CAP." In the 1991 budget, the federal government announced that it would continue the "cap on CAP" for an additional three years (i.e., until 1995–96). The legality of the federal action, challenged by the provinces, was upheld by the Supreme Court of Canada in September 1991.

The effect of the ceiling is to increase the provincial share of total program costs and to decrease that of the federal government: in 1991–92, the 5 percent restriction is expected to reduce Ontario revenues by $1.3 billion, converting a fifty-fifty

the type or location of the recipients' housing: seniors may use their income to purchase accommodation in a rest home or for any other purpose they choose.

"Non-hostel" Accommodation

Much of this chapter focuses on the hostel "system." Initially, however, we consider accommodation that is not funded under the hostel provisions.[5] If not assisted under these provisions, non-senior rest-home residents will receive their social assistance under the GAINS(D) or General Welfare Assistance (GWA) "room-and-board" rate. The alternative to a rest home is accommodation-only rooming houses, for which one receives support at the "renter" rate.[6] (See Table 7.)

The rents paid by those receiving the room-and-board or the "renter" rate are private-market transactions between proprietors and renters. Oral presentations before the Commission reported that room-and-board rates often begin around $300 per month and go up to and occasionally exceed the gross monthly income of persons on social assistance.[7] There is no legal requirement that boarders have any money left after paying rent; indeed, rents exactly equivalent to the GAINS(D) cheque were the norm in at least one community we visited. Proprietors might, on a purely voluntary basis, dispense to residents small amounts of money—perhaps $10 per month for bus fare or cigarettes.[8]

The amount of rent charged in rest homes seems to bear no systematic relation to supply and demand in local housing markets. In some cases, rents are virtually determined by social-assistance levels; limited only by rent-control ceilings where applicable, every dollar increase in benefits is passed through in higher rents, even when there is excess available accommodation. Such rents appear to reflect the power imbalance between proprietors and renters rather than housing-market conditions.[9]

Some rents reflect supply and demand within a specific subset of the housing market: poor-quality accommodation must often be shared among adults on social assistance who are unacceptable to many landlords. In still other cases, rents are set by some community norm, blending what is "traditional" and what is "fair": these situations tend to be found where rents are lower, communities smaller, and operators less entrepreneurial.

MORE MONEY FOR SOCIAL ASSISTANCE

"Social assistance rates are too low." This is, of course, the most common criticism of the entire system; and because of the huge cost involved, it is most difficult to rectify. Nevertheless, we accept the basic point: social assistance is seriously underfunded and benefit levels are too low. The Social Assistance Review Committee (SARC) and *Back on Track* have documented this persuasively. In the rest-home context, as room-and-board rates often leave no surplus for the personal needs of residents, there have been calls for blanket increases in the payment schedule. Although we shall highlight certain specific elements of the social-assistance system, we have fundamentally little to add to the adequacy debate.

Given that social assistance has been chronically underfunded, the speed of redress can never be fast enough and short-term increases can never be adequate. However, we are encouraged by and supportive of the initiative undertaken by the previous government, and continued by the present government, to re-examine the entire social-assistance system, particularly its adequacy.

RECOMMENDATION 47: That current initiatives to increase the adequacy of social-assistance payments, to vulnerable adults in particular, continue at the maximum speed possible.

federal/provincial agreement to a seventy-two–twenty-eight plan.

4 A single senior receives the basic OAS of $373.32 (October 1991). The federal Guaranteed Income Supplement (GIS) can raise the total as high as $816.97; and the Ontario supplement adds an additional $83 per month. OAS is a universal entitlement; the two supplements are based on a test of income. None of the income under OAS and the two supplements is considered to be social assistance.

5 Some municipalities choose not to use the hostel provisions of GWA. In communities that do participate in the hostel system, not all rest homes are funded as hostels, and not all beds will be contracted in any premises.

6 The major differences between room-and-board and "renter" accommodation are that the former offers a room and, usually, three meals; the rooming house ("renter") provides accommodation only, with or without access to shared kitchen or cooking facilities. Rest-home accommodation is funded under the room-and-board rate; renters receive accommodation only and are responsible for their own meals and other needs.

7 Note the example of the woman with developmental disabilities cited in the prologue.

8 The cost of accommodation in rooming houses appeared to fall in the $200–$450 range.

With a GAINS(D) cheque between $621 and $886 (the renter rate), $300–$400 a month would remain for food and other necessities of life. On a monthly GWA payment of $361–$626 (renter rate), there would be little, if any, money remaining after the rent was paid.

9 As social-assistance-reform initiatives have discovered, it is difficult to devise a payment system that will ensure that any specified sum (such as the Special Boarders Allowance) can be retained by renters.

10 As of September 1991, there were 30,923 boarders on GAINS(D)/FB. Shifting boarders (maximum $688) to the FB renter rate (maximum $886) yields a maximum monthly increase per person of $198, or approximately $6 million increase in total. In addition, there were approximately 14,000 boarders on GWA during that month.

11 More funds may ultimately translate into increased supply; but, in the short term, the clear and predictable outcome is higher rents.

12 Under paragraph 12(3)(b), authority is given to the director of Income Maintenance to determine the cost "of providing the applicant or recipient with board and lodging in the hostel and with personal needs."

During the public consultation, one municipal official suggested the straightforward abolition of the room-and-board category of social assistance; current recipients would be raised to the renter rate. Assuming the 31,000 persons now at the room-and-board rate were placed at the maximum point on the renter scale, social-assistance costs would increase by $6 million per month.[10]

We have one fundamental difficulty with this suggestion: there is no assurance, or even likelihood, that the increased social-assistance payments would remain in the hands of residents. In a tight housing market, any new money translates into higher rents, as a way to ration the available supply.[11] The same process is likely to occur even in a loose housing market: residents often lack the skills, information, and mobility to take advantage of the better housing that should become accessible with higher levels of income. Thus, there is little incentive for operators to use the higher payment to improve the quality of housing or lifestyle of the residents. Increased benefit levels are likely simply to translate directly into higher income for operators.

We are not suggesting that more money in the system is not desirable or even essential. However, in this time of economic restraint, we cannot recommend large blanket increases in monthly payments without clear assurance that the funds would be retained by the intended recipients.

Hostels

In some communities, hostel accommodation is available, funded under the *GWAA* Regulations.[12] There are two types of hostels in Ontario: emergency (or transient) and domiciliary (or long term).

EMERGENCY HOSTELS

There are approximately 4,300 emergency-hostel beds in the province, of which 2,300 are in Metro Toronto.[13] The emergency hostels, all of which operate on a non-profit basis, include special-purpose facilities for designated target groups, such as battered women, as well as general facilities offering temporary (including overnight) accommodation.[14]

It had been the intention of this Commission to exclude emergency hostels from the Inquiry as our focus is less on overnight than on long-term housing. However, as the economy deteriorates and homelessness and unemployment increase, some emergency shelters have become short-term and even long-term accommodation. Thus, our recommendations are intended to apply to permanent accommodation, regardless of how it is labelled or funded.[15]

DOMICILIARY HOSTELS

Domiciliary hostels emerged in Ontario after proclamation of the 1972 *Nursing Homes Act*. Some nursing homes could not meet the new standards, and municipalities were given permission to fund them as hostels under the *GWAA*. Their function was to deliver ongoing care to resident seniors requiring less than ninety minutes of daily nursing care. At its outset, the funding was exclusively for frail elderly persons; adults discharged from psychiatric settings were included later. (Domiciliary-hostel accommodation seemed an attractive and easy housing option for persons discharged from psychiatric hospitals when Homes for Special Care beds were frozen in 1985–86.)[16]

Adults with developmental disabilities were never formally included in the domiciliary-hostel program; but several hundred such persons currently reside in these settings. There are relatively few seniors funded under the domiciliary-hostel provisions.[17]

Most domiciliary hostels are private for-profit businesses.

13 Metro Toronto designates *all* its hostel accommodation as "emergency" and hence has no "domiciliary-hostel" beds. (Emergency beds used to receive a higher per diem, although this is no longer the case.) It may be that some beds, in Metro and elsewhere, serve a permanent domiciliary function, but they are nevertheless categorized as emergency housing.

14 These general facilities are for groups, including evicted families; refugees; transients and migrants; older single persons; and youth.

15 Under the *Landlord and Tenant Act* [paragraph 1(x)] a specific exclusion from coverage is given to "short-term accommodation provided as emergency shelter." However, not all accommodation labelled or described as an "emergency hostel" is necessarily excluded under paragraph 1(x). The status of any particular accommodation could be argued before the court.

16 Per diems in HSC beds are lower than those in domiciliary hostels.

17 OAS plus supplements would give a senior a monthly income of $899.97, which is usually enough to purchase accommodation in the private market without municipal financial assistance. Seniors resident in a domiciliary hostel before they turn sixty-five will often simply stay there upon reaching age sixty-five. Typically, they sign over their total monthly cheques to the hostel operators.

18 $33.40 x 30.416 days per
month = $1,015 per month.

19 Federal/Provincial Guidelines
with reference to the comple-
tion of CAP 30, Federal/
Provincial Cost-Sharing and
Financial Advisory Services,
November 8, 1986, p.5.

Hostels receive payment for eligible residents on a per diem basis. (The 1990–91 total provincial/municipal expenditures for emergency and domiciliary hostels have been estimated at approximately $58 million. The Ministry of Community and Social Services (MCSS) was unable to separate emergency from domiciliary costs, though one official suggested a fifty-fifty breakdown might not be far off the mark.)

Under paragraph 1(1)(j) of the GWA Regulations, a municipality may participate in the hostel program. If it chooses to do so, it must enter into an agreement with each supplier to provide room, board, and assistance "with personal needs"; payment is to be at or below a maximum per diem rate set by the province. (When the program began in the mid-1960s, the domiciliary-hostel payment was $5 per day; increases were ad hoc until 1987, apparently to offset inflation and in response to pressure from municipalities and operators.)

Since 1987, the annual increases in the domiciliary-hostel rate have been the same as those for FB and GWA. Effective October 1, 1991, the per diem ceiling was $33.40, about $1,015 per month.[18] (MCSS estimates that about 30 percent of the municipalities participating in the domiciliary-hostel program pay at this maximum, though the ministry has been unable to provide us with a provincial average figure.)

Because municipalities can pay any per diem up to the provincial ceiling, rate setting can be vulnerable to arbitrary decision-making: one operator noted to the Commission that his municipality had intended to give a smaller increase than the maximum; it was only through the exercise of "political connections" that the maximum was set.

According to the Canada Assistance Plan (CAP) guidelines[19] the per diem is intended to cover three types of services in addition to room and board:

1. "domestic services of an ordinary household nature," such as meal preparation, cleaning, heavy laundry, etc.;
2. "supervision of an ordinary household nature," such as

pointing out the need for haircuts, medical/dental appointment reminders, observance of house rules, etc.; and

3. "limited personal services," such as those temporarily required during minor ailments.

Unlike room-and-board or renter payments, the domiciliary-hostel payments are made by the municipality directly to operators.

Other than the means testing required for an applicant to qualify for social assistance, the province specifies no eligibility criteria for applicants to be funded under the hostel provisions. Nor must operators meet any provincial criteria to receive a hostel agreement.

The municipality may negotiate any or no conditions in contracts with prospective hostel operators. Thus, receipt of a contract and funding can be contingent upon operators' meeting certain conditions (such as fewer residents per room, or provision of a sitting room) or providing specific care as is identified by the municipality. In some cases, the condition may be compliance with a local rest-home by-law. However, the money can simply be paid by the municipality to warehouse vulnerable persons out of sight of the community.

A municipality will typically contract for only some of the beds offered in any given setting, and not all will be used or paid for at all times. According to MCSS, the precise number of domiciliary-hostel spaces in the province is not known. There are an estimated 9,250 beds in residences that hold municipal contracts. Less than 40 percent of these are subsidized under the domiciliary-hostel provisions; the balance is occupied by self-paying residents. In October 1989, approximately 4,550 domiciliary-hostel beds were occupied.[20] In February 1991, the ministry estimated there were approximately 3,500 domiciliary-hostel beds in Ontario.[21]

The low public visibility of the domiciliary-hostel sector in Ontario is perhaps surprising, given its large size—between 3,500 and 4,500 beds. With provincial and municipal spending

20 Of these about 2,250 residents (49 percent) had psychiatric disabilities. MCSS, *List of Emergency and Domiciliary Hostels by Area Office*, April 29, 1990.

21 These were occupied by approximately 2,200 residents with psychiatric histories, 800 frail elderly persons, and 500 persons with developmental and/or other disabilities. MCSS, Community Services Branch, *Domiciliary and Emergency Hostel Review*, February 1991, p.3.

In the survey on domiciliary-hostel accommodation conducted for this Commission, fifty-five municipalities reported they held hostel agreements with private operators, with some 7,445 beds in residences that hold hostels contracts. (See above, note 1, chapter 2.) Responses to our questionnaire seem to indicate underreporting as the figures err consistently on the low side compared to the MCSS estimates.

22 The Commission is surprised and disappointed that comprehensive information on the domiciliary-hostel system is not available from MCSS. Such an imperfect data base renders difficult not only discussion of the system and analysis of its operation, but also projections about alternative approaches and service-delivery models.

However, there is a major survey under way within MCSS, which is attempting to collect comprehensive descriptive and demographic data on the domiciliary- and emergency-hostel programs in Ontario, and information about the concerns of various stakeholders "particularly … provincial and municipal officials and hostel operators." MCSS, *Domiciliary and Emergency Hostel Review*, p.4.

of some \$30 million per year, the domiciliary-hostel system is a significant form of accommodation for vulnerable adults in Ontario.[22] (There is approximately a 20 percent constant vacancy rate in the domiciliary-hostel accommodation on a provincial basis.)

PROBLEMS WITH THE HOSTEL SYSTEM

The Commission has two fundamental objections to the domiciliary-hostel system as a funding mechanism.

First, a flat per diem is given to all operators within a community. Needs of residents, however, are individual. A uniform per diem leaves it to operators to decide what services individuals will get, based on their own subjective assessments of need and worth or merit. Many residents have described to the Commission how operators deny contracted services as a weapon of social control, moral judgment, or punishment.

The uniform per diem was originally established for convenience and because only limited care services were available or envisaged. Over time, services were added, usually at the behest of the municipalities. When the per diem was inadequate to cover needed services, it was left to the operators to determine their priorities: whether, for example, to sacrifice the special diet of one resident, forgo assistance with bathing for another, cut back on the cost of food, or privately subsidize the residents by doing tasks without compensation.

Such discretion, when exercised by operators with limited or no constraints on their actions, is simply bad public policy, for operators are virtually unaccountable. More important, operators should not be deciding service priorities, access, and individual needs; nor are they usually qualified or trained to do so. A flat per diem gives operators too much power and far too much responsibility. It would be better to assess individual needs and to supply services that are designed and funded accordingly.

The Commission's second objection to the hostel system is

that it disempowers residents. Undoubtedly, the hostel system meets some needs of residents in that they receive accommodation and meals, and for some the lifestyle is attractive. However, the domiciliary-hostel system is a response to the needs of bureaucrats—hospital-discharge planners and municipal welfare administrators—who must find accommodation for difficult clients and keep vulnerable adults off the streets. The system offers a convenient and easy pigeonhole for uncomfortable social problems: operators tend to accept most referrals, and the rest-home environment is a flexible catch-all that can hold almost anyone's needs and problems when there is nowhere else (or nowhere better) to go.

One municipal official has pointed out that the domiciliary-hostel program is virtually the only remaining open-ended, mandatory cost-shared housing program for adults. As long as individuals meet the GWA criterion of being "in need," they can be housed in domiciliary-hostel settings, and the costs will be shared twenty-eighty with higher levels of government. The municipality initiates the spending; the financial involvement of the provincial and federal governments is then mandatory.[23]

Finding affordable housing for economically vulnerable persons is very difficult; however, in order to house residents under the domiciliary-hostel system, municipalities must designate potential residents as needing both housing and care, whether or not this is actually the case. Operators are then paid to provide both accommodation and care. In some cases, the result is an expensive housing program, as it pays for care services that individuals may not need or want. Yet it is only by purchasing both the accommodation and care from operators that municipalities can gain access to the desired accommodation.[24]

The domiciliary-hostel system also meets the needs of operators, providing them with secure and consistent funding. There is a great financial incentive for operators to take almost any resident: filled beds generate per diems; empty beds do not.

23 The "cap on CAP," to which reference has been made, limits federal spending in response to municipal spending. The federal shortfall is picked up by the province.

24 The converse also applies: some persons are required to accept housing they neither need nor want in order to receive care services provided by the operator. This appears to be the case with some accredited alcohol- and drug-recovery programs funded through the hostel per diem.

25 One operator noted to the Commission that even control devices on water taps, though preventing scalding, did little to prepare residents for life outside, where they would have to regulate their own hot and cold water.

26 We note one case brought to our attention during the consultations: all residents were moved out of Murphy Manor in Sarnia so major renovations could take place. They were taken to a home owned by the same company in Windsor, where they stayed from November 1989 to July 1990. Subsequently, they were returned to Murphy Manor. When the receiver decided to close the home in Sarnia permanently in March/April 1991, all residents were expected to be gone within four working days of receiving notice to vacate. See *London Free Press*, September 24, 1990, and *Sarnia Observer*, April 10, 1991.

A domiciliary-hostel contract is between a municipality and individual operators; residents are effectively disempowered. In theory, residents can take control by leaving particular boarding homes and going elsewhere; in practice, however, individuals are often "placed" in specific settings. (Nevertheless, we were told that the competition among operators in one community is so severe that hostel residents are "recruited" at local coffee shops and given small inducements, such as cigarettes, to leave one home and enter another. Residents indicated there was no point in moving as "all these places are basically the same." We have also heard of financial inducements being offered in return for directing clients to certain settings.)

All in all, the domiciliary-hostel system substantially meets the needs of bureaucrats and operators. It does less for many residents.

Residents are typically provided with three meals a day, irrespective of their ability to meet this need independently. When overmedication occurs, individuals may be left to spend their days in bed, sleeping or listless. The all-encompassing atmosphere of the hostel leads to a passive, detached life for the residents. There are no incentives to accomplish anything and strong inducements to remain quiet and uninvolved.[25]

Nor is there any incentive for operators to train their residents to graduate to more independent living situations, for every time a resident leaves, the operators lose a per diem. Agency workers have told the Commission that at times they are not permitted to meet privately with individual residents because of operators' fears that the workers will encourage the residents to leave the home. We have also been told of groups of residents being moved, like pieces of furniture, from one setting to another, without consultation, acquiescence, or warning, when a home is closed temporarily or permanently.[26]

We do not suggest that this depersonalization of residents is universal: one operator showed the Commission a coach house behind her residence that she was planning to turn into a halfway house for residents, as a first step towards independent living. Such an approach is both admirable and noteworthy for its apparent rarity. A far more typical priority, certainly in the larger residences, is full occupancy; the needs of the residents are of secondary interest.

A system that funds care attached to residences, on a per diem basis, rather than people, based on their individual needs, that does so at a high price[27] and disempowers residents in the process is unacceptable.

> **RECOMMENDATION 48:** That the domiciliary-hostel program with its per diem funding of operators be phased out as soon as possible, and that the provincial government commit itself to end the domiciliary-hostel system within a fixed period.

The funding of hostels as if they were small institutions is at odds with recent government social-welfare initiatives.[28] Individualized needs assessment and program design, if not individualized funding, is a major step towards reasserting the unique worth, dignity, and legitimacy of every resident in every hostel. Moreover, as we shall see, such a change in approach need not be significantly more expensive than the status quo.

Ending the domiciliary-hostel program cannot be accomplished overnight; however, the government of Ontario should avoid building up the hostel system into a more substantial "institutional" presence. Short-term per diem funding must be maintained, but future spending should be re-directed to new programs that will provide housing and service alternatives for residents now in domiciliary hostels.

27 Compared to basic social-assistance rates.

28 Recommendation 244 of the Social Assistance Review called for the removal of the domiciliary-hostel program from social-assistance legislation, to be funded and regulated through separate residential-services legislation. It also said that support services to domiciliary-hostel residents should be provided on a "portable" basis.

29 During the Commission's early exploration of this question, we learned that the Regional Municipality of Ottawa-Carleton has made a specific request to MCSS that covers virtually identical ground. The Region notes that during the past few years a number of reports have been written, by community advocacy groups and the local Department of Social Services itself, proposing that alternative use of domiciliary-hostel funding be allowed. Such reallocation of funding is not currently permitted under GWA.

30 In some communities, the payment of the higher hostel per diem is tied to specific performance expectations (though enforcement is often lax). These might include fewer beds per room or meals meeting the standards of the Canada Food Guide. In these cases, there is a clear relationship between the higher per diem expenditures and an improved living situation for residents.

In other communities, however, the agreement may be vague or the performance requirements based on a by-law that applies to *all* accommodation, not just domiciliary hostels. In such cases, the receipt of domiciliary-hostel monies may impose few or no additional requirements upon operators.

31 To keep total spending constant is consistent with our explicit commitment not to view any changes as a cheap option to save money. In fact, a full and comprehensive system of community-based care delivery might cost more—but

An Alternative Approach

We now consider how we can move away from domiciliary hostels towards an alternative that is more resident-based and -centred. First, we look at reallocating existing funding. In this context, we explore how the $1,015 per resident per month in the domiciliary-hostel system might be better spent.[29]

Table 8 presents the differentials between the room-and-board and renter rates and the domiciliary-hostel payments. In the first two cases, residents receive accommodation, with or without meals; in the hostels, residents are also supposed to receive limited care services provided by the operators. The difference in cost roughly estimates the cost to the public of the care services to be provided by operators.[30]

It is a fair and critical question to ask if the government of Ontario receives fair value for this money. In some cases it appears that we do, but in others very little is received in exchange for the $327–$524 addional expenditure per resident per month. We must ask, in the interests of public policy, whether better service and higher-quality accommodation can be delivered for the same money.

We do not use the language of cost saving, for it was such an approach to deinstitutionalization that made a sham of earlier efforts. Rather, we focus on reallocation of expenditures. We do not hold out the elusive (and ultimately deceptive) carrot of major cost savings, in the short term at least.

The alternative approach begins by separating accommodation (and board) from care, while keeping total monthly expenditure constant.[31] Thus, the level of social-assistance payments would be based on the accommodation in which the person lives. The remainder of the $1,015 currently being spent on the hostel would then be available for care services, on a flexible and portable basis, delivered from outside community-based agencies.[32]

The differential between "rent" and total income would

Table 8
Differentials Between Domiciliary-Hostel Payments and Social-Assistance Alternatives

Domiciliary Hostel	Alternative	Payment	Per Resident Monthly Differential	Annual Differential
$1,015 (max.)				
	Room & Board:			
	GWA	$491	$524	$6,288
	GAINS(D)	$688	$327	$3,924
	Renter (max.):			
	GWA	$626	$389	$4,668
	GAINS(D)	$886	$129	$1,548
	Senior:			
	OAS+Supps	$900	$115	$1,380

depend on the housing alternative chosen. Some residents may wish to prepare their own meals, and would receive support at the renter rate; others may choose to remain in room-and-board premises. (The rental setting is more empowering to residents than is room and board, in that it places them in control of their own meal preparation, and provides them with more money to meet this need.)

If residents "moved" from a domiciliary hostel to a room-and-board setting under GAINS(D) (at $688 per month), $327 per month per resident ($1,015 minus $688) would become available for portable community services. If individuals moved to a setting such as a rooming house and were eligible for the maximum variable renter payment under GWA, they would receive $626 monthly, leaving $389 for community-based services.[33]

RECOMMENDATION 49: That as the phasing-out of the domiciliary-hostel program proceeds, funds currently spent on

deliver more—than the current hostel system.

32 The question of control over the reallocated funds is complex. As we discuss subsequently, our preference is for maximum resident involvement in making these decisions. In some cases, outside service agencies would need to be involved.

33 The personal-needs allowance of $112 must be paid in hostel settings; the social-assistance alternative would cover accommodation, food costs, and personal needs. The lower the cost of accommodation (or room and board), the more the individual has available for personal needs. The Special Boarders Allowance of $50 is

not paid separately from the basic room-and-board rate; for our purposes, it is simply included in the monthly total.

34 The Ottawa-Carleton proposal referred to a moderate-size residence of forty persons, which aggregates to over $150,000 per year (based on 1991 rates).

35 The maximum potentially available may be readily calculated. If a resident is moved from a domiciliary hostel to accommodation where he or she would be eligible for the GAINS(D) renter rate—the most probable alternative—the funds available for reallocation amount to $327 per month ($3,924 per year). Aggregated over 4,500 residents, this yields a total of $17.7 million dollars potentially available for community-based services. (All residents, however, will not move.)

the hostel system be made available for reallocation to accommodation (with or without meals), and to care services delivered from the community.

The amount of money available to a person may be inadequate for all needed services, for it may be costly and inefficient for an outside worker to visit one person in a residence. However, when services can be provided to a number of residents at the same time, the approach becomes more attractive. If ten residents in one home require assistance with medications, for example, a visiting nurse's aide can deliver the service on a relatively inexpensive per-resident basis.

For ten people, the available funds amount to $3,270 per month or $39,240 per year (based on the FB/GAINS(D) room-and-board alternative).[34] This is clearly a substantial sum of money and could provide support to residents while not increasing total government spending.[35]

ARRANGING HOUSING

A discharge allowance has traditionally been paid under social assistance to persons leaving institutions, such as hospitals, to establish a residence in the community. As of October 1, 1991, this has been expanded into a new community start-up allowance, available to any person who must "for his or her health and welfare" leave one and establish another permanent place of residence in the community. The new allowance continues to be dependent upon financial need and is limited to a maximum of $775 once in twelve months. It is often used to meet the last month's rent required by some landlords.

It is the Commission's understanding that this new community start-up allowance is being made available to persons leaving hostels to establish independent living in the community. We endorse this action and urge that it be established as a firm policy.

Residents may also wish that a community-housing agency assist in negotiating rent with potential landlords.

RECOMMENDATION 50: That the Ontario government fund non-profit housing agencies to assist in arranging housing alternatives for those residents of rest homes who wish to leave domiciliary hostels and desire assistance to go onto other forms of social assistance.

Such housing groups should not be limited to arranging non-profit housing, although it should be the preferred alternative. The demand for non-profit housing far exceeds the supply, and the cost per unit is high. In some cases, acceptable arrangements might be made with rest-home operators to offer room and board or accommodation only, perhaps even to current residents.

ARRANGING CARE

In many cases, groups of residents, with assistance if desired, may arrange for their own care needs. Former hostel residents might be hired to provide supports for current residents, for care needs can often be met through peer interaction and support, for which formal credentials are neither needed nor desirable. Care-givers must be acceptable to the care recipients, and former hostel residents may be most acceptable of all.[36]

RECOMMENDATION 51: That the Ontario government fund non-profit agencies and groups of current or former rest-home residents to assist residents, as desired, to identify their own care needs and arrange for these to be met in ways acceptable to themselves as they leave domiciliary hostels and go onto other forms of social assistance.

36 For example, the Consumer/Survivor Development Initiative, an anti-recession program of the government of Ontario, was announced in March 1991. Funding of $3.1 million was designated to assist in developing consumer/survivor job-creation strategies and long-term employment projects. Support services to residents of hostels could well fit within this program.

The Commission is aware that Recommendation 51 opens up the question of who is to determine if care needs identified by residents are "reasonable." Although we do not intend to enter into this broad debate, it is our general view that residents, with assistance if desired, are best able to identify their own needs; and that constraints on this approach should be used only in exceptional cases.

37 In some cases, another community-based agency may be contracted to deliver support services. As noted in chapter 4, Habitat Services in Toronto contracts with Community Occupational Therapy Associates (COTA), a non-profit agency, to deliver a life-skills or social/recreational program two half days a week in the boarding homes with which it has contracts. The workers are attached to the homes, and do not follow the residents if they move.

38 Specialized and individualized services currently being delivered, such as individual mental-health counselling, would not be directly affected by our proposals. These programs would continue to receive funding from the Ministry of Health or MCSS. It is possible, however, that the Commission's approach might generate greater demand for these services.

In other cases, a non-profit agency might deliver portable services for a group of residents, either in the home or in a community setting. Again, this care might involve personal support, life skills, or supervision, if and when needed.[37]

We note that if rest homes are covered under the *Landlord and Tenant Act* (*LTA*) as we recommend, residents cannot be required to use support services. It is essential that no community services be delivered to anyone who does not want them. Individuals, groups of residents, or community-based agencies would contract for or deliver community-based services to residents who may wish them, while respecting the right of the others in the setting not to participate.

It is assumed that groups of residents or, failing that, outside community agencies exist or can be created to administer the funds and broker, manage, or deliver the services. At present, it is individual operators, within the broad framework set by GWA, who decide residents' needs. Under the revised approach, groups of residents or community-based agencies would identify priorities within a given budget for care services. Service providers could include agencies such as local Canadian Mental Health Associations or local Associations for Community Living.[38]

It is essential that residents be actively involved in making choices among service needs and priorities. For clients to be disempowered by community-based agencies may be slightly more benevolent than being disempowered by commercial operators, but neither outcome is acceptable: residents must be empowered to participate in the decision-making that affects their lives.

One group of consumers with psychiatric histories suggested to the Commission that an intervening agency was necessary and desirable to assist in the empowerment process, but that consumers and ex-consumers should hold a majority of the seats on the board of directors of any such agency. Certainly such an agency should have an explicit commitment to increasing consumer involvement in policy-making, as expeditiously and to the maximum extent possible.

RECOMMENDATION 52: That all community-based agencies involved with housing or service provision in the move away from the domiciliary-hostel system have an explicit commitment to involve consumers actively in all aspects of decision-making to the maximum extent possible.

There may be some question whether this alternative approach is appropriate for *all* residents of domiciliary-hostel accommodation. In principle, the answer should be in the affirmative, as the portable services should at least duplicate care provided by operators.

However, some residents are quite happy in hostels and have no desire to move or otherwise change their living arrangements. In practice, the transition would be gradual: some residents will choose to leave domiciliary-hostel settings as effective alternatives are developed, but not all residents will choose more independent living.

Hostels have a valid and necessary role in a pluralistic housing environment, particularly as a home for those often rejected by group homes and other more supportive but demanding settings. Excellent operators, of whom there are many across the province, will continue to offer hostel accommodation to those who wish it, in the short term, at least.

We have assumed that outside portable services can meet the needs of residents as well as or better than those provided by operators. However, we do not envisage a situation in which operators will be prevented from providing care services, notwithstanding our strong preference for separating accommodation and care. In certain circumstances, operators may be better able to provide particular care services.[39]

Obviously, every dollar given to operators for care services is a dollar less for the development of portable community-based alternatives. However, there is—for the present—a

39 In rural or isolated areas, for example, the economic viability of portable services is limited; in addition, if the operators reside on the premises, it may be efficient to contract for certain care services if needed and desired. In areas where community-based services are not yet available or feasible, there may be little option but to contract with operators, though the priority should be the development of such services.

40 The Victoria Health Project, an innovative program in British Columbia, offers twenty-four-hour assistance and supervision for seniors in the home as needed. The Greater Niagara General Hospital has recently developed a quick-response team, based on the Victoria model, to serve the region. Brockville Psychiatric Hospital also has a twelve-person multi-disciplinary crisis-intervention team. The aim is to resolve the crisis in the community without hospital admission.

41 We have previously commended the Consumer/Survivor Development Initiative of the Ontario government. This program could well provide the needed peer support on an emergency or on-call basis. See above note.

42 Toronto's Gerstein Centre represents a response based on a consumer/survivor-centred approach. It provides non-medical community-based crisis service to people who have severe and persistent mental-health problems and are experiencing acute crisis. This is a viable alternative to consumer/survivor response teams.

need for certain care services to be provided by operators. Funding can be redirected only in a planned, phased-in manner as community services are developed. Nonetheless, redirecting increasing amounts of these funds, over time, to the non-profit providers of care services should be a priority.

RECOMMENDATION 53: That all new and reallocated funding of services for residents of hostels be directed towards non-profit community-based suppliers whenever possible.

RESPONDING TO CRISIS

Residents may have need of emergency intervention to deal with a crisis or life event. At present, when these occur in the middle of the night, operators' only recourse may be to call the police, who may or may not respond in an appropriate manner. The Commission is aware that "on-call" emergency-response teams are being developed to respond to psychiatric emergencies in the community, as well as to help seniors to remain living in their own homes.[40]

Of even greater potential value, in our view, would be the development of emergency-response teams composed of peers and persons with prior histories of psychiatric disability.[41] Such consumer/survivor initiatives may be the most effective means of assisting residents of rest homes in crisis; peer support may be more useful in many cases than medications and hospital-based teams.[42] Obviously, response teams that assume this formal responsibility should be paid a market wage; but the cost would undoubtedly be less than that of trained professionals operating from institutions.

RECOMMENDATION 54: That groups of consumer/survivors be utilized as paid first-line emergency-response teams in the event of resident crises in rest homes whenever possible.

If the consumer/survivor teams cannot be constituted appropriately, hospital emergency teams may provide an alternative.[43]

COSTING THE COMMUNITY ALTERNATIVE

MCSS has provided us with the current cost of delivering services to persons in the community but not in hostel. The MCSS data suggest it would cost approximately $40 million annually to deliver community services to 4,550 hostel residents—approximately $9,000 per capita—at the level of care provided to the elderly or adults with developmental or psychiatric disabilities currently in receipt of community programs.[44]

The $9,000 per resident would be generated in two ways: first, the funds available from reallocation of the hostel per diem would produce approximately $4,000 per resident per year ($325 per month), or $17.7 million annually if all current hostel residents were to move to GAINS(D). Additional or new funding totalling approximately $5,000 per resident per year ($22.5 million if all residents were to move) would be required to deliver the same quantity and quality of services as are delivered to persons considered to be in the same "consumer" categories, currently receiving MCSS and Ministry of Health (MoH) community programs.

The Commission finds $9,000 per resident to be a very high estimate. First, the needs of residents in hostels may well not be as great as those of recipients of MCSS community programs.[45] More important, residents may not *want* professionalized services of the type assumed by the MCSS figures.

We have stressed throughout this Report the importance of residents' making their own decisions about their own lives, and it has been made clear to us that many of them would prefer peer support and counselling to the interventions of professionals. As they would be actively involved in determin-

43 In either case, such outside support services may provide relief to rest-home operators, and ease the pressure on operators as isolated providers of ongoing care.

44 For example, an adult with developmental disabilities in the Supported Independent Living program receives community services valued at $19,200 per year; the assumption based on the MCSS data is that such an adult currently in a hostel would receive the same value of community services outside a hostel. A post-psychiatric resident of a hostel would receive $14,000 of community services, the mean value of community services per person served, now provided through MoH. The methodology and data are essentially the same as those used by MCSS in costing community-based services for the Rupert Hotel pilot project in Toronto. MCSS, *Cost of Community Programs Provided Under Supportive Housing* (Background Note for Rupert Hotel Pilot Project), n.d.

45 The adult with a developmental disability in a hostel may require less support than that provided through the SIL program. The post-psychiatric patient may not need community services to the value of $14,000 per year.

46 We must consider, as well, the question of economies of scale: the cost of services provided by MCSS and MoH includes travel time, as support workers move from one client to another. The alternative services envisaged here would be delivered to a number of people resident in the same physical location.

47 MCSS notes that a move to community-based services would produce mandatory standards higher than those required of hostel operators; these standards, they argue, would entail higher costs. To measure accurately the full care needs of hostel residents is, of course, a separate and complex issue.

48 We also note the current salary of a full-time COTA (community) worker in Toronto's Habitat program is about $25,000. Under our proposal, ten residents would have available some $50,000 per year, of which $10,000 would be new spending. Depending on the overheads, this sum would purchase somewhere between one and two full-time COTA workers.

49 The MCSS figures, cited in note 44, indicate a per capita annual cost of $2,900 for home-support services for seniors; $5,300 for residential counselling and supportive services in halfway houses; and $4,900 for "ministry purchase of counselling," a flexible category used to fund a wide variety of services, including services in some supportive housing.

ing their alternative-care programs, it is unlikely they would choose service providers with highly specialized credentials. The cost of such peer-provided services would be modest compared to the figures provided by MoH and MCSS.[46]

Moreover, the Commission does not advocate an *enrichment* of services as residents move to an alternative social-assistance category:[47] it is our wish to compare costs at a roughly constant level of care. Operators of hostels are paid about $350 per resident per month for limited care services; it is this modest level of care that we wish to duplicate for community-based delivery.

The Commission believes that an annual total of $5,000 per resident—or just over half the figure produced from the MCSS data—could provide appropriate community services.[48] This figure is based on MCSS per capita expenditure on community programs at the level we envisage.[49]

As before, the funds available from reallocation of the hostel per diems total just less than $4,000 per resident annually. Thus, it would be necessary to supplement available funds by about $1,000 per resident per year to roughly match the services currently received in hostels. Were all 4,550 current residents to move, new spending would total $4.5 million, an expenditure ceiling unlikely to be met.

The Commission wishes to stress that we envisage the move away from the domiciliary-hostel system to be incremental: as groups of residents decide they wish to live more independently, their hostel funding would become available for reallocation under social assistance and for purchase of community-based services. For each resident who chooses to make this change, it will be necessary for the government of Ontario to supplement current funding by $1,000 per year to roughly match the level of service currently provided in halfway houses and through MCSS purchase-of-counselling agreements.

This $1,000 is a small sum to enable a resident to move away from domiciliary-hostel accommodation.

RECOMMENDATION 55: That the provincial government allocate new funding of about $1,000 per year for the provision of community-based services for each resident who leaves domiciliary-hostel accommodation for another social-assistance status in the community. This funding is to be in addition to the reallocated hostel funding.

This proposal would have no immediate applicability in those communities that do not participate in the domiciliary-hostel program. However, consideration should be given to making additional funds available to these municipalities for community services to vulnerable people in rooming houses and room-and-board accommodation.[50]

We also recommend that all the money redirected to community care services be funded 100 percent by the government of Ontario.[51] Municipalities would continue to carry their 20 percent share of social-assistance spending under GWA, but they would, in effect, be free of paying for care services. If residents were placed under GAINS(D) rather than GWA, as would most likely be the case, there would be no municipal financial responsibility for accommodation or care.

RECOMMENDATION 56: That in the reallocation of domiciliary-hostel funding, the "care-services" portion be funded 100 percent by the Ontario government.

For those communities involved in the hostel program, actual cost savings may be substantial.[52]

The hostel program is the responsibility of MCSS; yet the reallocated spending, much of its directed towards those with psychiatric histories, may lie within the traditional community mental-health mandate of MoH. This Commission cannot resolve this jurisdictional dilemma, but stresses that the needs and wishes of the residents must be paramount and the ministries must reach an agreement acceptable to all concerned. We urge the ministries of Community and Social Services and

50 A funding formula could be developed, based on demographic information, to determine how many persons might have been in a domiciliary hostel if the municipality had participated in this program.

51 There is some question about how this "reallocated" funding would be administered: if the money were removed from social assistance, ongoing funding could not be guaranteed, as only social-assistance spending is both mandatory and open-ended.

52 Suppose the domiciliary-hostel payment is $1,015, and the alternative is room and board under GWA at $491. At present, a participating community pays a 20 percent share of the $1,015 ($203 per month) under GWA. If housing were separated from care services, the $491 payment under GWA would carry a 20 percent local share ($98.20). However, the amount now available for portable services ($521) would be funded 100 percent by the government of Ontario. Total governmental expenditure would remain the same, but the provincial share would increase and that of the municipalities decrease. If the resident moved to a provincial program such as GAINS(D), the municipality would save its entire share ($203).

Health to co-operate to ensure a successful transition from the domiciliary-hostel program a system of community-based care.

Some Short-Term Measures

Although we have recommended that the government move away from the domiciliary-hostel system, we wish to raise a number of the critical issues associated with the present system. Our responses may be considered interim steps pending the more fundamental restructuring of the accommodation and care of vulnerable adults.

Concerns presented to the Commission have often begun with the general observation that the domiciliary-hostel program is suffering from system overload: GWA was never intended to deal with an ongoing, long-term, hard-to-serve caseload. There have also been very specific requests, criticisms, and suggestions.

DOMICILIARY-HOSTEL CONTRACTS

In the domiciliary-hostel system, there are three interested parties: the resident, the municipality, and the operator. At present, agreements are between only operators and municipalities: if an agreed-upon service is not delivered, residents can only approach their municipality and hope it will act on their behalf.

The Commission's recommendations would make these residents tenants under the *LTA*. (Although funding the tenant, the municipality would not be a tenant.) The agreements between the municipality and its operators would remain commercial transactions: in return for providing certain accommodation and care to an individual resident, the municipality would pay a set per diem to the operator. Each resident would be a party to a lease, which may include a mandatory care package; the resident may also be a party to a contract for optional care services. These may be enforced by the resident, the lease through the *LTA*, and the optional service contract through contract law.

As agreements between municipalities and operators will determine the terms of the lease and optional care contract, there is a need for direct consumer involvement in the negotiations. Given consumers' individual vulnerability, the Commission recognizes that some form of collective participation and decision-making is essential. We note the growing importance, for example, of associations of psychiatric survivors and residents' associations in some municipalities. The thrust of the approach is that residents become empowered, not individually but collectively.

RECOMMENDATION 57: That residents funded under the domiciliary-hostel system be involved in negotiating the agreements for their accommodation and care between operators and municipalities.

VARIABLE PER DIEMS

Municipalities have the right to offer a variable per diem to operators, but few do so.[53]

RECOMMENDATION 58: That a variable per diem, with two or, perhaps, three levels of remuneration be used by municipalities, as both incentive and deterrent to operators.

Habitat Services in Toronto has three levels of payment. These do not represent differing qualities of accommodation—one-star living for some and three-star for others; nor do they

53 Operators can also be paid the per diem when the resident is temporarily absent, for example, in a temporary return to hospital or for a designated number of annual "vacation days." This program is extremely valuable, particularly to the residents, because it provides them with continuity and stability of housing.

54 Habitat has never experienced litigation as a result of lowering a payment level.

55 There would also need to be some appeal mechanism to protect operators against capricious actions by the municipalities.

56 Any system in which payment is linked to specified targets—"performance-based contracting"—runs a risk that goals formally tied to payment may be met, while non-contracted but presumably desirable goals will be ignored. The common "solution" is to identify as many important goals as possible and incorporate them into the contract. The result may be a very detailed and complex contract.

reflect variable calculations of individuals' "basic needs." All operators are expected to attain top-level standards. The two lower rungs provide incentives for operators new to the system, and offer financial assistance through modestly increased levels of payment as the accommodation and care move towards Habitat's standards.

Probably more important, failure to satisfy the conditions set out in Habitat's contract can result in a lowering of the per diem. When the problem is redressed, the per diem returns to its previous level.[54]

Such penalties are rarely applied, for the mere threat often brings about the desired change; but they have been used three times since April 1987, always with positive effect. Within one or two months, the operators had rectified the situation sufficiently that they were again receiving payment at the highest level. Habitat suggests that the threat of penalties is so effective a deterrent that there is limited need for actual imposition.

In some communities, when operators' actions are unacceptable, the only recourse for the municipality is to terminate a contract or remove the residents. Clearly not all failures to meet terms of agreements between municipalities and operators warrant such a drastic response. A full range of responses is needed.[55]

Some municipal officials have expressed interest in a variable payment system to reward different amenity levels. The presence of a room for social activities or ready access to a telephone for residents might be rewarded through a per diem incentive, as might an improved staff/resident ratio. This approach would sanction differing qualities of accommodation for residents in different settings, which may be unacceptable to some.[56]

Some municipalities are concerned that political and other non-relevant considerations might have undue influence in a variable per diem system.

A FAIR PER DIEM FOR HOSTEL OPERATORS

Many presenters have expressed the view that domiciliary-hostel per diem funding is inadequate to enable operators to deliver quality service to residents. They stress the insensitivity to regional cost variations inherent in a single, province-wide maximum per diem. Individual operators, the Ontario Long-Term Residential Care Association (OLTRCA), and the Aftercare Residential Association (ACRA) have all stressed that higher payments are essential. Operators in communities that participate in the domiciliary-hostel system have argued that payments are too low; operators in communities that do not participate have claimed unfair and inconsistent treatment from one community to another.

To determine if the per diem funding is "fair" may be an impossible task, as it involves highly subjective decisions about the meaning of equity. A proper assessment would require information on the resident mix, their needs, and the expectations placed on operators to meet these needs.[57] As well, it would require information on direct outlays for accommodation, meals, and care services (including the cost of food and labour), taxes and mortgage, other operating costs (such as insurance), and a reasonable return on investment.

It is the right and the responsibility of government to spend public money in the way that best meets public-policy goals. It is the view of this Commission that increased per diem compensation to operators is not the most efficient way to improve the quality of accommodation and care for residents.[58]

The operator of an excellent rest home pointed out that if her time was costed at any reasonable rate, she would be operating at a deficit; it was only by subsidizing the residents through "donating" her time that the operation remained viable. The problem is a common one: many small businesses

57 Information on client demographics and needs may become available from the hostel survey currently under way within MCSS.

58 A preferred response, as we have noted, is to move towards portable services, so that some of the care burden carried by owner/operators will be assumed by outside agencies. Per diem payments to operators may not increase in real terms, but demands on and expectations of operators will decrease.

59 By accepting lower wages than those to which they would otherwise be entitled, operators subsidize those who receive their services, as residents would have to pay higher charges if operators were to receive the going rate for their time.

60 We asked the Ontario Dietetic Association to provide us with their estimate of the cost of three meals a day to meet the minimal requirements of the Canada Food Guide. They indicated that no reliable figures are available for Ontario; moreover, they noted that the Canada Food Guide is not always a reliable measure.

We also learned from a major union in the field that most of its members work at or near minimum wage, and there is little reason to believe the non-union sector pays more.

61 Rest Home Industry Study (untitled), by R. C. Taylor and Associates, Management Consultants, prepared for the Rest Home Association of Ontario, Region 4 (Windsor), November 5, 1984.

62 This figure was arrived at by more than doubling wages, including those of a psychiatrist, psychologist, psychiatric nursing staff, mental-health workers, and recreation-and-craft instructor, all of which would be funded through the per diem. It is not clear why a psychiatrist would not be paid by the Ontario Health Insurance Plan (OHIP) on a fee-for-service basis.

in Canada would fall by the wayside were the owner/operators' time valued at a fair-market rate. This in no way diminishes the strength of the operator's claim, but simply places it in the broader context of the economic viability of small business, which is obviously beyond our mandate to explore.

In any event, mom-and-pop boarding homes are disappearing from the province, replaced by chain operations with absentee owners and paid on-site staff. As this process continues, the subsidization of residents by owner/operators will end.[59]

COSTING THE PER DIEM

There are two components to an appropriate per diem: capital costs and operating costs.

Many rest homes were bought and sold during the past few years, when prices and interest rates were high. There is no question that a fair return on a normal land purchase is due operators, but it is far less clear that a per diem should reflect the costs of highly leveraged properties, often with multiple mortgages. Although it is probably impossible to define "highly leveraged acquisitions" usefully, we do not believe there is an obligation for the government to finance speculative investments through increased per diems.

With respect to operating costs, this Commission considered attempting to determine a fair per diem, notwithstanding the caveats set out above.[60] However, such a study was soon deemed superfluous in light of what had been done before. A 1984 study by Ralph Taylor and Associates for the Rest Home Association of Ontario[61] proposed a "philosophy of care" for post-psychiatric residents including "tasks and projects such as self-help groups, recreation programs, etc." At that time, the hostel per diem was $21.55; the study produced a "per diem maintenance rate of $68.16 for a resident in a 40-bed rest-home facility dedicated to post-psychiatric care."[62]

Given the time elapsed since the study was produced, there is little point in pursuing its data further. However, it is worth noting that the philosophy articulated in that report is very much at odds with current service-delivery approaches.

A 1989 MCSS study[63] may be more useful, both because it is more recent and because ministry staff worked with all the stakeholders in an attempt to determine an appropriate per diem for ongoing maintenance costs (but excluding capital costs).[64] The report noted that its attempts to cost social services provided under the hostel per diem were "limited and do not completely address the health, nursing or psycho-social needs of the individuals who occupy these hostels since *hostels are not intended to be a new or alternative form of institution.*" (Emphasis added.)

The study concluded that the cost data then available did "not provide justification for any specific course of action" concerning an increase in the hostel per diem. "The per diem would appear to be sufficient to allow most hostels to provide basic room and board, which CAP cost-sharing was intended to cover … however, additional services which may be deemed necessary will have to be funded through a mechanism other than the per diem."

A LIMITED ROLE FOR OPERATORS

Operators have regularly indicated they are able and eager to offer care services, such as counselling for residents with psychiatric disabilities. They are prepared to hire staff and assume a significant role in improving the quality of residents' care and life, provided that adequate funding is forthcoming.

It is the view of this Commission that operators should not be encouraged to become comprehensive care-givers. Operators should be compensated for providing room and board and limited personal-care services. Any additional services that operators wish to offer must succeed on the open market.

63 *Toward a Rationale for Determining a Provincial Per Diem Ceiling for Hostels Funded by the Ministry of Community and Social Services,* Toronto, MCSS, n.d.

64 The report examined the per diem costs at other residential programs, including homes for the aged, homes for special care, homes funded under the *Homes for Retarded Persons Act,* and unregulated (non-domiciliary-hostel) boarding homes.

65 The Commission is not breaking new ground in this discussion. The clear preference of the present and previous governments is to separate accommodation from services and to have the latter delivered by outside, non-profit community-based agencies. The proposals concerning long-term care, discussed elsewhere, are consistent with this approach in that they stress portable services delivered into individuals' homes (which, in the present instance, may happen to be rest homes).

66 Operators also identify residents' personal crises, particularly those occurring in the middle of the night, as major demands on their resources. Although there is an undoubted need for some emergency-intervention capacity, we have indicated a preference for a peer-based approach.

Just because a private operator wishes to sell something does not obligate government to buy it.

If there is a perceived need or desire for counselling or other services, the appropriate government response would be the same as that to any other community-based demand for service. First, a community-based agency should assess the need for the service, preferably on an individual basis, for operators are not necessarily equipped or trained to conduct needs assessments.

For example, one rest home visited by the Commission marketed itself as an alcohol-recovery centre that offered counselling to residents. The Commission, however, saw no evidence of ongoing programming of any kind. Other homes purport to offer "nursing care"; the staff wear white uniforms, but their qualifications and the services they deliver to residents were less easily identifiable.

We do not wish to subscribe to an ethos of unnecessary professionalization, although the operator of the "alcohol-recovery" home appeared to have no meaningful training or experience that would equip him as a counsellor. The point is more fundamental: it is not the place of government to fund any and all services operators may wish to offer. Non-profit community agencies should be the preferred basis of care and service delivery; deviations from this policy should occur only in exceptional circumstances.[65]

Some operators may find this approach limiting; others, however, may view the narrowing of their responsibilities as liberating. The tasks that operators will be called on to perform will be restricted, and, one hopes, the demands on their time reduced. This may make their job somewhat easier and less stressful.[66]

RECOMMENDATION 59: That increased per diem funding for operators not be viewed as the appropriate way to improve the quality of life for rest-home residents, and that operators of domiciliary hostels be encouraged to move towards a role that approximates that of landlords as closely as possible.

We note recommendation 246 of SARC called for a higher per diem to operators in the short term. As we indicate above, we consider such an approach counterproductive in the context of moving away from the domiciliary-hostel funding approach.

This Commission is unable to recommend a major increase in the per diem hostel rate for several reasons:

1. the 1989 MCSS study cited above found no justification for such an increase, notwithstanding the acknowledged methodological and data limitations of its survey;
2. the current and future trend, which we strongly endorse, is to separate accommodation and care services;
3. it would be unwise to make major changes while the current census of hostels is under way, as we lack objective data of even the most basic descriptive type concerning domiciliary hostels; once this information is known, however, it does not follow that government should fund the various services that operators report they are providing; and
4. to strengthen the present system, even on an interim basis, would be at odds with the goal of ending the hostel system and its per diem payments to operators for the delivery of care services.

RECOMMENDATION 60: That no increases in the level of per diem funding to operator (in real terms) be considered at present.

WHO GETS THE CHEQUE?

A single monthly cheque for all GWA residents of a hostel is written by the municipality to the operators: this contradicts the Commission's central principle of resident empowerment, and cannot be supported.

We prefer that separate monthly payments be made by the municipality for each resident, co-payable to operator and resident, with both signatures required for deposit or cashing. To avoid the need to issue multiple cheques, it may be sufficient that each resident authorize payment each month; that is, operators will still receive a single cheque, but all residents will sanction payment of their share of the rent and cost of optional services.

> **RECOMMENDATION 61:** That the domiciliary-hostel payment system from municipalities to operators be modified so as to involve residents directly.

The Commission recognizes that this change would be more symbolic than substantive. If operators physically lay out a cheque for endorsement by each resident, the right to withhold one's signature is likely to be more theoretical than real. Be that as it may, symbols are an important part of empowerment.

By contrast, GAINS(D) cheques are payable to residents alone. They are typically received at the premises in the operators' presence and signed over on the spot. Any difference between the amount of the cheque and the rent is returned to the residents. Residents can, in principle, decline to sign over the cheque; but they rarely do so, for speedy eviction is sure to follow.

If coverage under *LTA* is extended to rest homes, as we have recommended, this will tremendously empower residents in this regard. Failure to endorse cheques—whether the individuals' GAINS(D) cheque or co-payable cheques from the municipality—will no longer lead to immediate eviction. Operators will have to begin proceedings under *LTA* based on non-payment of rent.

Thus, coverage under the *LTA* is likely to lead to greater resident empowerment, even under the present domiciliary-hostel system. A co-payable municipal contribution is likely to add little substance, but will be a strong symbol of residents' empowerment.

TERM OF CONTRACTS

The termination of agreements with individual operators is seen by some municipalities as difficult and potentially expensive. One municipal counsel has drawn our attention to contracts that give operators the right to accommodate domiciliary-hostel residents in perpetuity. He suggested that agreements should have finite terms, which could be renewed at the discretion of the municipality.[67]

RECOMMENDATION 62: That the *General Welfare Assistance Act* Regulations be amended to specify that no municipal hostel agreement with operators can exceed one year. Such contracts may be renewed annually.

A MAXIMUM SIZE

In some communities, hostels are built on the hospital model and function in effect as "institutions." Resident populations of more than 100 are not uncommon. In such environments it is difficult to think of hostels as homes.

It is our view that large and necessarily depersonalizing rest homes must be down-sized as soon and as fast as possible. It would be our preference to mandate a maximum upper limit to the number of residents in any domiciliary hostel anywhere in Ontario.[68] We do not believe that any resident of a rest home who is funded under GWA should reside in a mega-institution in the guise of community accommodation.

RECOMMENDATION 63: That the *General Welfare Assistance Act* Regulations permit hostel funding only to residences below a provincially determined maximum resident capacity.

This maximum resident capacity in hostels should be set by the minister and should be consistently reduced on a staged

[67] The Commission also notes that the Habitat contract with operators gives Habitat the right to terminate the contract on ninety days' notice without cause. This clause was "designed to prevent extensive discussion or litigation arising from the need to terminate a contract." Habitat also requires that a new contract be signed each year "and there is no stipulation that cause must exist or be proved if a new contract is not signed."

[68] We do note many luxury retirement homes are built on the model of apartment buildings with private individual suites and very large total numbers, and we have heard no concerns expressed about size in these settings.

69 The PNA is included in the monthly cheque received by the operators from the municipality, but in some cases it appears the money is not appropriately passed on to residents.

70 The PNA was increased from $100 to $112 in October 1991.

basis over a set number of years: the reduction rate can be monitored and adjusted according to the capacity of the community to absorb residents. No final maximum size need be set in advance, as this too can be monitored.

Personal-Needs Allowance

By far the most frequent complaint expressed by residents concerned their lack of spending money after payment of room and board. Persons not in hostel accommodation often have to sign over their entire social-assistance cheque and be left with nothing. Residents funded under the domiciliary-hostel provisions are entitled to a $112 monthly personal-needs allowance (known as PNA or "comfort" allowance) from the operators; but this small sum does not go far and, it seems, it is not always received.[69]

The issue once again is empowerment and control. Without adequate money for personal needs, individuals are vulnerable and powerless. It is a central task of the social-assistance system to ensure that residents of rest homes, including hostels, have sufficient funds to exercise discretion over how they wish to lead their lives. A PNA of $112 in hostels is woefully inadequate, and we endorse all moves to increase this sum.[70]

We are encouraged by a change in the *GWAA* Regulations, effective October 1991, which specified that the PNA is a right that must be paid; previous regulations were silent on this issue and the PNA was not always passed on by operators.

The October 1991 changes did not specify that the PNA be provided in the form of cash. Yet without such clarification, the PNA is not an unambiguous right. We have been told of cases in which the PNA is withheld by operators in exchange for essentials such as soap, toilet paper, and hygienic pads.

The Commission recommends that MCSS explicitly require that operators include specified basic necessities of daily living (in particular, soap, toilet paper, and hygienic pads) as part of the accommodation-and-board package for which they receive domiciliary-hostel per diem funding. Only by doing so can the withholding of the PNA from residents be precluded. This specification should be part of every agreement signed by every municipality with every operator.[71]

Furthermore, these basic necessities must be available in adequate supply, at all times, to all residents, without charge by operators. Ideally, these commodities should be available on an open basis to be used as needed by residents. If this proves operationally impossible, operators may dispense; but they must supply as much as is needed for the residents' use, whenever needed and without challenge.

> **RECOMMENDATION 64:** That the *General Welfare Assistance Act* Regulations be amended to require that all domiciliary-hostel agreements include a requirement that the operators provide, without additional charge, all needed supplies of soap, toilet paper, and hygienic pads.

Some operators sell cigarettes, candies, etc. in a canteen. Residents have alleged exorbitant overcharging as a way of "skimming" the PNA. Although operators are not obligated to operate a canteen, if they choose to do so there should be a cash transfer from residents to operators for each transaction. Given that the buyers are vulnerable, may be unable to do comparative shopping, and are not always informed consumers, operators should not charge prices in excess of those prevailing in the neighbourhood.[72]

> **RECOMMENDATION 65:** That if rest-home operators choose to offer a "canteen service," they may not charge prices above those prevailing in the neighbourhood.

There have also been numerous complaints expressed to the Commission that PNA funds are simply not distributed by operators,[73] or are used as a behavioural tool for operators to ensure residents comply with the operators' wishes. (On the other hand, residents may believe their money is being with-

71 Municipalities should, of course, be free to negotiate a broader definition of "essentials" as part of their domiciliary-hostel contracts with operators.

72 The Commission is not attempting to present a legal standard for excess pricing. The intent is to prevent exploitation or price gouging (as these terms are commonly understood).

73 The Commission visited one rest home where we were shown a detailed ledger with each resident's name and enumerated disbursements from the PNA: there was, for example, a $7 weekly debit for a haircut for each resident, yet it was obvious that most residents had not received this benefit in some time.

74 This approach will have a further benefit beyond empowering the residents in making decisions about their own lives: people from outside visiting the residence regularly will serve an added monitoring function, merely by virtue of their presence.

75 If the PNA is distributed by some outside agency, the municipality would issue one cheque to the agency covering and payments due the agency's resident clients. The agency would be responsible for passing on the $112 to each person.

held when, in fact, that is not the case. Even a package of cigarettes is so costly that $112 does not go far.) *GWAA* Regulations do not set out the manner of distribution of the PNA; as a result, operators often decide when, how, and under what circumstances the money will be distributed. This is fundamentally unacceptable.

Some residents may wish to take their $112 in a lump sum, and that is their right, unless they have been declared by a court to be incapable of handling their money. (Regardless of how it is spent, a personal-needs allowance is just that—a payment to cover personal needs as determined by individual residents.)

The personal-needs allowance is a right that cannot be dependent upon operators' good faith or good will. In practice, this necessitates an absolute ban on operators acting as banker or trustee of the PNA.

> **RECOMMENDATION 66:** That owners/operators/staff of rest homes shall neither dispense nor trustee a personal-needs allowance, under any circumstances.

Some residents will want their money held by a trustee and allocated periodically; in such cases an agency outside the residence must assume this task, visiting the home on a regular basis. Social advocates, possibly employed by the Advocacy Commission, may help groups of residents to locate an appropriate, independent trustee.[74]

If the PNA is paid to a trustee, there should be a requirement that it be used for personal needs, not to supplement the rent.

A direct-bank-deposit option was offered to all FB recipients in May 1991, and the feasibility of extending this to GWA is being studied. These changes may offer some modest financial protection to residents in hostels. We particularly recommend that the PNA be distributed as cheques payable to recipients, separate from the payment of the rest of their monthly social assistance.[75]

RECOMMENDATION 67: That the personal-needs allowance be paid separately from other social-assistance payment to recipients who qualify for it.

Under FB, a "pay-direct" system in which social-assistance money goes directly to operators is not permitted. However, a director of FB can appoint operators as trustees for social-assistance recipients, and the money will then go directly to the operators.[76]

This Commission prefers that some outside agency be approached by government (and compensated, directly or indirectly) to serve as trustee for residents in hostels when appropriate. If residents appeared unlikely to control their money wisely, their consent should be sought for an order of trusteeship. If residents refused consent and did not save enough money for accommodation out of their FB cheque, eviction would likely follow and the individuals might spend the month in an emergency shelter. Only if this happens a number of times should a trustee be appointed, but such a decision should always be appealable to the Social Assistance Review Board (SARB).

RECOMMENDATION 68: That the Ministry of Community and Social Services arrange with suitable outside non-profit agencies to serve as trustee for those residents who wish such a service. That where a trustee is appointed under Family Benefits legislation, the social-assistance recipient should be permitted to appeal the appointment to the Social Assistance Review Board. That the regulations to the *Family Benefits Act* prohibit the appointment of rest-home owners/operators/staff as trustees for rest-home residents.

76 This decision to appoint a trustee under the Family Benefits legislation is not appealable to SARB because it does not involve suspension or cancellation of, or ineligibility for, benefits.

PART III

Empowering and Protecting Vulnerable Adults

In Part I of this Report, we concluded that comprehensive regulation of rest homes on the nursing-home model was not the best way to achieve our goals of empowering and offering protection to vulnerable adults. We observed that the protection promised by comprehensive regulation is uncertain, the empowerment non-existent.

We now turn to our recommended alternative, and effective empowerment of residents is its foundation. Ours is a multi-faceted response, including the following general recommendations:

1. a Residents' Bill of Rights for rest homes, effectively enforced through a new Rest Homes Tribunal. This recommendation is premised on the availability of adequate advocacy supports, both informal—by relatives and friends—and those to be created under Bill 74, the proposed *Advocacy Act, 1991*; it also assumes the mandatory reporting of abuse in rest homes;

2. mandatory registration of all rest homes with the municipality;

3. minimum safety standards regarding health, fire, and the physical environment, and proposals to improve the accountability of local inspectors;

4. minimum staffing ratios for all rest homes and a minimum "competence" standard for staff who assist with medications; and

5. quality of care, above the safety minimum, to be attained through mandatory written contracts rather than municipal by-laws.

Each of these areas will be discussed in some detail in the following chapters.

We begin, however, with a brief look at two existing protections: the Criminal Code of Canada and the Ontario Human Rights Code.

8
Two Existing Protections

The Criminal Code of Canada and the Ontario Human Rights Code have traditionally been considered of limited relevance in the context of rest homes; however, within the past year, greater potential has been demonstrated through successful legal action. Indeed, they may represent important complements to the other measures we recommend, although they would certainly not be sufficient on their own.

THE CRIMINAL CODE

In early 1991, the operators of an unregulated rest home near Dorset, Ontario, were convicted of criminal neglect.[1] The charges stated that the operators, being responsible for the care of Crozier Manor residents, did by criminal negligence cause the death of one resident and bodily harm to another resident.[2] The former died as a result of scalding in a bath; the latter suffered severe injury from frostbite after wandering from the premises on a winter's night.

To obtain a conviction under the Criminal Code, the prosecution had to prove that the operators, by omitting to do anything that it was their duty to do, showed a wanton or reckless disregard for the lives or safety of these two residents. To

1 The home's residents were mostly people with organic brain syndrome (as a result of Alzheimer's disease and/or excess consumption of alcohol over a long period of time). *R. v. Berry and Berry*, unreported oral reasons for judgement of Ontario Court of Justice (General Division), District Municipality of Muskoka (Hogg, O. C. J.), dated February 18, 1991.

2 Contrary to Criminal Code sections 203 and 204.

171

3 *R. v. Berry and Berry*, (note 1 above), p. 19.

prove a legal duty existed, it had to be shown that (a) these residents were under the charge of the operators or staff; (b) these residents were unable to withdraw from that charge by reason of age, illness "or other cause"; and (c) these residents were unable to provide themselves with "the necessities of life."

It is not simply the operators' failure to perform that duty, or mere carelessness, but a "wanton or reckless disregard" for the life and safety of the residents that is culpable. Moreover, such disregard must be proven beyond a reasonable doubt, because this is a criminal offence.

It is not clear from the decision how one man came to be in the bathtub in which the water was too hot and how another was able to wander away from the residence. However, the court found that the residents were in the care of the operators, who "were under a duty to provide qualified and adequate care for those in their charge."

In his decision, the trial judge emphasized the "meagre or non-existent" training of the staff. The teenage sons of the operators and their friend were regularly left in charge of Crozier Manor; while they were in charge "there was improper and immature behaviour on numerous occasions." When the severely frostbitten resident was returned to the home, the alarm was sounded but no one responded: the two sixteen-year-olds in charge were asleep, and the alarm system may have malfunctioned.

Recognizing that accidents will occur, the court made a considerable effort not to impose an unfairly high care standard on the operators. "What is required is a reasonable standard of care."[3] However, the court found that agreeing to provide care to very vulnerable residents and then providing inadequate supervision may, in itself, constitute an act of criminal negligence.

In my view, taking all the evidence into account, the placing of a 16 or 17 year old boy in charge of some 30 residents of the type that have been described was placing the well being and the very lives of the residents at risk and under the circumstances to do so was an act of criminal negligence.[4]

The judge's opinion might place a future onus on operators of rest homes to make very clear what care responsibilities they are assuming and to ensure that these are met. It would not be the responsibility of the placement agency or family (if involved) to determine what responsibilities operators are assuming; rather, operators must make this clear. Because severe penalties may be imposed on operators convicted of criminal negligence, they may no longer accept residents— merely because they are able to pay—if they are unable to care for them adequately; operators may be obliged to promise no more than they can deliver.[5]

The Commission does not know how many charges of criminal negligence in rest homes have been laid and successfully prosecuted. The criminal law is a blunt instrument for protecting or redressing harm to residents in care situations; however, the worst offenders can be successfully prosecuted in certain circumstances. Certainly, the conviction in this case may become a deterrent to the worst behaviours of some rest-home operators.

HUMAN RIGHTS LEGISLATION

Two recent cases, one in Ontario[6] and one in Quebec,[7] demonstrate that vulnerable persons can sometimes obtain appropriate redress of their grievances under human rights legislation. Neither case dealt with rest homes as defined for purposes of this Inquiry; however, both show that complaints against operators of accommodation can be successful when operators violate the human dignity of residents.

The Ontario case dealt with a young woman who has

4 *R. v. Berry and Berry*, (note 1 above), p.18.

5 The role of the doctor at the local hospital was also of interest to the judge. The operator of the home "did not advise the doctor that none of the staff at Crozier had any care-giving training. The doctor therefore assumed, understandably so, that there were professional, trained caregivers present."

Such misinformation about the care provided in a rest home is unacceptable. Doctors in local hospitals must be better informed about the care services provided—and not provided— by rest homes.

Operators should ensure that all local hospitals have information about the extent of responsibility they have assumed along with the qualifications and training, if any, of staff. As well, hospitals should be able to access it independently through the on-line information system that the Commission has recommended. It is particularly important that all personnel in the emergency units of hospitals, including physicians, have this information and act accordingly. We discuss this further in Part IV.

6 *In the Matter of Ms K.A. v. Mrs. S.P.*, an unreported decision of the Board of Inquiry (London, Ontario), Ontario Human Rights Commission, dated January 8, 1991.

7 *Resolution COM-353-5.1*, Unreported decision of Commission des Droits de la Personne (Montreal, Quebec), dated January 25, 1991.

8 This case dealt with eighty-eight residents who worked without pay to operate and maintain a Montreal "living centre," which was operated on a for-profit basis and fully funded by government.

Unlike the Ontario Human Rights Code, the Quebec Charter of Human Rights and Freedoms expressly prohibits exploitation of persons with disabilities (Article 48, paragraph 1. "Exploitation" is defined by the Quebec Human Rights Commission as any advantage a person takes from another because of the handicap of the latter.

The Commission decision in favour of the residents was the first in Canada based on the systemic exploitation of a vulnerable group.

cerebral palsy involving some cognitive deficiency as well as ataxia (lack of muscle co-ordination). She also has bilateral cataracts, which impair her vision considerably.

In 1986, the woman, her mother, and her social worker decided that she would live independently, and she moved into a basement apartment. At first, relations between the sixty-eight-year-old female proprietor and the young woman were quite amicable, involving visits and shared coffee breaks. Then the young woman assumed a more independent lifestyle than the proprietor desired or thought appropriate.

The relationship degenerated, and ultimately the young woman moved out. During the period of acrimony, the proprietor asked her: "What's a retarded girl like you doing having a boyfriend?" Later she sent a note that began: "Listen retarded and listen good."

Section 2(2) of the Ontario Human Rights Code states that "Every person who occupies accommodation has a right to freedom from harassment by the landlord ... because of ... handicap."

The Commission found that the proprietor's actions violated the tenant's rights under this section.

Awards for general damages up to $10,000 can be made by the Commission to reflect "not only the mental anguish which wilful or reckless conduct may cause, but the injury to the complainant's dignity and self respect." The sum of $2,000 was awarded for this purpose. Special damages were also awarded to offset direct expenses, such as the cost of moving to another apartment.

In the Quebec case, the Quebec Human Rights Commission found that eighty-eight vulnerable residents had been systemically exploited by an institution.[8] It awarded $1 million in damages, the largest award for human rights violations in Canada.

Both cases clearly indicate that violations of human rights can be addressed successfully through human rights legislation. Indeed, remedies at present available through the Criminal Code and human rights commissions may deter certain unacceptable behaviours, and can provide redress if that conduct does occur. Although we should not rely unduly on these remedies, neither should we underestimate their potential to protect vulnerable residents.

We now turn our attention to other protections that the Commission considers essential for residents of rest homes. Foremost among these is the residents' bill of rights.

9
A Residents' Bill
of Rights

1 The bill became part of the *Nursing Homes Act* in 1987. In municipal and charitable homes for the aged, a bill of rights has been adopted as a matter of policy.

2 The bill of rights can be enforced only by laying a charge under the *Nursing Homes Act*. The charge is then heard in provincial court, like any other provincial offence, such as a violation of the *Highway Traffic Act*.

A bill of rights for residents of rest homes is the symbolic centre of this Report. It embodies the Commission's overriding principle that the residents come first, and that the needs and interests of all others are secondary. If the government of Ontario is able and willing to enact a meaningful and enforceable bill of rights, it will have gone a long way towards achieving the purpose of the Inquiry.

RECOMMENDATION 69: That a bill of rights for residents of rest homes be enacted as a matter of priority.

The Commission is well aware of the pitfalls. For example, a bill of rights exists for residents of nursing homes.[1] Community and advocacy groups had great expectations of that bill of rights, for its language is powerful. Yet there has not been a single prosecution under the bill, although we are told that threats to invoke it have had effect on occasion.[2] This raises doubts about the effectiveness of the bill, for without effective enforcement, it is little more than a statement of good intentions.

The Commission has heard about many problems and complaints that could be resolved through an effective residents' bill of rights for rest homes. Most have been expressed by residents themselves, directly or through peer support groups. The tone and content of these requests have been truly compelling: what these vulnerable adults are seeking is so modest, yet potentially so empowering.

The violation of the self-esteem and sense of security of vulnerable adults, particularly those with minimal incomes living in boarding homes, is of great concern to this Commission. Residents are asking only for rights that the rest of us take for granted: the courtesy of being called by one's own name, rather than by some pejorative label assigned by a punitive staff member; the right to remain in one's residence, particularly in winter, rather than being forced out into the streets from breakfast until dinnertime or at the whim of operators; the likelihood that personal items—such as a package of cigarettes or even one's own clothing—will not be stolen, searched, or disposed of without one's agreement or in one's absence; the control of one's spending money, without being ripped off by unscrupulous operators; the right to be free from sexual assault by operators, staff, and other residents.

The Commission is absolutely convinced that such events occur with depressing frequency in the rest homes of this province, that the stories we have heard are neither exaggerations nor the fabrications of disturbed minds. They were told to us with clarity and consistency, and with a passion that can come only from lived experience. A meaningful bill of rights can provide both an important symbol of the rights of residents and an effective means to ensure these rights.

Some infringements of the rights of residents are prohibited by statute: sexual assault and theft, for example, are criminal offences. Many other rights—a surprising number, in fact—will follow automatically with coverage under the *Landlord and Tenant Act* (*LTA*): the right to come and go as one pleases; the right to invite visitors into one's own home; the right to form a tenants' association or residents' council; the right to not be moved, individually or in a group, from one home to another, without consent; the right to be protected against eviction, either temporarily, as punishment, or perma-

3 Bill 108, the *Substitute Decisions Act, 1991* and Bill 109, the *Consent to Treatment Act, 1991.*

4 Anyone can distribute oral medications. The College of Nurses has guidelines for RNs and RNAs for the direct administering of medications and for the delegating of responsibilities to unregulated personnel. The guideline states that administering medication by intravenous injection or other parenteral injections is a skilled nursing act that may not be delegated; however, in practice such responsibilities are often delegated to unregulated staff. The College is currently examining these guidelines, which date from 1987.

5 The inability to demand and receive respect for one's human dignity without outside support may even be taken as a rule-of-thumb indicator of vulnerable status.

nently, at the whim of the operator. Indeed it is precisely to ensure these rights that we are so adamant that all rest homes in the province be covered by the *LTA*.

The right to manage one's property and make personal-care decisions is protected under pending legislation.[3] For example, the right to refuse medication or treatment and the right to control one's own money can be overridden only if the resident is found legally incapable. Even if a court appoints a guardian to make decisions on an ongoing basis, the guardian will have decision-making power only in those specific areas in which the person was found incapable.

The right to see and receive support from advocates accountable to the proposed Advocacy Commission may also protect vulnerable adults in Ontario. Provided that legal protections for the privacy of vulnerable persons are observed, advocates representing the Advocacy Commission will be able to enter rest homes without explicit invitation.

Under the proposed *Regulated Health Professions Act, 1991* (Bill 43), it will be illegal for persons not authorized by a health-profession act to administer medications through injections and inhalations unless authority is properly delegated.[4]

Some of the rights we would include in our bill of rights for rest-home residents extend further than the rights that accrue to other members of society. For example, the most general right we advocate is "respect for the basic human dignity of the resident." This, perhaps surprisingly, is not a right of persons living in their own homes in the community. Yet residents of rest homes must be assured such a right precisely because of their vulnerability. The general population typically possesses the options, power, and resources to demand and receive this dignity or to leave a setting in which this dignity is not honoured:[5] we command a measure of dignity through the power to withdraw our resources.

Vulnerable adults in rest homes do not generally have such meaningful options. It is therefore necessary for the government of Ontario to ensure, by legislative enactment, that vulnerable adults in dependent living arrangements are entitled to and receive courtesies and treatment that others are able to obtain on their own, i.e., to minimize or offset the imbalance of power within a rest-home setting.

Even though certain rights are assured to vulnerable adults through other means, reiteration in the bill of rights will emphasize that the rights the rest of us take for granted are guaranteed to those who live in rest homes. Moreover, in some cases, remedies through the bill of rights might be more accessible to residents than remedies through other avenues.

6 All rights are to be interpreted subject to non-interference with the rights, dignity, and privacy of other residents.

The Bill of Rights

The Commission has identified general areas of concern, which call for a response in a formal bill of rights; within each area, we indicate a number of specific rights that represents a minimum, rather than a comprehensive or exhaustive, listing. In conjunction with these specific rights, a statement of broadly worded rights should be developed to enable cases to be argued on an individual basis. This approach offers flexibility, with boundaries that can be defined with use.

We wish to emphasize that our use of language and terminology is not meant to be legally precise: we are setting out principles upon which we hope there can be substantial agreement. It is our recommendation that a small group be constituted as soon as possible, with speedy input from the major affected parties, to draft the precise legislative instrument.

A rest-home residents' bill of rights must ensure that operators and staff observe and uphold the basic rights of residents. The concerns that must be addressed in a bill of rights encompass the following:[6]

1. respect for the basic human dignity of the residents;

7 Agriculture Canada, Food Market Analysis Division, has compiled information on a "nutritious" and a "thrifty nutritious" food basket using sixty-four and forty-three foods respectively, drawn from eleven food groups. The minimum of the Canada Food Guide can be met with 1,000–1,400 kilocalories/day, which could lead to malnourishment for some people.

New guidelines being developed by Health and Welfare Canada will probably recommend a nutrient intake for energy of 1,800 kilocalories for women aged fifty to seventy-four and 2,300 for men in that age range. Women and men over seventy-five need 1,700 and 2,000 kilocalories respectively. Persons with psychiatric histories tend to require more food, as medications increase their levels of hunger, as may anxiety, and boredom.

8 The right to come and go is particularly controversial. Some residents of rest homes tend to wander, and operators contend that without the authority to restrict residents' freedom of movement they cannot be responsible for their safety or security. The resolution of this issue depends in part on the duty of care that operators assume with respect to residents. We have found that most operators do not accept a legal duty of care for residents. More important, however, is our view that operators and/or families ought not to make personal subjective assessments of the competence of residents. If guardianship

2. a safe, secure, and clean living environment:
(a) clean and private bathing and toilet facilities including, without additional charge, sufficient soap, toilet paper, and hygienic pads;
(b) a secure and locked storage area for personal effects, and the key to it;
(c) a key to the home (unless there is open twenty-four-hour access), and to one's bedroom and bathroom, each of which must have a lock;
(d) a secure, locked area for storage of medications;
(e) meals, as contracted, that meet the minimum standards of the Canada Food Guide[7] and are served at appropriate times; operators must accommodate reasonable needs of residents (for example, with sufficiently flexible scheduling of meals to meet work or comparable needs of residents);

3. personal rights:
(a) the right to be treated as competent in all areas of decision-making in accordance with the law. This includes decision-making in all personal and financial matters, the freedom to come and go, and a prohibition on operators' requiring residents to sign in and out;[8]
(b) the right to dress and to decorate one's own living area as one wishes;
(c) the right to designate someone to receive any and all information to which the residents have a right of access;
(d) the right to know who owns and operates one's residence (including the names, addresses, and phone numbers of owners and operators);[9]
(e) residents shall not be required to do work or services for or on behalf of operators;
(f) residents' right to privacy shall be respected at all times; this includes prohibitions on intrusion into residents' living areas, except as provided under the *Landlord and Tenant Act*, and on interference with residents' personal belongings;

(g) no physical search of the residents;

(h) no restrictions on communication by telephone and mail, or on access to print or broadcast media, including the right to send and receive written correspondence unopened;

(i) the right to unimpeded access to independent advocates, lawyers, or physicians at any time;

(j) the right to receive visitors, including staff from community-based programs;

(k) the right to form a tenants' or residents' association and to meet without the presence of owners, operators, or staff;

(l) the right to be addressed by name and in non-patronizing language;

4. confidentiality:

(a) if files or records on residents are kept, the right to complete access by the residents to all information contained therein;

(b) no information about residents shall be released to any third party except with the written consent of the residents; residents shall have the right to correct any misinformation held or released by operators and to attach a statement of their position on an issue to that of the operators;

5. sexuality:

(a) the right to engage in consensual sexual behaviour that does not interfere with the dignity and privacy of other residents;

6. religion:

(a) the right to engage in religious practice in any manner that does not interfere with the dignity and privacy of other residents, and the right not to engage in religious practice;

7. consent to treatment:

(a) the right to be considered competent to accept or refuse treatment in accordance with the law;

orders have been made, then the guardians (who cannot be the operators) may authorize the operators to restrict the residents' movements; operators may accept the responsibility, or not, on terms negotiated between the parties. Without a guardianship order or a duty to care, there is no legal authority for anyone to detain individuals; indeed, doing so may be considered unlawful confinement. Movement on the part of residents of a rest home can be constrained only by the legal process under current or newly proposed provincial legislation or if the residents' movements would constitute a danger to the life or safety of the residents and the operators have a legal duty of care.

9 This information must be posted prominently within the residence.

10 The Commission recommends a standard for the competence of persons who assist residents to take medications. See chapter 12.

11 The telephone number of the Advocacy Commission should be posted prominently in every rest home. Operators should be required to provide residents, at the point of entry, with printed information, prepared by the Commission, concerning advocacy and their rights.

(b) the right to be free within the premises from pressure or coercion to accept or refuse medical treatment, including psychiatric treatment;

(c) the right to self-medicate in accordance with the law;

(d) if someone assists with medication, the right to one's own medication—not another's—received from a competent person[10] according to the prescribing doctor's or pharmacist's instructions;

8. restraint and seclusion:

(a) the right to be free from punitive restraint or detention measures. This includes a prohibition on the use of binding, tying, chemical, and/or other similar restraints, and locked rooms and enclosed spaces;

9. abuse:

(a) the right to freedom from physical, verbal, emotional, and sexual abuse;

10. advocates and other outside supports:

(a) the right to have unimpeded access to independent advocates (as specified in the proposed *Advocacy Act, 1991*);[11]

(b) the right to have access to community support services and the right to choose the supplier of one's purchased goods and services;

(c) no one shall impede or deny entry to a residence of any person or advocate invited into the premises by the residents.

Therefore:

RECOMMENDATION 70: That the residents' bill of rights include rights in the following general areas: respect for the basic human dignity of the residents; a safe, secure, and clean living environment; personal rights; confidentiality; sexuality; religion; consent to treatment; restraint and seclusion; freedom from abuse; advocacy and other outside supports.

A copy of the bill of rights should be provided by the operator to every resident on signing a lease or moving into the rest home. It should contain an explicit statement that nothing in the lease or contract for optional services can override the rights contained in the bill of rights.

Finally, we stress the requirement of "respect for basic human dignity of the resident" as the crucial point: basic human dignity *must* be respected. A variety of concerns not specifically enumerated elsewhere can be argued on this basis.

No legislative enactment can guarantee that violations will not occur: there is no way to ensure that a Crozier Manor or a Cedar Glen will never happen again. But we do believe that a clear and strong endorsement of these rights and an effective enforcement mechanism will make clear that behaviours and actions that we have tacitly condoned will no longer be tolerated in the province of Ontario.

MANDATORY REPORTING

In any discussion of enforcement of residents' rights, the first matter to be raised is, inevitably, mandatory reporting of abuse.

The concept of a legal obligation to report abuse has generated considerable heat, even within individual community groups. Some have argued an analogy to child welfare: there is a legal obligation to report child abuse, although only a professional can be prosecuted for non-reporting.

Others claim that such a requirement would be infantilizing. A middle position opposes mandatory reporting concerning people living in their own homes, but accepts the idea for those in settings such as rest homes, where significant power imbalances occur.[12]

It is, therefore, not without some ambivalence that this Commission recommends mandatory reporting of abuse in

12 This argument is compatible with the idea of the rest home as the individual's own home. It merely adds a condition that the rest home is a particular type of home, in which power imbalances occur (and should be redressed).

rest homes. Physical abuse of vulnerable persons is clearly a criminal offence, to be dealt with by the police. Emotional and other abuses that violate the proposed bill of rights will become the concern of the Rest Homes Tribunal (which we discuss next).

We acknowledge that many policy and operational issues ensue from this recommendation, and that we do not deal with them here. However, we see the requirement to report abuse, however defined, as a strong and clear public statement that certain types of behaviours are unacceptable. Although educational and voluntary programs are necessary and desirable, they are unlikely to bring about sufficient change. Attitudinal and behavioural change will come about expeditiously only when encouraged by the moral force of the law.

We believe that most people, if given protection from sanctions, would report abuse even in the absence of a legal requirement to do so. Consider, however, a frail senior in a rest home subject to abuse but reluctant to have a relative report for fear of reprisal. The disagreement between the vulnerable person and the relative may be settled more easily if the relative is able to argue that the law demands that the abuse be reported. The issue then becomes obeying the law rather than reporting abuse. As well, a specific legal mandate may be necessary to protect rest-home staff, who might otherwise decline to report for fear of losing their jobs.

We understand that this debate has a highly symbolic aspect: abuse of vulnerable adults is undoubtedly intolerable; but equally so is the infantilization of residents.

RECOMMENDATION 71: That there be a legal requirement to report abuse of residents of rest homes. That there be a legal prohibition of sanctions or retaliation by operators and staff against the allegedly abused resident and any person who reports the abuse of a resident in a rest home.

The question remains: how and to whom to report abuse, and what responses are possible? It would be to the Rest Home Tribunal that many allegations of abuse and violations of the bill of rights would first come. It is to this body that we now turn the discussion.

A Rest Homes Tribunal

This Commission has made an effort to avoid the creation of new bureaucracies and regulatory processes, while stressing government's responsibility to ensure that basic rights of rest-home residents are respected and minimum health and safety conditions are enforced.

In our view, there must be an easy and accessible way to ensure these basic rights are respected, and minimum standards enforced.

The Commission therefore recommends the creation of a Rest Homes Tribunal (RHT), whose primary mandate will be to ensure compliance with the rest-home residents' bill of rights.[13]

RECOMMENDATION 72: That a Rest Homes Tribunal be created. That the Rest Homes Tribunal assume administrative, mediative, and adjudicatory responsibilities with respect to the rest-homes residents' bill of rights.

The RHT should have authority to deal with the full range of alleged violations of the bill of rights. It is hoped that the RHT would offer a user-friendly and informal atmosphere, in which issues could be resolved expeditiously.

The RHT would undertake mediation and adjudication, but each arm would function independently. Thus, a complaint under the rest-homes bill of rights may involve a two-stage process: first, RHT staff would offer the parties relatively infor-

13 Some submissions have argued that the tribunal should also review decisions of local regulatory authorities, such as fire inspectors. The implications of such proposed responsibility are complex and will be considered separately, in chapter 10.

mal mediation. If matters were not resolved, an adjudicatory proceeding would follow.

> **RECOMMENDATION 73:** That in dealing with the bill of rights, the Rest Homes Tribunal staff first offer an informal mediation process, followed by a second adjudicatory stage if necessary.

We assume that, in many cases, when operators or staff have complaints drawn officially to their attention, unacceptable behaviour would cease and the issue would be closed. However, mediation would depend on the willingness of residents and operators to participate. One attempt at mediation would be the norm, unless both parties felt further activity would be beneficial.

Complaints about violations of the bill of rights would be made directly to the RHT by residents or other persons. Usually complaints about the treatment of a specific individual resident would be dealt with only if that resident were the complainant or consented to the complaint being dealt with by the RHT. However, in some instances complaints would proceed to the RHT at the request of advocates or other concerned persons, when, for example, residents had been systematically intimidated by operators, as was the case at Cedar Glen.

Residents could make complaints with or without the assistance of advocates or other support persons. Advocates appointed under the proposed advocacy legislation must be available to assist residents in lodging complaints and to make them aware of the existence and function of the RHT. As well, the complainant must have the assistance of appropriate social and legal advocates throughout the complaint process and during mediation. If the case comes to adjudication, residents must have access to legal representation, including legal aid clinics and legal aid certificates.

> **RECOMMENDATION 74:** That rest-home residents have

access to advocates under the proposed Advocacy Commission and, if eligible, access to legal representation under the Legal Aid Plan to pursue complaints before the Rest Homes Tribunal.

Residents or staff who make complaints must also be protected from sanctions and retaliation by employers, operators, and staff.

RECOMMENDATION 75: That there be legal prohibition of sanctions or retaliation by operators, employers, and staff against residents and staff persons who make complaints to the Rest Homes Tribunal.

It is important that the RHT be readily accessible to residents and to informal advocates. There must be an 800 telephone number so that complaints can be reported, anonymously if desired, from anywhere in the province. In all complaints of alleged rights violations, an advocate should be informed, as well. The 800 number should access all services provided by the RHT; as such it must be operated on a twenty-four-hour basis, to deal with emergencies.

RECOMMENDATION 76: That there be an 800 telephone number, staffed continuously, for easy and rapid access to the Rest Homes Tribunal.

We also recommend that a sign with the 800 number be posted in each rest home in a highly visible location. Printed information concerning the RHT and the use of the 800 number should be prepared, provided to the public on request, and posted at or near the residents' entrance of all rest homes.

RECOMMENDATION 77: That printed signs with the 800 number be posted in every rest home and that literature concerning the Rest Homes Tribunal be readily available at all rest homes.

The RHT should establish rules of procedure, including the size and composition of hearing panels, while attempting to create a non-intimidating, non-courtlike atmosphere. Decisions should be based on a preponderance of evidence as presented before the RHT. Decisions should be appealable to the Ontario Court (Divisional Court) only on matters of law.

We note that the model for dispute resolution recommended here is unlike that of the Ontario Human Rights Commission: in effect, "ownership" of human rights complaints and determinations of priority and approach pass to the Human Rights Commission from the individual complainant.

The "private-law" model that we recommend places the onus on individual residents, with assistance, to pursue complaints; it would thereby be more empowering than alternative models that de-emphasize the active involvement of the complainant in determining the outcome.

Our proposal, however, is critically dependent on sufficient legal and social advocates to assist residents in the pursuit of their complaints. There must be an adequate number of advocates; there must be free and ready access by vulnerable adults to their services; and the advocates must be competent in their tasks and responsive to the wishes of the residents. The need for supports to vulnerable adults is a crucial, and recurring, theme in this Report, for without such assistance a resident-centred approach may amount to little in practice.

PENALTIES AND SANCTIONS

The range of penalties available to the RHT should be wide, suited to the range of offences. The RHT should be able to issue a mild reprimand, order that the violation cease, order that operators or staff do what is necessary to comply with the bill of rights, and award damages to residents.

Legislation should authorize the RHT (or the responsible

minister on the recommendation of the RHT) to suspend or revoke the registration of the rest home and/or to order the takeover of the operation of the rest home for a limited period.[14] The RHT could direct a specific ministry to assist with rehousing residents in an acceptable alternative location should premises be subject to closure. The sanctions should also include the temporary or permanent suspension of persons (owners, operators and/or staff) from the rest-home business in Ontario.

The concept of graduated penalties is crucial: an incremental approach permits appropriate penalties short of closure. (Closure would be applied only as a last resort because of the dehousing effect.)

However, the response to certain violations, such as sexual assault, may demand a mandatory zero tolerance: the RHT may decide that a single criminal conviction for sexual assault would automatically permanently bar guilty parties from the industry.

RECOMMENDATION 78: That the Rest Homes Tribunal have available a wide range of penalties and remedies appropriate to the severity of a violation.

When certain violations—such as criminal offences causing bodily harm—are alleged, the RHT should be able to temporarily suspend the accused from involvement with the rest home pending the outcome of court proceedings. The findings of any court, civil or criminal, would be admissible before the RHT.

In the most serious cases, those that involve serious health risks or potential serious physical injury, the RHT must have both the capacity and the obligation to act rapidly. Complaints for which retroactive redress would be insufficient demand a speedy response. In such circumstances, the RHT must have the authority to issue orders without notice; questions of ultimate responsibility and liability would be resolved subsequently.

14 The provisions could be modelled on the *Health Facilities Special Orders Act (HFSOA)*. That legislation allows the minister of Health to take strong action when a health facility falls below minimally acceptable standards — where "the physical state of the [premises] or the manner of operation is causing or is likely to cause harm to or an adverse effect on the health of any person or impairment of the safety of any person ...," [section 3, *HFSOA*]

15 The facts of each particular case, and the recorded frequency of violations committed in the rest home by individual staff members, should make clear whether the violation was an aberration for which the home should not be blamed, or part of systemic management behaviour.

16 In Part IV, we discuss the desirability of all information on penalties being provided on-line to hospital-discharge planners and placement co-ordination services (or service co-ordination agencies).

17 The complaints register could be modelled on the register maintained under the New Home Warranty Program. In this program, home builders are ranked as average, above average, or below average in resolving complaints. It is important that the complaints register permit comparison between rest homes in a way meaningful to the consumer. For example, the number of complaints could be given as a proportion of resident days or the number of beds in the residence, and the percentage of successful mediations of complaints might be noted.

RECOMMENDATION 79: That the Rest Homes Tribunal possess the capacity to order emergency responses and interventions, including the power to order the temporary takeover of a residence, when the Rest Homes Tribunal believes that the rest home is being operated in a manner that presents a serious risk to the health of residents or a serious risk of physical injury to residents.

All penalties assigned by the RHT, whether to operators or to individual staff persons, along with a brief summary of the facts of the case, should be permanently recorded and readily available to the public.[15] It is crucial that a list of persons banned from involvement in the industry be readily accessible to operators, local registration offices, and the broader community.[16]

RECOMMENDATION 80: That all decisions and penalties of the Rest Homes Tribunal be widely and easily available to the public at large.

All complaints should be permanently recorded. The history of complaints against a particular rest home, and the resolution of each complaint, should be readily available to any member of the public via computer bulletin boards, information systems, and at public libraries. Obviously, the individual residents' privacy should be protected in such records.

The Commission therefore recommends that a complaints register be established for the rest-home industry.[17] Some homes will develop a good record in resolving residents' complaints, while others will be seen to be less successful. When complaints are resolved through mediation, this should be noted in the complaints register. The complaints register should be part of a computerized data base, maintained by the RHT, that would also include a record of all adjudicatory decisions made by the RHT.

RECOMMENDATION 81: That a complaints register that is readily accessible to the public be maintained by the Rest Homes Tribunal.

ADMINISTRATIVE RESPONSIBILITY AND DESIGN

The choice of which government ministry should be responsible for the RHT is an important one.[18] The RHT should operate independently of the major service-providing ministries, particularly the Ministry of Health (MoH) and the Ministry of Community and Social Services (MCSS). It should also be independent of the Ministry of Housing and the Ministry of the Attorney General. Because of its developing expertise through the proposed *Advocacy Act, 1991*, the Ministry of Citizenship seems to be a logical home for the RHT.

RECOMMENDATION 82: That the Ministry of Citizenship be vested with responsibility for the administration and funding of the Rest Homes Tribunal.

We must ensure that the legislation establishing the RHT does not fall foul of section 96 of the *Constitution Acts, 1967–1982* by conferring on it jurisdiction similar or analogous to that traditionally exercised by a judge of a superior court. The potential infringement arises because the RHT would consider some complaints in the area of landlord-tenant law. The remedies of landlord-tenant law, such as eviction orders, are historically within the exclusive jurisdiction of federally appointed judges.[19]

However, an administrative tribunal's powers may be upheld as part of a wider regulatory scheme, even though, if viewed in isolation, they are judicial in nature *and* have been exercised historically by judges of superior courts. In the context of the proposals contained in this Report, the process and

18 The Macaulay Report (*Directions: A Review of Ontario's Regulatory Agencies,* 1989) discussed, among other issues, the appropriate relation of independent agencies to government. It contains much information that will be useful in the development of the RHT's structure.

19 The Supreme Court of Canada held in 1981 that Ontario's *Residential Tenancies Act* was invalid because it violated section 96 by empowering the tribunal under that legislation to evict tenants and to order landlords and tenants to comply with the rent-control legislation. See *Reference re Residential Tenancies Act [1981] 1 S.C.R. 714.*

powers of the RHT are distinguishable in a number of ways from those of section 96 courts.

For example, mediation is an important aspect of the RHT's process; it would only be when mediation is refused or fails that the complaint would go to adjudication. In addition, the residents' bill of rights would include many items (such as the residents' right to be treated with basic respect) that are outside landlord-tenant law. The remedial powers of the RHT would be distinct from court powers in landlord-tenant disputes: only the RHT could, for example, suspend operators from the business, or forbid the employment of a named individual in any rest home.

It should be emphasized, however, that the Commission is not recommending that the RHT be given the power to order the traditional remedies of landlord-tenant law. If landlords want an eviction or residents want the termination of a lease or abatement of rent, for example, the proper forum is the landlord-tenant court. In other words, the RHT's jurisdiction in landlord-tenant issues should be seen in the wider context of protecting the rights of rest-home residents under the bill of rights.

This distinction raises the second concern, that of the relation of the RHT and other avenues of recourse, for certain conduct may contravene both the proposed bill of rights and the *LTA* or the Human Rights Code, each of which has a discrete enforcement mechanism and remedies.

On the basis of our preliminary consideration, we prefer that the RHT's jurisdiction extend to all complaints brought to it that allege breaches of the residents' bill of rights. We have reached this conclusion for two principal reasons. First, the RHT would be designed—in its expertise, process and powers, including remedies not currently available—to respond to the needs of a specific and particularly vulnerable population. The Commission intends that members of the RHT possess specialized knowledge of vulnerable adults in rest homes and of the rest-home environment. (The existing enforcement machinery—the courts, for resolving tenants' rights disputes, and the Ontario Human Rights Commission, for resolving complaints of discrimination—is more general, and more restricted in remedial powers than the RHT.)

In addition, expeditious disposition would be critical to the success of the residents' bill of rights, and we intend that complaints brought before the RHT typically be resolved speedily. Finally, it is crucial that complainants, assisted by their advocates, take charge of their own cases, which does not happen in complaints brought under the Human Rights Code.

Moreover, if separate tribunals have *exclusive* jurisdiction over closely related issues that arise from disputes in a single setting, the likely result is needlessly frustrating and costly jurisdictional wrangles that could undermine the efficiency of the regulatory scheme.[20] An alleged breach of the residents' bill of rights might overlap in part with other statutory regimes (particularly the Ontario Human Rights Commission); some remedies sought before the RHT might overlap with those available under those other statutory schemes. In such cases, the complainant should decide to pursue a remedy through the RHT or elsewhere, on the understanding that once an issue has been decided by an appropriate body, the same remedy may not be sought in another forum.

20 It would be undesirable to require complainants to divide their complaints into severable parts, and to seek relief from more than one tribunal, unless residents are seeking remedies of different sorts. For example, some violations of residents' privacy could be pursued in two fora, but for different remedies. In some cases, a charge could be laid against the landlord under the *LTA*; the matter would then be pursued as a quasi-criminal matter in court, perhaps resulting in a fine upon conviction. As well, the matter might be pursued before the RHT with the aim of obtaining an order that the specific conduct cease.

Advocacy

Social advocates are vital for the empowerment of residents of rest homes. Bill 74, the *Advocacy Act, 1991*, currently before the legislature, proposes a formal program of advocacy services for all vulnerable persons. The program would be operated by an independent Advocacy Commission funded by the provincial government. We wholeheartedly endorse its role and mission.

We have described the main features of the proposed social-advocacy program; however, we wish to comment on the advocacy initiative itself.

First, the number of advocates has not yet been finalized, but it seems clear that demand for services will exceed the capacity of the provincial government to respond. A working estimate of 600,000 vulnerable adults in Ontario has been used for planning purposes for the *Advocacy Act, 1991*. Our own research with census data has suggested that some 47,500 vulnerable adults live in unregulated accommodation. Although all vulnerable adults will not need formal advocacy services, the potential demand is considerable.

Obviously, the Advocacy Commission will need to establish priorities for its services. It is our view that adults are particularly vulnerable when residing in settings where care is provided by operators and staff.

> **RECOMMENDATION 83:** That the Advocacy Commission consider identifying settings in which the receipt of advocacy services will be deemed a priority. The rest home as defined by this Commission should be one such setting.

The successful implementation of the residents' bill of rights and the RHT are particularly dependent on advocacy—legal and social. As the Advocacy Commission's mandate is primarily social (i.e., non-legal), advocacy staff will make referrals to legal advocates, including legal clinics operated under the Ontario Legal Aid Plan.

Our approach to resident empowerment assumes that sufficient advocates—social and legal—will be accessible to people living in rest homes. Without their involvement, the rights of residents will be merely theoretical. Many residents of rest homes, particularly those on limited incomes, have few family or other supports. They will be dependent on advocacy should they need assistance.

If advocacy services are not funded and developed in an effective manner, it may be necessary to resort to comprehensive governmental regulation of rest homes, notwithstanding our many reservations about such an approach. A system that relies on government regulators and inspectors would be superior to a system based on advocates in which too few advocates are available. Rights are not a reality if the means to enforce those rights do not exist.

There is also a second overriding need, which those working on the advocacy program are sensitive to: we must ensure that advocates do not become one more set of intrusive social workers, making decisions on behalf of residents. There is a fine line between assisting individuals in identifying and articulating their wishes and unilaterally deciding what is best for them. Disempowerment can be brought about by benevolent intentions.

RECOMMENDATION 84: That the Advocacy Commission ensure operational procedures are in place so that empowerment of the individual remains the central goal of the program.

INFORMAL ADVOCACY

Informal advocates can play a key role in empowering and protecting vulnerable adults in rest homes. Informal advocates may be friendly visitors—family, friends or relatives, local school, church or community groups—or tradespeople working on the premises.

Operators who run quality operations should welcome the regular involvement of the wider community. Volunteers can lessen the isolation that afflicts so many residents. Friendly visiting and programming of events—such as day trips in and around the community or shopping at the local mall—can restore a connection to the outside world that so many residents lose through extended hospitalization or abandonment by friends and family. The comings and goings of visitors can only accelerate the process of integrating residents into the world outside the rest home.

As well, pressure on operators to provide such programming and pressure on government to fund operators to do so should be significantly reduced.

These informal advocates could monitor and report possible abuses or violations of standards or rights to the RHT or other appropriate public authority (such as fire inspectors). Physical abuse or severe neglect would be readily noted by anyone entering the premises. Indeed, the mere presence of outside parties—whoever they are—may serve as a check against unacceptable behaviours. Therefore, one goal of this Inquiry is to encourage as many individuals and agencies to be on rest-home premises as frequently as is feasible.

Many community groups would be amenable to such "friendly visiting" if their activities were encouraged. We recommend that church and other community groups be encouraged to undertake regular visits to residents of rest homes and to offer programming for interested residents. We also recommend that MCSS (or the Ministry Citizenship) make available a small amount of money to such groups to defray direct outlays in connection with such visiting.

> **RECOMMENDATION 85:** That church, community, and other voluntary groups be encouraged to visit rest homes regularly, thereby serving as informal advocates. That limited funding be available to such groups to defray direct costs in connection with such visiting.

At present, community groups may enter rest homes only with the permission of operators; with coverage under the law of landlord and tenant, the right of entry will be effectively ensured, provided that a resident extends an invitation. In addition, we have reinforced this right of access under the residents' bill of rights.

We also commend the Good Neighbours initiative of the Office for Seniors' Issues. Currently, thirty-four regions, cities, towns, and villages in Ontario are involved with the initiative, which has as its slogan, Take Time to Reach Out. The intention is to promote community awareness of the value of people helping one another, and the development of informal neighbourhood support networks for frail, isolated, and vulnerable persons who live in the community. As rest homes are to be considered part of the community rather than institutional settings, the Good Neighbours initiative should be encouraged to promote awareness of the needs of rest-home residents.

RECOMMENDATION 86: That the Good Neighbours initiative promote awareness of the needs of rest-home residents.

10
Safety Standards

Throughout this Report we have stressed the twin goals of empowerment and offering protection to vulnerable adults in Ontario. Minimum standards with respect to health and safety are in place for the general population and the housing in which they live. However, the application of these standards to rest homes and their residents has been uneven, and in some cases non-existent. At times the omissions result from the lack of formal definition of a rest home, and the absence of an obligation for these homes to make themselves known to municipal authorities. The inconsistent application of minimum standards often results from differing concepts on the part of local regulatory authorities as to what a rest home is or is not, and what population it serves.

In this section, we consider the three major areas of public regulatory concern for the population at large: public-health protection; fire safety; and safety of the physical environment (which includes the Building Code and municipal occupancy by-laws). We examine these areas in the rest-home context and make recommendations that should result in universal effective coverage and consistency from site to site. Because the rest home is a setting in which care is delivered, we also explore the rationale for minimum staff ratios. First, however, we shall make recommendations for minimum standards and the mandatory registration of all rest homes.

Minimum Safety Standards

1 See note 41, below.

We believe there must be absolute minimum standards of housing quality in rest homes, and operators should not be permitted to offer accommodation that falls below this line.

> **RECOMMENDATION 87:** That the principle of a minimum standard for housing quality for rest homes based on protecting the lives and safety of residents be adopted, and that no operator be permitted to offer accommodation that fails to meet this minimum.

We draw the line low, given repeated and legitimate fears that all standards reduce the supply of housing for the most vulnerable persons. Indeed, we are recommending standards that protect only lives and personal safety. Housing below these minima is unhealthy, dangerous, or unsafe. Therefore, these standards must be enforced, even if the result is the dehousing of vulnerable persons. Surely one of the lessons to emerge from the tragic Rupert Hotel fire in Toronto is that in some cases dehousing is better than the alternative—which, in that case, was death.

We recommend that every assistance and encouragement, including financial aid, be given to operators to meet the minima. We particularly endorse the use of low-rise rehabilitation funding from the Ministry of Housing.[1]

There will be cases in which operators are unwilling or unable to meet minimum standards, however low they are set, and some loss of housing will inevitably occur. Although we do not desire loss of housing, in such cases the result is proper and necessary. Some housing is so dangerous that it is truly unfit for habitation.

Finding acceptable alternative housing for those evicted owing to unsafe or dangerous conditions should be a priority for the local authorities, even when this entails jumping the housing queue; if residents are not guaranteed rehousing they

2 We recall that residents at Cedar Glen were individually invited to leave and were guaranteed rehousing, but many feared to act. Eventually, the residents were simply removed and the operator closed the premises.

3 We assume that advocates and others will be vigilant in assisting residents to bring unsafe and unhealthy situations to the attention of the appropriate regulatory bodies.

will resist leaving unsafe premises and, indeed, may return illegally, raising the prospect of forcible removal.[2]

Residents cannot be expected to assess whether housing is unsafe or dangerous: we cannot assume they have the technical expertise to distinguish the unsafe from the merely unaesthetic; as well, many are reluctant to speak out because of their personal vulnerability: they may fear reprisals by operators; they may, understandably, feel any housing is better than no housing; or they may favourably compare their current residence to life in a psychiatric hospital.

Enforcement and corrective action must be rapid, when minimum standards are not met. Work orders in areas that affect personal health or safety cannot be permitted to accumulate over extended periods of time. We have stressed the importance of a timely response and the development of mechanisms to ensure this outcome.[3]

Mandatory Registration

In order that minimum standards be enforced, all rest homes must be known to regulatory authorities, such as the health, fire, and building inspectors. To this end, we are recommending a system of *mandatory registration* for all rest homes as defined by this Commission.

At the outset of this Report, we recommended a legal definition of the rest home. These two simple steps—defining and registering—will end the current situation in which "hidden" or "invisible" rest homes, particularly for low-income people and often in rural areas, operate unknown to or ignored by various public bodies.

A legal definition combined with mandatory registration will enable regular and systematic visitation and inspection by local regulatory bodies. For example, public-health inspectors and nurses often do not visit rest homes regularly, in part because of the ambiguity about what a rest home is. Once definition and registration are in place, mandatory and regular visits and inspections become an explicit responsibility of public-health units.

It is our intention that registration be simple and straightforward, primarily for identification. (This registration would be done by a municipal clerk or similar municipal authority.)[4] Registration should be given to rest-home operators who apply and meet the conditions specified below. Discretionary judgments should be limited to whether a particular premises fits the legal definition of a "rest home."[5]

Registration should not be transferable or assignable; and no property rights should be conveyed. (This approach stands in contrast to the system of granting nursing-home licences, which become valuable assets that can be bought and sold.)

RECOMMENDATION 88: That a system of mandatory registration for all rest homes be introduced as soon as possible. That all rest homes be required to register with the municipality in which they are located. That municipalities be permitted to charge a modest fee for registration.

Registration of rest homes should be contingent on filing documentation concerning both the safety of the premises and the fitness of owners and operators. Registration should not be contingent on meeting minimum standards. Compliance with standards should be noted at the time of registration, but it is the responsibility of the relevant regulatory authorities to enforce standards.

RECOMMENDATION 89: That any owner or operator seeking registration for a rest home shall be required to produce the following documents to the municipality in which the dwelling is located:

1. a certificate from the fire inspector attesting to compliance with the relevant sections of the Fire Code, or noting all outstanding work orders;

4 In the parts of Ontario where there is no municipal government, the province will have to assume direct responsibility for registration.

5 The only other discretionary judgment will be that of the Rest Homes Tribunal in interpreting applicants' criminal records. See below on the CPIC check. Currently in some communities, municipal licensing committees make subjective judgments about the "suitability" of operators or premises: it is this type of approach we wish to avoid.

6 It is not intended that this process will be time-consuming or complex. All necessary information can be forwarded on-line, as it is recorded for the municipality's use.

7 We note, for example, that the operator of Crozier Manor in Dorset who was convicted under the Criminal Code (discussed in chapter 8) was simultaneously operating a rest home in Kent County. At present, the local authorities in Kent would not have this information formally drawn to their attention.

2. a certificate from the building inspector attesting to compliance with the relevant sections of the Building Code and applicable local property standards by-laws, or noting all outstanding work orders;

3. a certificate from the local board of health attesting to compliance with the applicable sections of the *Health Protection and Promotion Act*, or noting all outstanding orders;

4. a certificate from the local police containing the results of a Canadian Police Information Centre check on the operators; and

5. a certificate from the Rest Homes Tribunal that affirms the operators are not at present banned from the industry and that the Rest Homes Tribunal holds that any convictions indicated by the Canadian Police Information Centre check do not constitute a bar to involvement in the industry.

When these conditions were satisfied, the clerk would issue a certificate of registration, to be posted prominently within the residence.

All registration information concerning the premises and the owners/operators should be forwarded by the municipality to the Rest Homes Tribunal (RHT), which should maintain a central data base.[6] The central data base is necessary so that multiple ownerships can be readily identified: if individuals are barred from the industry in one community, information on their involvement elsewhere in the province can be retrieved immediately and the notice of their being barred sent to affected municipalities and advocacy units.[7]

THE CPIC CHECK

The Canadian Police Information Centre (CPIC) is a computerized data base maintained by the RCMP on behalf of police forces across Canada, who contribute the records. It assembles criminal records of individuals but does not judge the nature or severity of offences. Those using the data system must interpret for themselves the meaning and implications of specific convictions.

Access to the system is strictly controlled. Besides law-enforcement authorities, certain agencies whose roles are complementary to law enforcement may be provided CPIC information.[8]

Individuals willing to undergo a CPIC check must consent in writing to the release of information and must have their fingerprints taken. The fingerprint form and the request are forwarded to the Ontario Provincial Police in Toronto, who access the RCMP files and release available information regarding criminal convictions to the agency specified in the consent form.

The Commission recommends that everyone seeking registration as an owner/operator of a rest home in Ontario be required to undergo a CPIC check. We make this recommendation in response to the very few cases in which, for example, individuals convicted of assaulting residents immediately resume operation of rest homes.

The number of cases in which the CPIC check would produce a record of convictions will undoubtedly be small, and we regret the imposition on the vast majority of potential registrants. However, the public interest does require this limited information about the criminal histories of all applicants for registration. The CPIC check is a clear statement that operation of a rest home—or, indeed, any other business in which care is provided to vulnerable persons—is a privilege rather than a right.

A report indicating an absence of criminal convictions would be submitted by the OPP to the municipal clerk as part of the registration process. If the CPIC check uncovered previous criminal convictions, the RHT would assess the implications of the individual case. Certain offences may not bar reg-

8 Current Ontario users of the CPIC system (in the category that could include rest homes) include the Ontario Racing Commission, the Liquor Licence Board of Ontario and the Ministry of Transportation, with respect to licensing school-bus drivers. For example, the Ministry of Transportation reviews the CPIC information on each case. The ministry is particularly looking for convictions under the *Narcotic Control Act* and for sexual offences. If the convictions are minor or time has elapsed, a licence would be granted. Though the ministry cannot ban individuals for life, they can continue to refuse to give licences. There is an appeal process, initially within the ministry and subsequently to the Human Rights Commission, the ombudsman, or the courts.

istration; others, particularly if they occurred in the recent past, might result in a decision to refuse registration at that time. The RHT may subsequently permit registration when the applicant demonstrates the character suitable to own/operate a rest home.

The RHT may also wish to decide that certain types of criminal convictions would lead to a permanent bar from the industry. We are reluctant to recommend absolute and permanent penalties, but it would be up to the RHT to establish its own criteria. Over time, the cases that accumulate would serve as precedents for members of the RHT and potential registrants.

RECOMMENDATION 90: That every person seeking registration as owner/operator of a rest home be required to undergo a Canadian Police Information Centre check prior to registration.

RECOMMENDATION 91: That if an applicant has previous criminal convictions, the Rest Homes Tribunal determine the suitability of the applicant to own or operate a rest home and whether the applicant shall be permitted to register the rest home.

FULL DISCLOSURE

It will be essential to "pierce the corporate veil" so that the actual owners and operators of a rest home be known. Limited corporations and partnerships should be required to provide full information—names, addresses, and phone numbers—on all shareholders or partners holding more than a specified minority interest. Such information must accompany each application for registration and be posted prominently in each rest home.

RECOMMENDATION 92: That full information on the names, addresses, and phone numbers of all owners and operators holding more than a specified minority interest accompany an application for registration of a rest home and subsequently be posted prominently in the home.

Any change of ownership of a rest home should entail new registration, complete with all required documentation, irrespective of registration by the previous owner.

After the initial registration of a rest home, an annual renewal should be required. This would simply entail the payment of a modest fee, and would serve the sole purpose of informing various authorities that the premises are still in operation as a rest home.

RECOMMENDATION 93: That registration be obtained upon any change of ownership and renewed annually.

It is not our intention that registration be refused or revoked, as nursing-home licences can be. Thus, there would be none of the associated administrative or court proceedings, or threat of proceedings, to terminate operators' right to do business.

No municipality or licensing body could remove the right to operate a rest home because of a failure to comply with standards contained in other regulatory legislation. Rather, all violations and infractions should be cited and remedied under the relevant health-, fire-, building- or property-standards legislation.[9]

It is the view of the Commission that municipal licensing is superfluous where there is effective enforcement of the available penalties for violations of the relevant regulatory legislation.[10] To ensure that basic standards are met, the relevant regulatory officials would be encouraged to meet on a regular basis, and to share their information.

RECOMMENDATION 94: That all municipal inspection and enforcement bodies be encouraged to keep all infor-

9 Each regulatory authority (fire, building, public health) possesses a series of sanctions, including the right to close premises.

10 Elsewhere we recommend measures to ensure that powers be exercised appropriately and that the safety of residents be protected. Violations of the basic rights of residents would be protected in the bill of rights. Remedies for violations of those rights, including closure of the rest home, could be pursued through the RHT.

mation about rest homes in such a manner that it can be easily shared. That these bodies share the information on a regular basis.

No annual re-inspections should be required, as it is our intention that inspections occur regularly and unannounced as part of the ongoing monitoring of rest-home premises.

We do not envisage a need for a lengthy implementation period for this system.

> **RECOMMENDATION 95:** That all rest homes be given a six-month period to register after the enactment of the legal requirement to do so.

After six months, unregistered rest homes should be subject to closure, based on a complaint that any person could lodge with the RHT. The RHT may then hold a hearing; if an unregistered rest home were in operation, the RHT might order closure of the premises or a temporary trusteeship pending removal of the residents, to be followed by closure. RHT orders should have the effect of a court order to be enforced by the sheriff.

In any procedure to close an unregistered rest home, the interests of residents must be protected; any costs associated with their move to alternative accommodation should be fully chargeable against the operators. The costs of the closure itself should be recoverable from the operators.

> **RECOMMENDATION 96:** That there be a range of penalties for a rest home that operates without registration, including an order by the Rest Homes Tribunal to close the premises with the cost of relocation of the residents chargeable to the operators.

Staffing Issues

Minimum standards apply not only to the physical conditions of the home but for the staffing of the rest home, as well. Inadequate numbers of staff, irrespective of their qualifications, is one of the more troubling situations reported to the Commission. We have been told of residences housing large numbers of frail and bedridden seniors, where one or two teenagers are left in charge at night, on weekends, or on holidays, with no one else available or on call.

STAFF RATIOS

What is an appropriate staff-to-resident ratio depends on the purpose for which staff are present. We do not recommend a minimum staffing level based on the care needs of residents, even if this were possible to determine on a universal basis. To do so would create a major cost burden for operators and would endorse their role as providers of care rather than as landlords.

In the Commission's view, the purpose of a mandatory minimum staff ratio is to prevent serious harm to residents, in cases such as fire, serious personal crisis, sudden illness, or accident. The ratio should be sufficient to respond to any crisis that has the potential to cause serious harm to one or more residents. The ratio should be determined on the assumption that the staff would not be expected to treat an illness, but they would be expected to know the appropriate professional to contact, and to make the contact quickly.[11]

RECOMMENDATION 97: That staff in rest homes be viewed as serving a safety rather than a care-giving function.

[11] If a staffing ratio were premised upon a care function being served, then presumably the richer the ratio, the better the quality of care. In such cases, an individual assessment of each of the premises and the functioning level of its residents would be almost essential.

12 Many day staff are engaged in tasks such as food preparation or laundry, even though the regulatory intent may be for them to deliver care.

13 One community proposes a staff ratio of one-to-five and another of one-to-seven, averaged over twenty-four hours. Assuming payment at minimum wage and without benefits, the cost of one staff person per twenty-four-hour day is approximately $150. Under the hostel provisions of GWA, total daily income to operators for five residents is about $160. Virtually all income from five GWA residents would go into the salary of the one mandatory staff person, with little left over for food, housing, or compensation to operators.

14 In Hamilton, for example, a current proposal would require one night-staff person for up to twenty-five residents. For twenty-six to forty residents, the night-shift requirement would rise to two staff. Above forty, one staff person must be added for each fifteen residents.

The minimum staff according to the ratio must be on the premises at all hours, for if the purpose of staff is to respond to crises, this function must be guaranteed to residents at all times.

Once a staff ratio is specified, its enforcement would be quite straightforward: a simple head count—of staff and residents—and a check of records could determine compliance. Non-compliance could be reported to the RHT.

Calculating a proper staff ratio for safety purposes would involve tradeoffs between ensuring safety and cost. Individualized assessment of rest-home residents is not feasible, given rapid changes in population mix and the technical and administrative complexity of assessment. Instead, we recommend that a single consistent staff-to-resident ratio be determined for all rest homes.

RECOMMENDATION 98: That a minimum staff-to-resident ratio be mandatory in all rest homes at all hours. That only adults over the age of sixteen count in meeting this ratio.

Some mandatory minimum ratios set out in municipal by-laws permit averaging of staff ratios over a twenty-four-hour period: more persons are present during the day than at night.[12] Because our minimum staff ratio reflects only a safety function, this minimum must be operative at all times, on all shifts. Averaging over shifts should not be permitted.

Some of the ratios required or proposed in municipal by-laws strike us as costly. Given the limited incomes of some residents, it appears that only by using staff for "household" purposes can these ratios be met.[13] From the Commission's perspective, there is little point in requiring high staff ratios, only to have the staff doing laundry; operators would require laundry services, in any event.

The ratios for evening or night-shift duty in some by-laws seem to reflect safety needs and to minimize care-giving expectations.[14] As such, these ratios are probably in the desirable range for a provincial minimum staffing ratio.

The administrative responsibility for staff ratios should be assigned to municipal fire inspectors.[15] Operators would have to maintain a staff log book to document compliance with the ratio, and it would be the role of the fire inspector to ensure compliance.

RECOMMENDATION 99: That administrative responsibility to ensure staff ratios in rest homes are met be given to municipal fire inspectors.

ASSISTING WITH MEDICATIONS

Of the concerns that arose again and again, those surrounding medications in rest homes were among the most pressing. Current practice varies widely. In some settings we visited, particularly where a nurse is present, the system for the distribution of medications is on the hospital model, complete with log books, records, etc. Other homes we visited frankly scare us. Often, case material refers to teenagers or adults unable to read labels dispensing to residents without knowing or paying attention to who is getting what. There have also been many references to medication cabinets not kept locked or secured, and to systematic improper dispensing being used as a behavioural tool by operators.

The more rigorous the standard required of operators, the greater the need for them to maintain complete records and for inspectors to apply a formal enforcement mechanism with penalties. Such regulation, of the type that occurs in nursing homes, implies an assumption of substantial responsibility on the part of operators and staff. However, the greater the responsibility and potential liability, the less likely operators will be to become involved. At the very least, operators have a right to compensation commensurate with the responsibility and liability they are being asked to assume. Without com-

[15] This assumes the safety function would primarily focus on evacuation in case of fire. There are also other safety concerns, such as certain behaviours on the part of residents. Thus, administrative responsibility might be assigned to public-health inspectors instead. In either case, the responsibilities are modest.

16 This does not mean that the staff must be able to communicate in the residents' own language, but they must be able to understand if residents are requesting or refusing the medication.

17 In Part IV of this Report, we suggest how competence may be ascertained.

18 We prefer to see this responsibility lying with the prescribing physicians and pharmacists. We do not recommend mandatory staffing of rest homes by nurses or other medical personnel. In small rest homes, a requirement for an RN or an RNA, even if only at specified hours, would be prohibitively expensive. In large homes where costs can be spread over substantial numbers of residents, an operator may desire, and deem it economically feasible, to have qualified nursing staff on-site at certain hours at least.

pensation, operators will refuse to be involved with medications; residents will be expected to self-medicate, and those who need assistance will not receive it.

This is not an acceptable approach or result. Therefore, staff and operators' responsibilities with respect to medications must be clearly defined and restricted.

Operators may choose to assist with medications. If they do so, they must have the consent of the residents (or substitute decision-makers) and their responsibilities must be narrow, but precise. Staff must be aware of and respect the residents' legal right to refuse medications unless there is a court order to the contrary.

All staff persons involved in any aspect of medications must be "competent" in this service. The Commission does not wish to impose a high standard that would professionalize or medicalize this assistance.

RECOMMENDATION 100: That any staff person who is involved in any aspect of assisting residents to take medications must be "competent" to do so. In assisting a resident in taking medications, "competence" means, at a minimum, that assistance can be provided only by someone who is:

    1. sixteen years of age or older;
    2. able to read and follow the directions on the bottle or package; and
    3. able to identify, recognize, and communicate[16] with the resident.

A requirement to meet this standard of competence has been incorporated into the residents' bill of rights.[17]

Ensuring that medications are not counter-indicated or making other quasi-medical judgements is not a responsibility we can realistically assign to rest-home staff without tremendous cost and liability implications for operators.[18]

Rest-home staff must merely be capable of ensuring that

the designated recipient receives the prescribed medications in the prescribed dosage at the prescribed time.

RECOMMENDATION 101: That any operator providing assistance with medications be responsible to ensure that the medications, as prescribed, are delivered to the correct person in the prescribed dosage at the prescribed frequency.

The staff and operators' responsibility is limited to following the instructions provided by the pharmacist or prescribing doctor, and does not entail any clinical or medical judgements.

A requirement that operators offer a secure locked area for the storage of medications has been incorporated into the residents' bill of rights. In general, residents should not be required to keep their medications in this locked area, because they have a right to control their own medications. In some cases, however, to ensure group safety—for example, to lessen the risk of theft—a common locked area for medication may be necessary.

RECOMMENDATION 102: That operators be required to offer a secure locked area for the storage of medications.

Health Protection

The protection and promotion of health in rest homes has proven to be a complex issue, for protecting health and assigning a proper role to public-health authorities presupposes a definition of what constitutes a rest home, and who, if anyone, has responsibility for its residents.

Were rest homes to be viewed as first-stage nursing homes, for example, it would be appropriate that they assume a major health-care role. Many submissions and presentations

19 A majority of the members of the board are appointed by the municipality. The senior staff person for each board is the local "medical officer of health," who must be a medical doctor.

have argued that only RNs should be permitted to assist with medications and/or that every rest home should be required to have RNs or RNAs on staff. The cost implications are rarely discussed, as the case is usually made on the grounds of empirical need: large numbers of frail elderly persons receive inadequate or minimal health care.

We have set out our view that the rest home ought not be viewed as a first-stage nursing home, and that care be increasingly delivered on an in-home portable basis by community-based agencies. We also bring this general approach to the discussion of the protection of the health of residents in rest homes.

There is a limited mandate in existing provincial legislation relating to the role of public-health authorities in protecting and promoting the health of residents in rest homes. The *Health Protection and Promotion Act (HPPA)* is administered by the Ministry of Health; services are delivered through local boards of health.[19] Within each health unit are public-health inspectors and public-health nurses, with different professional training and roles.

Sections 5 and 10 of the *HPPA* are particularly relevant to the work of the Commission.

SECTION 5

The mandatory programs and services for local boards of health are set out in section 5. These include "family health," "home-care services," "nutrition," and "public-health education." Standards for these activities are set out in *Mandatory Health Programs and Services Guidelines* (Ministry of Health, April 1989).

The *Guidelines* are concerned primarily with health promotion and education rather than with the direct provision of health services. For example, the goal of "healthy elderly" requires health education on topics such as the aging process, nutritional needs, prevention of and coping with chronic disease, and health benefits of physical activity.

Section 5 also mandates some direct health services to a few specific groups, such as "infants, pregnant women in high-risk health categories and the elderly" and the "provision of preschool and school health services."[20] In general, however, public-health nurses do not monitor individual health, nor do they inspect schools and child-care centres.

There is no explicit legislative mandate for public-health nurses to provide health services in rest homes under the *HPPA*. To a large extent, any role they assume is decided locally. Not surprisingly, then, there are wide variations in this role across the province: in some communities, particularly those with comprehensive rest-home by-laws, public-health nurses actively and regularly visit rest homes; in other communities, nurses may be unaware that particular rest homes exist. Nonetheless, the primary role set out for public-health nurses under section 5 is that of educators. (Public-health nurses have indicated that they are not comfortable with inspection and enforcement responsibilities.)

Section 5 also mandates public-health inspectors to provide services and programs to ensure sanitary conditions and to prevent or eliminate health hazards.

SECTION 10

Section 10 of the *HPPA* sets out two separate inspection duties to be performed by public-health inspectors: inspecting premises used as a "boarding house or lodging house" for health hazards; and inspecting food premises for health hazards.[21]

Neither section 10 nor the *Guidelines* are specific about *what* is to be inspected in boarding houses, but the focus is clearly on the physical setting, not the residents. The section is interpreted to encompass the general sanitation of the

20 Most health boards also operate the Home Care program, which delivers nursing services to people in the community. These services are usually provided by an agency under contract to the Home Care Program, never by public-health nurses.

21 A "health hazard" is defined as "a condition of a premises that has or is likely to have an adverse effect on the health of any person."

22 Section 20 of the *HPPA* requires that every person who owns a residential building shall provide sanitary facilities or a privy for the residents. Thus, the practice at Cedar Glen of residents being required to use buckets in their rooms rather than toilets in the bathrooms would have been a legitimate concern of the public-health inspector.

23 This contrasts with a requirement that public-health boards determine a minimum inspection frequency for food premises.

24 The food-premises-inspection mandate applies generally to the "sanitary storage and preparation" of the food served; there is no concern with its nutritional characteristics or dietary sufficiency.

premises (for example, the presence of rodents and the hygiene of washrooms).[22]

The terms "boarding house" and "lodging house" are not defined in the *HPPA*. A broad interpretation of the terms would include simple room-and-board situations and perhaps even student residences or accommodation-only premises. The *Guidelines* do not require regular visits to boarding houses, probably because of the potentially broad definition, and there is no requirement that boarding and lodging houses, however defined, make themselves known to municipal authorities. Public-health inspectors often perceive no expectation to conduct regular inspections; therefore, rest homes, as defined by the Commission, are not regularly or frequently inspected by public-health authorities under section 10.[23]

The second duty under section 10—the duty to inspect food premises for health hazards—covers *all* food premises. A specific regulation under section 10 explicitly includes (but does not define) boarding houses. This regulation is extensive, detailed, and gives strong authority to inspectors with respect to all matters regarding the physical plant (e.g., flooring, lighting, ventilation, cupboards); the sanitary equipment; food handling; food quality (e.g., pasteurized milk and inspected meat); and the cleanliness of persons doing food preparation.[24]

However, boarding houses that provide food service to fewer than ten residents are excluded from the food-premises regulations, whose standards are clearly targeted at large operations. (They would be prohibitively expensive and technically impossible in many smaller settings.)

Therefore, there is no specific food-premises standard for smaller boarding houses. However, the general duty to inspect premises for health hazards does apply to boarding houses serving food to fewer than ten residents. The duty, under section 10, to inspect sanitation in boarding houses, would apply to kitchens in smaller premises; but there are no specific standards or guidelines.

If the medical officer of health or the public-health inspectors find a health hazard while inspecting a boarding house or food premises, they have extensive power to order corrective action, including vacating the premises; closing part of the premises; the performance of work specified in an order; removing the hazard; and cleaning or disinfecting the premises.

Where compliance is not forthcoming, the medical officer of health may see to it that the order is carried out, with costs recoverable from the owner. All orders by public-health inspectors and local medical officers of health are appealable to the Health Protection Appeal Board and then to Divisional Court.

Like public-health nurses, inspectors tend to prefer persuasion to confrontation. Moreover, public-health bodies are reluctant to engage in adversarial court proceedings, which are time-consuming and costly.[25]

Public-Health Officials

Many submissions to the Commission recommended or made reference to a set of inspection guidelines for local health boards issued in 1976.[26] These guidelines, which are quite extensive in their coverage, are no longer applicable under the current public-health legislation, which came into effect in 1983; however, the guidelines are still used by some local health boards.

Some public-health officials believe that these guidelines were appropriately scrapped, as they have no basis in public-health practice. The Commission has examined them for content, irrespective of their relevance to public health. They represent a form of comprehensive regulation (in which enforcement powers are given to local public-health units)—with all the concomitant disadvantages that we referred to in chapter 4. As a result, we are unable to recommend their adoption or to endorse the role they give to public-health authorities.

25 There is also some concern that the takeover power is too vague and that action under it might not be upheld in court.

26 They were produced by a "task force on rest homes, lodging houses, group homes and like facilities" and deal with matters such as space requirements, sewage disposal, bed sizes, ventilation, lighting, heating, and record-keeping.

Some municipalities have given the public-health unit and the medical officer of health an extensive inspection mandate well beyond inspection of food premises and general sanitation, including administration of medications, nutritional standards, and nursing care. To the extent that this mandate is embodied in a municipal by-law, it is probably beyond the authority of the municipalities, as we have noted earlier. More to the point, however, we deem it inappropriate to give a broad mandate to public-health authorities, as we are reluctant to create medicalized mini-institutions with comprehensive regulation on the nursing-home model.

PUBLIC-HEALTH INSPECTORS

Section 10 of the *HPPA* gives public-health inspectors (PHIs) the duty to inspect premises used as boarding or lodging houses. We recommend that the rest home as defined in chapter 3 be included within the meaning of "boarding and lodging houses" in the *HPPA*. We have also recommended a system of mandatory registration so all rest homes become known to local authorities. Taken together, the duty to inspect boarding houses, and in particular "rest homes," becomes operational and meaningful.

> **RECOMMENDATION 103:** That the Ministry of Health develop relevant standards and guidelines for the regular inspection of rest homes, as defined by the Commission, under section 10 of the *Health Protection and Promotion Act.*

Even should these inspections be limited to matters of sanitation, the standards would establish what is to be inspected, how often, and in what manner. Like all other inspections, these *must* be unannounced if they are to be effective. The protocol should also contain a procedure for responding to complaints from individuals or referrals from the RHT (based on complaints received by it).

The effect of this change would be to make regular and unannounced visits to rest homes a mandatory part of PHIs' responsibilities.

Moreover, once there is a clear definition of a rest home, and registration of all such premises, the PHIs' duty to inspect food premises (based on the detailed standards) would include all rest homes serving food to ten or more residents.

RECOMMENDATION 104: That the duty to inspect food premises under section 10 of the *Health Protection and Promotion Act* include regular inspections of all rest homes serving food to ten or more residents.

We recommend that the Ministry of Health (MoH) consider the development of guidelines for all premises serving food to three to ten persons. We also recommend that the ministry explore the relative merits of an approach based on specific standards and one with a more general approach.[27]

RECOMMENDATION 105: That the Ministry of Health consider the development of guidelines that would apply to all premises serving food to three or more and fewer than ten persons.

PUBLIC-HEALTH NURSES

We support the continued primary role of public-health nurses (PHNs) to promote health, with some informal representation on behalf of residents.

The general mandate to provide health services under section 5 of the *HPPA* extends to residents of rest homes, as to all members of the community. Once rest homes are covered under the *Landlord and Tenant Act* (*LTA*), the full range of

27 The Commission has not explored whether it would be more effective to develop a detailed set of standards for small premises or to rely on the existing general duty to inspect all premises for sanitation. If any such standards are to be developed, they must apply not only to rest homes: a traditional room-and-board setting and a care-providing residence should also meet the same minimum standards for the cleanliness and safety of food premises.

28 The *Guidelines* focus on consumer groups or specific health problems rather than on settings in which programs should be offered. However, programs for the "well elderly" and other health-promotion programs are essential both to residents and to operators of rest homes.

In general, PHNs provide services to non-profit service providers and agencies. The Commission recommends that rest-home operators also be eligible for appropriate health education and promotion services.

29 They will be expected to contact the Advocacy Commission or the Office of the Public Guardian, as appropriate, either directly or by notifying the RHT, which would then refer the case to the proper body or bodies. A violation of the residents' rights should be investigated by the advocate, as a matter of urgency, if there is suspicion of abuse or intimidation. Alternatively, the Office of the Public Guardian may conduct an investigation to determine if the person is not capable of personal decision-making, in which case a guardian may be appointed by a judge. See also the earlier discussion on mandatory reporting of abuse in rest homes, chapter 9.

programs offered by PHNs becomes accessible to residents at their request.

In addition, however, PHNs should conduct regular outreach programs in rest homes. Such services should be added to the *Guidelines* under the *HPPA*. "General Standard—Equal Access" under the *HPPA* requires that public-health programs and services be "accessible to people in special groups for whom barriers exist." Rest-home residents should be recognized as a special group under this Standard.[28]

RECOMMENDATION 106: That rest-home residents be recognized as a special group for the purpose of equal access to mandatory public-health programs under the "General Standard—Equal Access" in *Mandatory Health Programs and Services Guidelines* under the *Health Protection and Promotion Act.*

It is not, nor should it be, within the mandate of PHNs to provide nursing care to individual residents. The individual health of residents is best served when the PHN works in the role of educator with operators, staff, and residents.

Let us consider a brief example, in which an individual resident of a rest home is malnourished or in need of medical attention. The response should be the same as it would be if the event occurred in a private home in the community. If the resident is competent and making an informed choice to decline medical-model care, that choice must be respected. On the other hand, the cause may be rooted in poor-quality food provided and/or fear of reprisal from the care-giver if the problem is raised by the resident.

PHNs are not responsible to provide health care to individual residents or to enforce a particular standard of health-care provision by rest-home operators.[29] However, PHNs cannot ignore the observable health needs of residents, or abuse. Like all members of the community, they are obliged to report abuse in rest homes.

Indeed, PHNs and public-health nutritionists, where available, can be particularly valuable in dealing with resident nutrition. The Commission has recommended a minimum nutritional standard as part of a bill of rights; violations can be pursued through the RHT. It would not be the nurses' role to enforce this standard, although they would be encouraged to try informal representation to the operators, inform residents or their advocates of appropriate recourse and/or report their concerns to the RHT.

There has been some question as to whether the Canada Food Guide or the new standards being developed by Health and Welfare Canada are suitable for residents of rest homes.[30]

> **RECOMMENDATION 107:** That public-health officials, in conjunction with the Ontario Dietetic Association, explore appropriate minimum nutritional standards for residents of rest homes.

Whatever the outcome, PHNs and nutritionists should offer advice and education to operators and staff in the planning and preparation of proper meals. This service should be required under the *Guidelines* for the *HPPA*, analogous to the requirement to provide effective nutrition education for care-givers of preschoolers in group settings.

> **RECOMMENDATION 108:** That public-health nurses and nutritionists offer nutritional services to rest-home residents and operators as part of their mandatory provision of health services. This requirement should be incorporated into the "Program Standard—Nutrition Promotion" in the *Mandatory Health Programs and Services Guidelines* under the *Health Protection and Promotion Act.*

Medications in Rest Homes

Some submissions have argued that operators and staff have no responsibilities with regard to medications; if they do

30 See above, note 7 in chapter 9.

31 We do not wish PHNs to assume a formal responsibility concerning medications, for to do so would assign to the public sector the costs and burden of following up the private entrepreneurial activities of individual doctors.

assist, they do so as a courtesy to residents, who are responsible for their own medications. Others have called for qualified medical personnel on all premises to control distribution of all medications. Some have recommended that PHNs formally approve any system used to assist with medications, or that they inspect to ensure a proper system is being used.

As we discuss elsewhere, formal responsibility with respect to medications should lie with the prescribing physicians and possibly the pharmacists, but not with PHNs.[31] Their role remains one of education, information, and informal representation. Part of their role should be to offer assistance in the development and maintenance of a system in which medications are stored safely and distributed correctly, and to offer assistance with staff training.

> **RECOMMENDATION 109:** That public-health nurses offer assistance to rest-home operators in developing appropriate systems for assisting residents with their medications, and that they offer training to rest-home staff in utilizing an appropriate system.

PHNs should not be responsible for inspection or formal approval of systems being used. They would, however, be encouraged to report possible breaches of the standards specified in the Report by operators to the RHT or Advocacy Commission if they are unable to resolve matters informally. In this way, PHNs will help to ensure that residents' rights concerning medications are protected; the ability to report, however, will lend great authority to their recommendations and suggestions.

Protection from Fire

It is widely believed that the Fire Code, an extensive regulation under the *Fire Marshals Act*, sets standards for protection against fires in all rest homes in Ontario. This assumption is erroneous, although it was expressed in many submissions to the Commission. In fact, section 18 of the *Fire Marshals Act* provides the only provincially legislated protection for rest homes: it gives the fire marshal power to act, in certain hazardous circumstances, even if the Fire Code is not applicable.

The Fire Code is currently being revised by the Office of the Fire Marshal; the status of rest homes under these proposals has not yet been clarified. We shall recommend specific inclusion of rest homes under an appropriate section of the revised Fire Code.

The Fire Code: Part 9

The sections of part 9 of the Fire Code, which set out fire-protection standards for existing buildings, are commonly referred to as the "retrofit" sections. They specify the upgrading necessary for some types of buildings constructed before 1976. (Since 1976, all newly "constructed"[32] buildings have been subject to the fire protection provisions of the Building Code, which are generally higher than the standards in part 9 of the Fire Code.)

Each section of part 9 sets out the standards required in a specific type of building.[33] The standard of fire protection that applies to a particular type of building is based on two primary considerations: the physical structure of the building, and its intended usage or the characteristics of the occupants. Higher standards are set for buildings occupied by persons who would require assistance to exit the building in case of fire. As well, higher standards are set for buildings with more than a certain number of floors or surface area.

Two sections of the existing Fire Code are relevant to the present discussion:

Section 9.3 of the Fire Code deals with "boarding and rooming houses" in which (a) the residents "do *not* require

32 See note 45 below.

33 Each section sets out standards in four areas of concern:
1. fire containment: for example, construction materials for walls and ceilings, and fire-resistance ratings of walls, ceilings, and fire separations. (The fire-resistance rating is the time that a material will withstand exposure to fire and heat under specified conditions);
2. means of egress: for example, the number, location, and access to exits from various parts of the building;
3. fire alarm and detection: for example, the requirements for fire and smoke alarms;
4. fire suppression: for example, access for fire fighting, extinguishers, and standpipe and hose systems.

34 The 600 m² refers to ground coverage only, not the total floor space.

Section 9.3 also applies to smaller Homes for Special Care (between three and ten residents) if nursing care is not required.

35 Section 9.7 also applies to other classes of premises subject to the same MCSS legislation, but it adopts for these premises the standards of 9.3 (small non-care-providing group homes), 9.4 (larger care-providing group homes and facilities), 9.5 and 9.6 (larger non-care-providing group homes and facilities), as appropriate.

care or treatment due to age, mental or physical limitations"; and (b) the premises are neither more than three storeys high nor cover more than 600 m² of ground.[34]

Section 9.4 applies to specific "health-care facilities" such as hospitals, nursing homes, homes for the aged, and larger Homes for Special Care. This section contains the highest standards.

The Office of the Fire Marshal has drafted new regulations for part 9 that will apply, if proclaimed, to new classes of existing buildings:

Draft section 9.5 would apply to residential buildings with up to six floors. Buildings covered under section 9.3 (small boarding homes not providing care) or 9.4 (health facilities) are excluded; specifically included are residential buildings containing boarding, lodging, and rooming accommodation for more than three persons. Boarding accommodation for persons who require care, which is excluded from section 9.3, is not specifically excluded here.

Draft section 9.6 would apply to residential buildings of more than six floors. It specifically includes buildings that contain boarding, lodging, and rooming accommodation for more than ten persons. Boarding accommodation in which the residents require care is not excluded.

Draft section 9.7 provides standards for group homes providing accommodation with care for fewer than ten persons, licensed under specific Ministry of Community and Social Services (MCSS) legislation (such as the *Developmental Services Act* or the *Child and Family Services Act*).[35] The proposed standards for these small care-providing group homes are more rigorous than the current section 9.3: higher-rated fire separations and higher standards for means of egress are required so occupants have more time to evacuate in case of fire.

INTERPRETATION

In summary, the Fire Code does not apply to buildings built

after 1975, provided that they continue to comply with the standards for fire safety contained in the Building Code.[36] Currently, the Fire Code retrofit sections apply to small boarding homes and rooming houses in which the residents do not require care (section 9.3), and to regulated health-care facilities (section 9.4). Proposed for coverage are residences subject to specific MCSS legislation, in particular small MCSS-funded group homes where care is provided (section 9.7), and low- and high-rise residential buildings, including those that "contain boarding, lodging, and rooming accommodation" (sections 9.5 and 9.6).

Strictly interpreted, section 9.3 excludes rooming or boarding houses in which the residents require care, even if no care is delivered by operators or community agencies.[37] Being ill-equipped to conduct a needs assessment of residents—for that is what section 9.3 might require—the fire marshal's only practical alternative is to base decisions on whether care is actually provided by operators.

Under the current Fire Code, there is no specific protection for rooming or boarding houses in which the residents require care, only the general protection of section 18 of the *Fire Marshals Act*. (If certain very hazardous conditions exist, the fire marshal may order structural alterations and the installation of safeguards such as alarms and extinguishers. This power has seldom been used, although it is undoubtedly available with respect to rest homes as defined by this Commission.)

Moreover, there are no specific definitions in the Fire Code of what constitutes a boarding, lodging, and rooming house, or of residents *not* requiring "care or treatment."

The exclusion of premises in which residents require care, found in section 9.3, is not repeated in proposed draft sections 9.5 or 9.6. However, these proposed sections may be intended to include only larger rooming houses, such as Toronto's Rupert Hotel.[38]

Because rest homes have not yet been precisely defined

36 Where a change in use of a building "constructed" after 1975 has occurred, the Fire Code and/or the Building Code may apply.

37 Thus, section 9.3 does not necessarily distinguish between a rooming house, in which the operator provides no care, and a boarding home, in which care is provided.

38 "Real" hotels are subject to separate legislation, the *Hotel Fire Safety Act*.

39 Decisions about the number and location of fire exits or fire-resistance ratings of construction materials used in rest homes, for example, are ultimately empirical reflections of the general tradeoff between safety, cost, and housing supply.

and because residents' care needs are not known, there may have been uncertainty about how to treat them when revising the Fire Code. One observer before the Commission has suggested that rest homes be covered under section 9.4 (health-care facilities); another suggested draft section 9.7 (small MCSS group homes). Both these standards are more rigorous than those of section 9.3 and draft sections 9.5 and 9.6, which generally require higher standards for the same types of premises as they increase in size.

The exclusion of boarding homes where care is provided has led some municipalities to enact by-laws containing fire-safety requirements specifically directed at such boarding homes. These standards are, in many cases, higher than those of the Fire Code.

PROPOSED REVISIONS

No system of fire protection can absolutely guarantee the safety of the individual. All are based on probabilities: the more rigorous the standards, the higher the likelihood that a greater proportion of people will be able to escape a given fire. (Fire stations are not located on every block in every neighbourhood, but rather are positioned so that a response can be made to most fires within a specified number of minutes.)

Although the ideal is to maximize the probability of safe egress for the maximum number of people at all times, we make tradeoffs in our policy choices. The higher the standards, the greater the cost of compliance—and the greater the likelihood that low-income housing will be diverted to other uses.

The Office of the Fire Marshal is currently revising the Fire Code. Although we cannot comment on the technical issues, we believe it is the appropriate role of this Commission to contribute to the general discussion, in the expectation of facilitating the resolution of the issues.[39]

In this regard, we have previously indicated that in setting mandatory standards we believe the general tradeoff should tend to protect scarce low-income housing, bearing in mind that there must be a minimum standard for fire safety below which no rest home should operate.

RECOMMENDATION 110: That as a matter of general policy, residents of rest homes should have the same protections under the Fire Code as are provided to persons in rooming houses.

We have argued that there is no clear distinction between residents of rooming houses and of rest homes. Any person may be in one or the other setting, dependent on capricious factors including geographic location; the willingness of the municipality to subsidize (and thereby create places in) domiciliary-hostel settings; personal preferences, either for care services or for the greater autonomy of accommodation-only settings; and availability of places on any particular day.

As services are increasingly delinked, i.e., delivered to residents by community-based agencies rather than operators, the more rest homes will resemble rooming houses. The decreasing distinction between a rest home and a rooming house may be expected to bring with it a diminishing need to impose higher fire standards on one than on the other.

We are also very concerned about the possible dehousing effect of new, higher standards. Rest homes should not be required to meet the standards imposed on health-care facilities (section 9.4) or proposed for MCSS group homes (draft section 9.7). Many rest-home operators could not meet these standards without incurring substantial costs (which would also fall to government should it choose to assist financially). Many operators would leave the industry and convert the premises to other uses, become accommodation-only premises (subject to the lower standards contained in section 9.3, draft section 9.5 or 9.6), or ignore the new, high standards.

As well, the high standards of section 9.4, intended for

"institutional occupancies," impose requirements that conflict with the homelike environment of smaller rest homes. High fire-safety standards were frequently criticized during the Commission's consultations for creating an unnecessarily sterile and cold living environment.

> **RECOMMENDATION 111:** That the standards required of rooming houses as set out in section 9.3 and draft sections 9.5 and 9.6 of the Fire Code be required of rest homes.

> **RECOMMENDATION 112:** That the exclusionary reference to premises in which the residents "do not require care or treatment" in section 9.3 of the Fire Code be eliminated, and that the terms "boarding, rooming and lodging accommodation" as used in section 9.3 and draft sections 9.5 and 9.6 be interpreted to include rest homes as defined by this Commission.

The section of the Fire Code—section 9.3 or draft sections 9.5 or 9.6—that would apply to a particular building should be determined by number of floors and ground cover.

IMPACT

Buildings constructed since 1976 would be unaffected by these changes as they are covered by the generally higher standards of the Building Code. Communities with municipal by-laws containing fire-protection standards for rest homes should also be substantially unaffected, as most of this housing should be at or near required levels. The greatest impact would be felt in communities that do not have municipal by-laws, for it is here that the gap between current practice and new standards will be widest.

The Office of the Fire Marshal did an impact analysis of meeting the standards proposed in draft sections 9.5 and 9.6,

and estimated an average province-wide cost of approximately $500 per dwelling unit for buildings constructed prior to
1976.[40]

The standards proposed for rooming houses (under draft
sections 9.5 and 9.6) have been criticized by some community
groups because of the probable adverse impact on housing
stock. We cannot assess the suitability of particular standards:
our concern is that the *same* standards be required of rooming houses and rest homes, as defined by the Commission,
and our general sympathies lie with those concerned to protect low-income housing.

> **RECOMMENDATION 113:** That the fire marshal explicitly
> recognize the possible adverse effect on the rest-home stock
> of any higher standards under consideration.

Such an approach, if adopted, might alter the way fire safety
is conceptualized. In place of a straightforward technical analysis about square metres and fire ratings, the assessment
would become a cost-benefit analysis that explicitly acknowledges the competition between social goals, such as housing
availability, and costs. The tradeoffs and choices would
become more value-based (and difficult), and less technical.
We further suggest that affected community groups be actively
involved in deciding these tradeoffs.

> **RECOMMENDATION 114:** That community housing
> groups be involved in any decision-making process con-
> cerning higher fire-protection standards for rest homes.

Some substandard housing stock can be brought up to an
acceptable level at acceptable cost. Owners of these premises
should be encouraged and financially assisted to upgrade.
Although we clearly cannot determine what constitutes an
"acceptable" cost in any specific case, we do endorse the
principle that public funds be used to aid private operators of

40 Included were apartments,
which would probably
involve higher costs than
rooms in a rest home; both
would certainly be higher
than the cost per roomer or
boarder.

41 This program provides forgivable loans to owners of older low-rise apartment buildings and rooming houses to upgrade to the minimum standards set out in municipal property maintenance and occupancy by-laws. The maximum for rooming houses is $5,000 per bed unit. Loans are secured by a mortgage held by the Ontario Mortgage Corporation. There is no repayment for the first five years; thereafter, loans are forgiven at the rate of 10 percent per year, provided that certain conditions, such as the property remaining rental property, are met.

42 The by-laws may also deal with certain fire-safety matters that are not covered in the retrofit sections of the Fire Code, such as a requirement for periodic fire drills.

43 The City of Toronto Solicitor has raised this problem with respect to Toronto's Housing Standards By-law, which regulates fire standards in rooming houses and rest homes: "The City Solicitor believes there is some doubt as to whether Section 29a of the Housing Standards Bylaw is in effect in light of Section 18a(4) of the Fire Marshals Act ..." Section 29a deals with the requirements for fire-alarm systems in rooming houses. (From Joint *Report of Commissioner of Buildings and Inspections and the Fire Chief to Neighbourhood Committee*, November 12 and 13, 1990).

44 The safety/housing supply tradeoff is relevant even in determining a minimum floor, and this of course can change over time.

rooming and boarding houses to meet new standards enacted in the Fire Code.

In particular, we recommend that the Low Rise Rehabilitation Program of the Ministry of Housing be funded to assist owners of registered rest homes to meet the new fire-safety standards for rest homes under the Fire Code.[41]

RECOMMENDATION 115: That the Low Rise Rehabilitation Program of the Ministry of Housing permit that funding be made available to operators of rest homes for upgrading purposes, including meeting retrofit fire-safety standards.

MUNICIPAL FIRE-SAFETY BY-LAWS

The Commission has noted that many municipalities have established their own standards for fire safety in rooming and/or rest homes through municipal by-law. Some are more stringent than those contained in section 9.3 or proposed in draft sections 9.5 and 9.6.[42] The legal validity of aspects of these municipal by-laws may be questionable. Subsection 18a(4) of the *Fire Marshals Act* states that "the Fire Code supersedes all municipal by-laws respecting fire safety standards."[43]

It is our view that a provincial minimum below which no residence should operate comes close to an absolute floor.[44] A provincial minimum should not vary from region to region, nor should municipalities be permitted to enact higher or lower standards for all rest homes.

Municipalities that wish to have higher standards of fire protection for residents funded in domiciliary hostels are, of course, free to negotiate higher standards with operators, in their hostel agreements under the *General Welfare Assistance Act (GWAA)*. Indeed, municipalities can require high standards for entire premises if even one bed is funded, as the terms of such agreement can be any that the parties freely negotiate.

> **RECOMMENDATION 116:** That where a municipality
> desires higher standards in a domiciliary hostel than those
> contained in the Fire Code, they should be negotiated on a
> contractual basis between the municipality and operators
> of the rest homes.

Local municipalities can best judge the quantitative impact of
higher fire-safety standards on the supply of housing in their
communities. However, we wish to ensure that higher standards are not used as a means of restrictive or exclusionary
zoning.

We are concerned that the adverse impact on housing
stock be minimized. If a community ties the receipt of hostel
funding to compliance with higher standards, housing at the
minimum safety floor set in the Fire Code would remain available for residents on a self-pay basis. This would then create
different qualities of housing, with some at higher levels and
others at lower levels.

This outcome is optimal in that it maintains the integrity of
the Fire Code as a province-wide constant bottom line. Minimum standards will not vary from block to block or community
to community. Higher standards can be obtained, but only voluntarily on the part of operators, presumably in exchange for
compensation, for example, through the domiciliary-hostel system.

The Rupert Hotel Inquest

The Commission has examined carefully the many thoughtful
recommendations of the Rupert Hotel fire coroner's jury, and
we have benefited from their important work.

Some of the recommendations are very significant, among
them the power to order twenty-four-hour fire watches with

45 "Construction" includes the material alteration or repair of a building, regardless of age. Section 10 of the Act applies to all buildings that an inspector finds to be unsafe, regardless of age.

the cost added to the operators' municipal tax bills. This power exists at present, but its wider use would undoubtedly lead to the rapid redress of serious violations of fire-safety standards without dehousing residents. Other recommendations are more troublesome. A requirement for central monitoring of fire-alarm systems, for example, estimated to cost about $1,500 per residence, raises concerns on both technical and cost grounds.

The Commission endorses the general thrust of the jury's recommendations, although we cannot comment on specifics in the absence of fuller information on cost and technical feasibility. We note that the Office of the Fire Marshal is seriously considering many of the jury's recommendations, and we endorse this action.

> **RECOMMENDATION 117:** That whatever new fire-safety standards may emerge from the Rupert Hotel inquest apply not only to rooming houses, such as the Rupert Hotel, but also to rest homes as defined by this Commission.

Ultimately, however, the jury's recommendations must be resolved by interested parties taking into account the safety/ housing-stock tradeoff, the need for appropriate province-wide minimum safety standards, and the need to minimize the adverse effect on housing availability.

The Physical Environment

Standards affecting physical conditions in Ontario rest homes are set in two ways: the Ontario Building Code regulates construction standards, and municipalities may set standards for occupancy and maintenance.

The *Building Code Act* was proclaimed on December 31, 1975. All buildings constructed[45] in the province since that time must conform to the construction standards contained in the Ontario Building Code, a regulation under that Act. The Building Code is "essentially a set of minimum provisions respecting the safety of buildings with reference to public health, fire protection and structural sufficiency.... Its primary purpose is the promotion of public safety through the application of appropriate uniform building standards."[46]

The retrofit sections of the Fire Code apply to buildings constructed before 1976; the Building Code, with its generally higher standards, determines fire-safety requirements for buildings constructed since then. The Building Code also regulates construction aspects such as structural design,[47] heating, and ventilating and air-conditioning equipment.

Of particular relevance to this Inquiry are the Building Code standards for such things as the ratio of residents to washrooms, sleeping-room size per person, heating capacity sufficient to maintain a minimum room temperature,[48] minimum window sizes for room area, and lighting requirements.

The Code sets standards for buildings according to their use or intended use. There is one standard for "institutional occupancies," and another, generally lower, standard for "residential occupancies."

"Institutional occupancy" (Division 2) indicates that the use or intended use is for shelter by persons "who require supervisory care, medical care or medical treatment ... "[49] Examples of buildings that may be included in this classification are nursing homes, hospitals, and children's custodial homes.[50] "Supervisory care" is probably strictly interpreted, as most group homes are *not* designated as "institutional occupancy."

The other classification, "residential occupancy," indicates that the use or intended use is by persons "for whom sleeping accommodation is provided but who are not harboured or detained to receive medical care or treatment or are not involuntarily detained." Examples of buildings that may be included in this classification are apartments, boarding houses, group homes, hostels, houses, retirement homes, and rooming houses.[51]

46 From "A Guide to the Use of the Code" in Ontario Building Code, 1990 (Office Consolidation).

47 The loads to be used in design calculations and design requirements for wood, concrete, steel, glass, etc.

48 There is no requirement that this minimum be maintained. The *Municipal Act* (section 210, paragraph 69) gives municipalities the power to define what is "adequate and suitable heat" in rented accommodation.

49 Division 1 intended uses include those "by persons who are under restraint for correctional purposes and are incapable of self-preservation because of security measures not under their control."

50 These examples are given in Appendix A of the Building Code.

51 The examples are again taken from Appendix A of the Building Code.

52 Under the *Building Code Act*, the inspector's decision can be appealed.

53 Bill 112 received first reading in the Ontario Legislature in the spring of 1991, and is due for second reading. Although the current *Building Code Act* applies to all buildings in Ontario, buildings that have not been "constructed" since 1976 do not have to meet the standards contained in the Ontario Building Code. These buildings were usually constructed to standards contained in municipal building codes.

The Code does not define the examples given for the two types of occupancy; the examples are generic. Thus, a "nursing home" would include a nursing home licensed under the *Nursing Homes Act*, a home for the aged operated under the *Homes for the Aged and Rest Homes Act* and, possibly, an unregulated rest home, depending on the type or amount of care to be given.

When an application is made for a building permit, an inspector decides, on a case-by-case basis, whether the intended use is "institutional" or "residential."[52] Presumably, most rest homes, as defined by the Commission, fall within the "residential occupancy" classification.

The Commission recommends that "rest homes" be added to the examples of "residential occupancy" in the Appendix to the Building Code. We do so because "hostels" and "retirement homes," listed in the Appendix of the Code as "residential" occupancies are subsumed in the Commission's definition of a rest home. As well, the Commission does not view rest homes as institutions. Were rest homes to be designated "institutional," construction costs would rise, thereby limiting the creation of housing for vulnerable people.

> **RECOMMENDATION 118:** That rest homes, as defined by the Commission, be included in the list of examples of "residential occupancies" in Appendix A (at A-3.1.2.A.) of the Building Code.

Bill 112, the *Building Code Act, 1991*, extends the coverage of the present Act: it will require compliance with the applicable code and standards when any building's use changes.[53] This means that the owner of a building might be required to upgrade a building if its use changes, even if there is no "construction." Under Bill 112, a building converted to a rest home could be required to meet the "residential," "institutional," or any newly proposed standard. The first outcome—a "residential" designation—would be welcome; the Commission considers the "institutional" category to be inappropriate. (A possible intermediate classification with new standards for rest homes is discussed below.)

MUNICIPAL OCCUPANCY BY-LAWS

Once the premises are constructed, there is no formal procedure to confirm that the premises are indeed being used for their stated purpose. The actual use of the premises may be regulated by municipal occupancy and maintenance by-laws under section 31 of the *Planning Act*. Some municipalities enact broad property standards by-laws to ensure adequate maintenance, cleanliness, and repair of all types of residential housing. Some municipalities also enact by-laws specifically for rest homes under which the homes must meet certain standards such as minimum room sizes, and a specified ratio of bathrooms to residents. Other rest-home by-laws simply require compliance with the Building Code; usually this is interpreted as imposing the standard for "residential occupancies."

There is some question about the legal effect of municipal by-laws that set occupancy standards *higher* than the applicable construction standards in the Building Code. Section 27 of the *Building Code Act* states that the Code "supersedes all municipal by-laws respecting the construction ... of buildings."

The distinction between "occupancy" standards (as determined by municipal by-laws) and "construction" standards (as determined by the Building Code) is problematic. Municipal by-laws dealing with, for example, bedroom size per person or the ratio of washrooms to residents are not dealing directly with construction. However, municipal by-laws that required a higher standard for "occupancy" of a rest home than that required for its "construction" under the Building Code might

54 The issue becomes particularly complex if the standards in the municipal by-law do not require a structural change in the building, but as a consequence of the standards imposed, fewer people can reside in the premises than would have been permitted under the Building Code standards.

55 For cases that deal with the effect of section 27 on municipal by-laws, see *Minto Construction Ltd. v. Gloucester* (1979 8 MPLR 172 (Ont. Div. Ct.); *Toronto v. Shields* (1985) 29 MPLR 207 (Ont. C.A.) and *Evans v. Toronto Terminal Railways Co. et al.* unreported decision of Ontario Court (General Division), delivered April 15, 1991.

56 In Hamilton, the lodging house by-law requires that a bedroom comprise 110 square feet for one person, 180 square feet for two, 270 square feet for three, and 320 square feet for four persons: these numbers correspond exactly to the Building Code standard for "institutional occupancies." In Windsor, the rest-home by-law requires 600 cubic feet per resident, with 80 square feet floor coverage if there is only one resident in a bedroom. In Toronto, the Personal Care Rooming Houses by-law is silent on the issue, but the Housing by-law applicable to all residential housing requires that a bedroom comprise 40 square feet per person and the premises comprise a total floor area in habitable rooms of at least 100 square feet per person. We also compared the ratio of residents to toilets in

well be considered to be imposing a "construction" standard in disguise, as it might necessitate alterations to the existing construction.[54] There is no case law to resolve this particular issue.[55]

In the Commission's view, if a building is legally constructed for its intended use according to the Building Code's classifications and standards, municipalities should not be permitted subsequently to impose higher standards for the same use.

How high a municipality can set its standards for occupancy of a rest home in view of section 27 of the Building Code cannot ultimately be resolved without a clear determination of whether rest homes are subject to the "institutional" or "residential" standards in the Building Code. Given our belief that rest homes should be considered "residential" premises for the purpose of the Building Code, it follows that municipalities should not be permitted to impose standards for occupancy higher than those of the Building Code "residential" standards.

Let us consider one specific example. The Building Code specifies that a bedroom intended for "residential occupancy" must comprise seventy-five square feet for one person, 100 square feet for two people and an additional fifty square feet for each additional person. Under section 27 of the *Building Code Act*, municipalities lack authority to alter this ratio in a by-law relating to the construction of "residential" premises. We have considered the space requirements of various municipal by-laws in Ontario. The municipal occupancy standards for rest homes range from standards lower than the Building Code "residential" standards up to the Building Code "institutional" standards. Others cannot be easily compared to the Building Code requirements.[56]

We cannot comment on the suitability of any minimum standard set out in the Building Code or municipal by-laws; however, there is also no clear or consistent pattern across municipalities. We do not value consistency for its own sake, and even the administrative ease of a single standard is merely one among many considerations. Of greater concern are the purposes to which local discretion may be put. For example, one community may require a greater floor space for every resident on the grounds of compassion and human dignity; another may demand the same high requirement because land is inexpensive and it costs little to give everyone ample room. A third community, however, may use the same requirement as an exclusionary measure, to keep out less desirable types of housing and residents, by making it uneconomical to operate or too expensive to construct a rest home within its boundaries.

Thus the question is not of the standards themselves, but of motive. Local autonomy cannot become a tool for exclusionary housing practices: this is non-negotiable in the eyes of the Commission. Acceptance of unfettered local autonomy necessitates acceptance of all its motives and outcomes. As some of these are unacceptable, the Commission recommends that municipal discretion continue to be circumscribed by the overriding jurisdiction of the Building Code.

> **RECOMMENDATION 119:** That the Building Code be endorsed as a single provincial construction standard, and that municipalities not be permitted to impose higher standards for the occupancy and/or maintenance of rest homes than those required by the "residential-occupancy" standard of the Building Code.

Some concern has been expressed that there are only two relevant occupancy classifications in the Building Code. It is felt that the "residential-occupancy" standards may be too low for some types of housing now subject to them but that the "institutional-occupancy" standards may be too high and costly.

Interest has been expressed in the development of new, intermediate standards for group-home-type living arrangements[57] in which there are centralized facilities (such as kitchens), unrelated persons sharing living and sleeping space, supervision required, and vulnerable residents. The

the Building Code and the three municipal by-laws. Each was different.

57 This might be comparable to the standards proposed for draft section 9.7 of the Fire Code discussed earlier.

Commission has no position on the optimal number of occupancy classifications in the Building Code, though two does seem low, and there may be a persuasive case for a third option. Our concerns are somewhat different.

When determining the premises to which any new standards will apply, adequate account should be taken of the increasing trend to delink care services from accommodation. To include a building within one category of the Building Code because supervisory, social, or medical services are delivered in-house, yet to exclude the identical building across the street because services are delivered from community-based agencies does not make sense. The Commission believes that any new standard should be equally applicable to rest homes and rooming/room-and-board accommodation, whatever the source of needed care.

ASSESSMENT

Many submissions to the Commission have indicated concern about physical standards in rest homes. Some of the most frequently identified areas for which provincial standards have been requested are set out below. They are followed by the ways in which the Commission's proposals offer a response.

1. space requirements:
    (a) total capacity of residence;
    (b) bedrooms: cubic air space and/or floor space per resident; space between beds; ceiling heights; special restricted or prohibited use of basements as bedrooms;
    (c) size of dining and sitting rooms related to capacity of residence; requirement to have a sitting room;
2. ventilation requirements:
    (a) window size and opening size in bedrooms related to bedroom floor space;
3. toilets/showers:

(a) location and number related to capacity of residence;

4. water supply:
   (a) temperature-regulating device;
5. lighting:
   (a) minimum levels;
6. residence air temperature:
   (a) minimum level;
7. waste disposal and sewage;
8. secure area for belongings.

In considering such issues, the Commission began with the given that we lack the technical expertise to devise or assess specific standards. We examined a number of the municipal by-laws as well as those proposed by the Ontario Long-Term Residential Care Association (OLTRCA) and community groups, and found that there was no widely agreed upon set of standards.

We also began with the assumption of an inverse relation between standards and housing supply: higher standards increase costs, which tend to result in dehousing vulnerable residents. Our strong preference is to protect low-income housing, while recognizing a minimum floor below which no rest home should operate.

We are satisfied that most of the specific issues raised above are treated through our proposals. Most or all luxury retirement homes are assumed to meet or exceed Building Code minima. The power to regulate minimum temperatures exists under the *Municipal Act* (section 210, paragraph 69); the requirement for a secure storage area is dealt with in the residents' bill of rights proposed by the Commission. Most of the other items are dealt with in the Building Code. The proposed *Building Code Act, 1991* (Bill 112) should ensure that any newly established rest homes will meet at least the "residential-occupancy" standard of the Code.

The Commission is satisfied that the Building Code (and

58 See discussion on by-laws and contracts in chapter 4.

Bill 112) specify an acceptable set of minimum conditions. If any particular "residential" standards in the Code are unacceptable, the appropriate response is to alter the Building Code. We do not consider it desirable for individual municipalities to require standards higher than those in the Building Code, and we support the "residential-occupancy" standard as suitable for rest homes as well as accommodation-only premises, such as rooming houses.

Problems may arise when municipalities have no occupancy and maintenance by-laws. A requirement that all municipalities have by-laws was rejected because they might set standards so high as to be exclusionary or so low as to be ineffectual. A requirement that all municipalities share one standard for the occupancy and maintenance of rest homes (such as the "residential" standard in the Building Code) was also rejected because of the potential cost and the likelihood of dehousing vulnerable residents. We thus endorse continued municipal jurisdiction in this area, provided that standards are not set higher than those of "residential-occupancy" standard of the Building Code.

In some areas—such as a requirement to have a sitting room or a prohibition on basement bedrooms—the Building Code is silent. Municipalities may act in these or any other areas using contracts with owner/operators receiving funding through the domiciliary-hostel provisions of General Welfare Assistance (GWA). The municipality may negotiate contractual terms that require any rest home in which even one bed is funded through these provisions to meet any conditions it wishes in the entire building.[58]

Some rest homes, we readily acknowledge, will exempt themselves from these higher standards by declining or being unable to contract with the municipality. Some of these will offer lower-quality housing, which would be unavailable to vulnerable low-income residents if a higher standard was required for all rest homes by municipal by-law. We consider this outcome to be quite acceptable.

Enforcing Minimum Standards

Each regulatory authority possesses a substantial array of remedies, from minor reprimands to closure of premises. No one has indicated to the Commission dissatisfaction with these responses. The problems, as presented to the Commission, lie not in the content of the responses, but rather in their application and enforcement.

First, many people have criticized inspections announced in advance: indeed, such prior warning subverts the inspection from a serious assessment of whether minimum standards are being met.[59] It is our very strong opinion that all inspection or regulatory visits must be unannounced to ensure they have effect.

> **RECOMMENDATION 120:** That all inspection visits to rest homes be conducted on an unannounced or surprise basis.

Second, many concerns have been expressed about the failure of regulatory and inspection authorities to act on complaints in an appropriate manner. Some complaints are not acted on at all; in others, there is merely a pro forma investigation, often with a substantial time lag. Some remedies ordered are considered inadequate by the complainants; in other cases, the follow-up or enforcement of a remedial order is deficient. In addition, there seems to be considerable regional variation in the adequacy of enforcement, with particular problems in unincorporated municipalities.

Each of the three inspecting authorities of primary interest to this Commission has an internal appeal mechanism: the Fire Code Commission; the Building Code Commission; and the Health Protection Appeal Board. However, their focus is on appeals of inspection orders; as well, only owners and operators affected by an order can appeal. This means that an inspector's decision not to make an order is not appealable;

[59] This view is confirmed by the Commission's own experience in which all official visits to rest homes were arranged in advance. The dominant smell in the homes was typically that of disinfectant, and in some cases bedrooms were so neat as to suggest no one actually slept there!

nor do residents of a rest home have the right to appear before the appeal tribunal. Thus, they are not able to appeal an order or a penalty that they believe to be inappropriate.

Some submissions to this Commission argued that a tribunal (perhaps the RHT) should have power to review any local inspection-unit decision—procedural or substantive—that affects a rest home. The decisions of front-line inspectors could be appealed to the tribunal, and the tribunal would have the power to order anything that the inspectors could have ordered, including closure of the premises.

The relation between the tribunal and the current appeal bodies would have to be clarified, but the tribunal would be more user-friendly, giving ready access and standing to any individual who files a complaint. It would also operate outside the "culture" of professional fire, building, and health inspectors.

Some see this to be advantageous, but others note that it risks lacking credibility within the professional culture. It would also be costly to duplicate existing appeal systems. Front-line staff, who would have to oversee the implementation of any remedies ordered by the tribunal, suggest that this model is too adversarial and counterproductive.

Two alternatives have been suggested to the Commission as more likely to be effective: a provincial inspectorate could be established within the provincial ministries responsible for fire, building, and public health. Persons dissatisfied with local responses could approach the relevant inspectorate. Provincial inspectors could investigate, hear all interested persons, mediate when appropriate, and make any appropriate orders that the local inspectors could have made.

This approach would be less adversarial, and would operate within the norms and culture of the inspection system. This may, of course, be disadvantageous, in that the relationship between local inspection units and the provincial inspectorate may be too cosy to produce an impartial reconsideration of local decisions. It might also cause some municipalities to neglect, de-emphasize, or vacate the inspection field: they may be reluctant to inspect what the province might well reinspect.

The other alternative calls for the creation of a separate unit within the current appeal commissions to deal specifically with rest-home settings and, over time, to develop familiarity with and expertise in the problems in this area. Residents would be given the right to appeal both inaction by public inspectors and orders they deemed inappropriate; owners and operators would retain their present appeal rights.

Designing institutions and processes to ensure compliance with regulatory standards is rarely simple, as it requires a careful assessment of the objectives and priorities of the program. Any compliance mechanism selected to realize these objectives is likely to have both strengths and weaknesses.[60]

So it is with the options to secure compliance with fire, health, and building standards. The advantages of an independent quasi-judicial tribunal include the openness of the adversarial process, and the independent decision-makers' impartial duty to base their decisions on the material produced at the hearings. The disadvantages include the delays and expense of any "judicialized" process, and the counter-productive tensions typically aroused by adversarial procedures. This latter point is particularly important when the dispute involves parties in an ongoing relationship, as local enforcement officials, residents, and operators are likely to be.

The "inspectorate" approach may be less formal and legalistic, and consequently quicker, less expensive, and, in a sense, more accessible to vulnerable persons. However, the bureaucratic process is less open, and subject to the suspicion that the decision-makers are more responsive to the views of the officials under review than to those of the complainants.[61]

The application of any model for regulatory compliance to a specific context requires a sustained attention to administrative detail that is best undertaken following this Inquiry. This task should be the responsibility of the ministry charged with

60 Another model suggested to the Commission was that of the Employment Practices Branch (EPB) in the Ministry of Labour. This unit recovers back pay, vacation pay, etc., owed to employees from employers and generally does so in an efficient and expeditious manner. We briefly explored the potential applicability of this model to the rest-home sector, but did not pursue the issue, as the EPB largely deals with matters that are quantifiable (compensation owed) and in which the facts are often not in dispute.

61 See "Policy Implementation, Compliance and Administrative Law" (Law Reform Commission of Canada, Working Paper 51, 1986). See also M. L. Friedland, editor, *Securing Compliance: Seven Case Studies* (University of Toronto Press, 1990).

the implementation of this Report, in consultation with interest groups and the ministries responsible for health, fire, and building inspections.

> **RECOMMENDATION 121:** That the ministry responsible for rest homes ensure an effective and speedy appeal procedure is in place with respect to inaction or decisions by public inspection authorities responsible for minimum standards in rest homes.

We, therefore, make no recommendation on a preferred means for securing compliance with minimum fire, health, and building standards. However, rest-home residents should be ensured ready and easy access to an effective and speedy mechanism for reviewing the decisions, action, or inactivity of front-line enforcement officials. This goal would be equally important if the proposals in this Report were to be extended, as we think that they should be, to other congregate living environments, including rooming houses, nursing homes, group homes, and, eventually perhaps, all residential tenancies.

> **RECOMMENDATION 122:** That in matters within the jurisdiction of Fire Code Commission, the Building Code Commission and the Health Protection Appeal Board, any residents or their advocates shall have the same formal standing as is given to the owners/operators.

We also recommend that the compliance mechanism be able to examine not only the adequacy of any order made by inspectors but also their failure to act. Such inactivity would include, for example, a fire inspector's decision not to make an order to remedy apparently hazardous electrical wiring, a failure by a health inspector to respond to or to investigate a complaint about the filthy condition of a kitchen, or a failure by a building inspector to follow up within a reasonable time a complaint about the dangerously dilapidated state of the premises. None of these forms of official inertia is currently subject to appeal.

RECOMMENDATION 123: That the mandates of the appropriate appeal tribunal or provincial inspectorate be extended to include non-response and untimely responses on the part of front-line inspectors.

This Commission is very strongly of the view that legal review protection should be as available to the intended beneficiaries of the program—the residents of rest homes—as it is to the operators of the premises. The law cannot merely protect operators from unjustified official intrusions; it must also ensure that the beneficiaries of statutorily created rights receive their entitlement.

As we anticipate that rest-home residents will make use of any expanded rights to seek a review of inspection orders, we recommend that steps be taken to ensure that current appeals bodies have members familiar with rest-home settings. Should the mandate be extended to allow standing to all residential tenants, the appeal boards should be composed of members familiar with a variety of residential settings.

RECOMMENDATION 124: That persons familiar with residential tenancies, including residents, be appointed to the Fire Code Commission, Building Code Commission, and Health Protection Appeal Board.

Once rest homes are covered under the *LTA* and the proposed *Rent Control Act, 1991* (*RCA*), residents will have means not currently available to them to enforce health and safety standards. Under the *LTA* tenants may apply to a judge to enforce landlords' responsibility to maintain premises in a good state of repair and to comply with health and safety standards. Under section 96, tenants may obtain court orders requiring landlords to comply with municipal work orders. In some cases, tenants will be able to get an abatement of rent until the landlords have complied.

As well, under the proposed *RCA* (section 23) tenants may apply to the chief rent officer for an order reducing their rent when maintenance or repair in the premises is inadequate. And under section 39, a rent penalty may be imposed for non-compliance with work orders regarding the standards of maintenance in the premises, i.e., landlords may not increase the rent until the work is done and the order is rescinded. We view the *LTA* and *RCA* as part of the solution, in addition to and not in lieu of the proposals made immediately above.

PART IV

Related Issues

In this final part of the Report, we examine a number of broader issues relevant to rest homes. We consider the role of professionals and human resources in three contexts: education/training needs; the medical role; and referrals and placements into unregulated accommodation. We also summarize our recommendations with respect to provincial/municipal relations. The Report proper concludes by asking once again the critical question: "Would all this have prevented Cedar Glen?" An appendix then briefly revisits long-term care and comments on certain current proposals in that area.

We begin, however, with the one critical issue that we have not yet discussed: housing, its supply and availability to vulnerable adults, and the fundamental conundrum that without greater choice in housing options, there will be limited effectiveness for any system of resident protection.

11

Housing: Supply and Choice

The Commission's Discussion Paper stressed housing supply as "a necessary condition for any real and effective solution" to many of the problems encountered by rest-home residents. Neither a regulatory system for protecting vulnerable adults nor empowerment and informed consumer choice is likely to be effective unless there are housing options and alternatives. Residents' power to leave unacceptable settings serves as the ultimate sanction to operators. Yet as the Social Assistance Review Committee (SARC) bluntly observed, there "is simply not enough affordable housing for people who need it."[1]

Housing "supply" and housing "choice" are not the same thing, although the distinction is often subtle. Residents have repeatedly stressed that vacancies mean little if the quality of all housing is the same. Choice is merely theoretical if the characteristics common to all boarding-home accommodation outweigh the differences between particular premises. In many communities, there appears to be a small number of high-quality rest homes. Not surprisingly, these premises are difficult to enter, as residents do not tend to move out. Most other rest homes are seen as virtually interchangeable and of a uniform low quality. There is little incentive to move from one unacceptable place to another.

1 *Transitions*, Queen's Printer for Ontario, Toronto, 1988, p. 467.

2 Those who, for example, are unwilling to attend treatment sessions.

3 These needs include the need/wish to be left alone, to live anonymously without particular interaction with one's neighbours.

4 In one northern city, the Commission heard about the experiences of women with hearing impairments and psychiatric histories: the communication problems in standard rooming houses were acute, often resulting in exploitation and/or dehousing.

Thus the issue is not solely one of supply. Residents vary widely in their needs, interests, and preferences, and in their capabilities to function independently; moreover, these needs, interests, and preferences change with time. There must be a variety of housing types to complement individual interests, preferences, and capabilities. More important, there must be flexible, portable services available to meet individuals' needs.

The Commission has been repeatedly told that the rest home fills an essential place in the housing spectrum (in the short term, at least). Group homes run by non-profit agencies, even were they available in adequate numbers, cannot meet the needs of all. Rest homes often take the "difficult" cases, those residents whose behavioural or other problems render them unsuitable for or unacceptable to treatment-oriented facilities.[2] Treatment centres often "cream off" the prospective residents who are most motivated and capable of personal growth and development; the difficult cases are left for the rest homes.

The ease of access and lack of criteria for housing people in rest homes leads to inappropriate housing arrangements. People who should receive housing and services tailored to their needs are instead warehoused. As well, rest-home operators may be providing—and being paid to provide—either more or fewer services than are needed and desired.

What is required is a range of housing types and service options that better corresponds to the needs and wishes of individual residents.[3] The need for appropriate housing and social supports among vulnerable adults with multiple disabilities is particularly severe.[4]

Although non-profit housing is typically preferred for many vulnerable adults, it is not without problems. For example, the current emphasis in non-profit housing is on generic provision rather than premises targeted to specific groups; different populations live in neighbouring apartments in the same building. Both the 1989 Ministry of Housing consultation on housing for seniors and this Commission heard about tensions resulting from the integration of persons with developmental or psychiatric disabilities into seniors' housing.

This Commission sees this problem as one of supervision and support services rather than an issue of housing. The anxieties of frail seniors must be eased in any way not demeaning to others; however, the real solution lies in better supports for all vulnerable adults. Segregated housing merely localizes the symptoms; it does not solve the problem.

5 Housing for people with special needs includes housing for vulnerable adults as defined by this Report.

Special-Needs Housing

It is now widely understood that public policy must further the development of a spectrum of special-needs housing.[5] There are three conceptually distinct forms of such housing: institutions; supportive community living; and fully independent living accommodation.

Figure 2
Spectrum of Special-Needs Housing

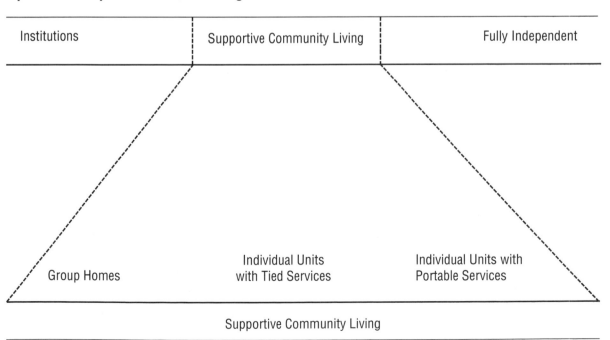

Institutions	Supportive Community Living	Fully Independent

Group Homes | Individual Units with Tied Services | Individual Units with Portable Services

Supportive Community Living

6 Bert Perrin Associates, *Discussion Paper on Supportive Housing*, presented to the Ministry of Housing and the Ministry of Community and Social Services, August 14, 1990.

7 CHSSD is a joint Division of MoH and MCSS. The term "supportive housing" refers only to the development of new, non-profit rental accommodation to which MoH, MCSS, or CHSSD has made a commitment to fund support services. (These ministries also offer community support services to individuals in their own homes.) Residents in supportive housing may also receive community services funded by these ministries/division in addition to the services funded by the supportive-housing initiatives.

The second category obviously covers a wide housing range, varying in degree of independence and integration into the community from group homes supplying all support services to individual living units to which all services are delivered from the community.

It is a concern of the Commission that this range has been severely truncated in some communities because of the convenience of the rest-home option. The result is that people are living in rest homes because appropriate community services are not being developed to support more independent living.

The number of people who would be unable to live in a supported community setting given adequate and appropriate support services is relatively small.[6] The rest home, at its best, represents but one point on the housing spectrum, and should not serve as a convenient catch-all for people who could receive more appropriate support in other housing arrangements.

The Importance of Supportive Housing

"Supportive housing" is an initiative to provide housing and support services to people with special needs in non-profit rental housing. The Ministry of Housing is responsible for developing non-profit housing programs. The ministries of Health (MoH), Community and Social Services (MCSS), and the Community Health and Support Services Division (CHSSD) commit funds for resident support services in these housing projects.[7]

The Commission attempted to ascertain the total supportive housing and funding in Ontario; however, the three ministries involved do not have data bases with common definitions for supportive housing. Therefore, it is difficult to determine how many new supportive-housing units have been built, what the target is, how many persons live in supportive housing, and what constitutes the expenditures in this area.

RECOMMENDATION 125: That current efforts at coordination among the ministries responsible for supportive housing be intensified, and that they develop a single, common definition of "supportive housing."

8 Norpark Research Consultants, Inc., *Research Study of Supportive Housing Initiatives*, a report prepared for MCSS and MoH, August 1991.

9 Ibid., p.22.

In the appendix to this chapter we present information concerning the development of supportive housing in Ontario.

SERVICE PROVIDERS AND HOUSING PROVIDERS IN SUPPORTIVE HOUSING

There is only limited information available on who actually delivers services in supportive housing and the extent to which housing provision has been delinked from the provision of services.[8] MoH was unable to provide this information with regard to its supportive-housing program. MCSS provided the following extrapolations from a sample of its supportive housing:[9]

1. in 46 percent of MCSS projects, the housing provider was the sole provider of support services;
2. in 70 percent of MCSS projects, all or most of the support services were provided by the housing agency;
3. in 16 percent of MCSS projects, all support services were provided by an agency other than the housing provider.

The separation of housing and delivery of support services has been identified as a central tenet of this Inquiry. One consequence of delinking is that housing could become more generic with operators of care-providing homes becoming more like traditional landlords. To the extent services are needed and/or wanted, they should be provided by those with expertise in delivering services, not by those who skills lie in providing housing.

The provision of accommodation and care by the same

10 As we discussed in chapter 5, many supportive-housing providers claim exemption from the *LTA*, usually on the grounds that they provide housing for the purpose of care and/or receive funding under health or social-services legislation.

11 If a service ministry has budgeted for services for persons in X units, it cannot continue service for a person who leaves a unit, as the funds must serve the new resident of the vacated housing unit.

providers (linking) also raises the issue of the *Landlord and Tenant Act* (*LTA*). The Ministry of Housing expects compliance with the *LTA* by supportive-housing operators. With coverage under the *LTA*, tenants would no longer be required to accept services as a condition of remaining in supportive housing.

The ministries that fund supportive services have permitted the linking of housing and services and thus provided the basis for supportive-housing providers to claim exemption from the *LTA*.[10] The Ministry of Housing has not yet developed a standard formal agreement incorporating its expectation concerning *LTA* coverage. Moreover, the legal consequences of such expectations and agreements are unclear. The Ministry of Housing could enforce its expectation through its control of operating funding to the housing providers, but appears not to have done so.

The tying of service funding to a particular housing unit makes such services non-portable: if residents leave the supportive housing, services do not follow them. If they decline the particular services attached to the housing, they may be unable to obtain them from another agency, as it might not be funded to provide services to such residents. Thus, linkage seems to be a budgetary consideration as much as a matter of public policy.[11]

In the long term, the only solution is a system of fully developed community services. If these were in place, there would be no need, for budgetary reasons, to ration services by tying them to particular units of housing. All individuals would be able to obtain services, wherever they chose to live.

In the short term, particularly in an era of budgetary constraints, this scenario is not attainable. It does, however, suggest the direction we must move in. Ultimately, expanding community-service funding is the surest way to delink services from units of housing.

There is also a risk that supportive housing may evolve into new mini-institutions when services are tied to housing rather than to people. If services moved with the people there would, in theory at least, be no need to allocate specific operating funds to particular units of housing.

These areas must be explored as ministries develop their commitment to portable services and experiment with individualized funding. If, as the above data from MCSS make clear, housing providers in nearly half the current supportive housing are the sole providers of support services, then delinking and portability are still a long way off.

> **RECOMMENDATION 126:** That the ministries involved with supportive housing recognize the importance of delinked service provision to such housing.

Using Land More Intensively

A number of initiatives from the Ministry of Housing in recent years have encouraged more intensive uses of land to increase the supply of available housing. We wish to comment on two such initiatives, identified during our consultations.

FREEING UP UNUSED LAND

In the mid-1980s, the province adopted a policy of selling its surplus lands in order to maximize revenue to the provincial treasury. In 1987, this approach was superseded by the Housing First policy: surplus land of ministries and some Crown agencies that was suitable for housing was to be made available for that purpose. At least 35 percent of the housing units developed in any year were to be "affordable." As of mid-1991, approximately 5,000 housing units had been created under this initiative.

In June 1991, a joint Green Paper from the Ministry of Housing and the Ministry of Government Services put for-

12 The Commission also endorses any moves the federal government or the municipalities may make concerning the disposal of their surplus Ontario land, and urges both Ottawa and the municipalities to move expeditiously in this regard.

13 Accessory apartments are defined as self-contained units created by converting part of or adding on to existing homes. They include, but are not limited to, basement apartments. Ministry of Housing, *Land Use Planning for Housing: Policy Statement* (July 13, 1989).

14 Between 1971 and 1985, new local zoning by-laws and the increase in property values resulting from gentrification led to the loss of 7,000 rooming-house units in Ontario. *More Than Shelter ...*, p.4.

ward a Housing Priority policy:

> Previously in practice sites only tended to become available for ... housing use when it was decided that no other provincial uses were feasible. In future sites will be considered for housing use as soon as they are surplus to the needs of an individual ministry or agency. (p.4)

The Green Paper acknowledges the modest contribution of such initiatives: housing production on government sites is unlikely to constitute more than 5 percent of total housing production in any year. Nevertheless, the Commission endorses the Housing Priority initiative, and supports other moves to free surplus government land for affordable housing, including housing provided by non-profit community suppliers.[12]

ACCESSORY APARTMENTS AND ROOMING, BOARDING, AND LODGING HOMES [13]

The Commission received a number of comments about the geographic concentration of housing for vulnerable adults. In one community we visited, virtually all rest homes are located in one neighbourhood, and we have the sense that a similar finding would emerge in many other cities, as well.

Housing for discharged psychiatric patients tends to locate near provincial hospitals when possible, and large houses suitable for boarding homes tend to cluster in certain areas. Restrictive and exclusionary zoning practices in many communities further concentrate housing for vulnerable adults.[14]

Accessory apartments provide an important source of inexpensive housing, even in communities where municipal zoning rules render them illegal. This illegal status often disempowers residents, as lack of coverage under the *LTA* may subject them to capricious behaviour and precipitate eviction by landlords.[15] We wish to indicate strongly, and unequivocally, that we find exclusionary zoning practices by local governments both offensive and unacceptable.

Such zoning practices have also been prohibited since the July 1989 housing *Policy Statement* of the Ontario government: this document saw the creation of rooming, boarding, and lodging houses (RBLs) as key to affordable housing, and required that municipalities permit these forms of intensification "as-of-right" in all areas that meet certain criteria.[16] (The principle of as-of-right zoning eliminates the right to consider neighbourhood preferences, the criterion traditionally used by municipalities to determine where accessory apartments and RBLs would be permitted.)

We support without qualification the principle of as-of-right zoning for both accessory apartments and RBLs.[17] We also endorse Ministry of Housing attempts to bring municipalities in line with the government's housing *Policy Statement* but fear current efforts may prove ineffective: 104 named municipalities were to have had official-plan and zoning changes required to implement the housing *Policy Statement* in place by August 1, 1991. No municipality met the deadline with respect to accessory apartments and RBLs; none has made the changes to date.[18]

It is now time for the Ontario government to take further action.

RECOMMENDATION 127: That the Ministry of Housing amend the *Planning Act* to make accessory apartments and rooming, boarding, and lodging houses an as-of-right use in all zones where residential uses are permitted.

As-of-right zoning will inevitably spread accessory apartments and RBLs more widely around a community. We have received requests that we recommend a minimum spatial distribution of such accommodation; but formal action may be unnecessary as the barriers to a more even distribution in the

15 If accessory apartments are illegal, they formally do not exist; thus, they are typically not covered under *LTA*. If a landlord wishes to evict a tenant, he may notify the municipality, which declares the apartment "illegal" and shuts it down, thereby evicting the tenant. The landlord is then free to rent to a new tenant. Some illegal apartments are in serious violation of the Fire or Building codes, but tenants fear to complain because they have no security of tenure.

16 The three criteria are: need, sufficient services, and capacity of site.

Prior to 1989, RBLs were typically either prohibited outright or restricted to specific sites by municipal zoning by-laws. If permitted, the accommodation was usually restricted to a limited number of unrelated persons.

Bill 128, passed in 1989, prohibited discrimination based on family status or relationship in zoning by-laws. Since Bill 128, municipalities have experienced difficulty in defining RBLs without reference to family status.

17 Municipal licensing and by-law activity cannot become a "back door" to exclusionary zoning through the imposition of unreasonably high standards. Hence, the constraints on municipal authority to license and set standards through by-laws, as set out in Part III, are even more important if as-of-right zoning is adopted.

18 At least one recent case before the Ontario Municipal Board (concerning student

accommodation in Guelph) suggests that the OMB may not have given sufficient weight to the *Policy Statement* with respect to rooming houses.

community are removed. We see no need for such restrictions with respect to accessory apartments, but, depending on how RBLs are ultimately defined by the Ministry of Housing, some measures to limit undue geographic concentration of RBLs may be appropriate.

It may also be desirable for the Ministry of Housing to limit concentration on single premises (for example, one accessory apartment per site). The *Planning Act* will have to be amended to give the minister of Municipal Affairs authority to establish, by regulation, physical standards for accessory apartments and RBLs: the intent will be to ensure adequate standards but to prevent standards so high as to exclude such uses.

APPENDIX:
Supportive Housing in Ontario

MINISTRY OF HOUSING

The Ministry of Housing's contribution to supportive housing is largely in the form of operating and subsidy payments to housing providers. These payments are intended to bridge the gap between the actual cost of providing the housing[1] and the rents paid.[2] The Ministry of Housing also provides development loans for non-profit housing projects and, under the Homes Now program, some mortgage financing.

Table 9 contains information on the four current Ministry of Housing programs/initiatives related to non-profit housing.

It is difficult to determine the expenditures (operating and subsidy) for the supportive-housing units built as a subset of all non-profit housing. The Ministry of Housing data base does not use the definition of supportive-housing clients used by the service-providing ministries. It has figures only for a cate gory it calls "client type: special."[3] Units specially modified for seniors are not counted.[4] The Ministry of Housing estimates that approximately 16 percent of all post-1986 non-profit housing units[5] are supportive housing, according to their definition, which excludes seniors. Under the four indicated housing programs, as of June 1991, there were a total of 7,190 units of supportive housing in Ontario; these include 1,219 units for persons with psychiatric disabilities and 1,021 units for persons with developmental disabilities.

Table 10 contains data on the Ministry of Housing estimated annual operating expenditures on post-1986 supportive housing.[6] They indicate a significant increase in the recent past, with total expenditures reaching some $35.6 million in 1990.

1 This includes mortgage payments, management, and other operating expenses.

2 Both subsidized and "market" rents. Both involve subsidies, though the latter is set closer to what should be the hypothetical market rent for the particular unit, and thus has a smaller subsidy.

3 "Special" includes "developmentally, physically, and psychiatrically handicapped individuals, homeless, victims of family violence, low-income single persons."

4 This is in contrast to MCSS and CHSSD, who fund supportive-housing support services to seniors.

5 Housing units are "bed counts" rather than a count of living units, since the projects built include group homes and hostels.

6 These figures omit some projects that have not yet submitted a budget to the ministry, as well as those recently occupied or not yet complete. Thus, the figures are approximate only. They are also probably an underestimate of true expenditures, as most projects would include seniors' units, which are not counted.

Table 9
Ministry of Housing Expenditures on Non-Profit Housing

| | ($ in Millions) | | |
Project	Operational Subsidy Payments (1991–92)	Capital Payments	Loans for Project Development
Federal/Provincial (F/P)	$264.6[1]	—	
P-3000	$ 29.9	—	$ 6.6[3]
P-3600	$ 15.8	—	
Homes Now	$ 91.1	$ 2.9[2]	

1 Includes federal contribution

2 The 1990–91 figure was $0.84

3 The 1990–91 figure was $17.3

4 This is defined in Ontario as "unable to afford the market rents in the project without paying more than 25 percent of income for rent."

5 The capital cost per unit must be consistent with the maximum unit price (MUP) guidelines established by Canada Mortgage and Housing Corporation. The current MUP in Toronto is $84,000 for hostel accommodation and $107,000 for studio or bachelor apartments.

6 The federal and provincial governments share sixty-forty the subsidy cost for households that cannot afford to pay more than 30 percent of their income for rent. The province subsidizes 100 percent of other rent-geared-to-income units as well as the market rent units.

7 See note 11.

8 These are defined as not able to afford more than 25 percent of household income for housing.

Program Descriptions:
Federal/Provincial Non-Profit Housing Program (F/P)
(a) This is a federal/provincial initiative to help non-profit- housing agencies and municipalities produce housing for persons with low-to-moderate incomes.
(b) At least 40 percent of the units must be allocated as "rent-geared-to-income"[4] (RGI), with the remainder available to those with "eligible household incomes" and/or those who can pay the market rents.

(c) Capital financing is arranged through private-sector lending institutions.[5] All non-profit units receive operating subsidies of the difference between the actual cost of providing the housing and the rents paid by tenants.[6]

Special Housing Initiative 3,000 (P-3000)
(a) These projects are primarily directed at the most disadvantaged members of society: homeless persons; battered spouses; adults with physical, developmental, and/or psychiatric disabilities; and low-income single persons. Mixed-use projects may include seniors and families. There must be a minimum of 40 percent rent-geared-to-income units.
(b) Both operating and subsidy costs are funded 100 percent by the Ontario government. Capital costs are arranged with private- sector lending institutions as above.[7]

P-3600
(a) This initiative was designed to create 3,600 units of mostly "regular," non-profit housing.

Homes Now
(a) The aim of this initiative is the creation of 30,000 affordable rental units over several years. About 70 percent of the units will be for "rent-geared-to-income" tenants.[8]
(b) The program provides funding for the purchase or lease and renovation of existing properties, and new construction.
(c) The Ministry of Housing will pay $300 million annually to subsidize rents and operational costs, with no federal contribution.
(d) Canada Pension Plan funds totalling $3 billion are being used as a source of low-cost mortgage financing for these projects. Other capital is earmarked for the renovation of leased properties. The capital cost per unit for new and acquired projects must be consistent with the maximum unit price set by the Ministry of Housing. (In other projects the MUP is set by CMHC).

Table 10
Ministry of Housing Operating/Subsidy Expenditures on Post-1986 Supportive Housing ($ in millions)

Program	1988	1989	1990
F/P[1]	$ 4.3	$ 9.8	$ 15.0
P-3000	$ 2.1	$ 11.4	$ 16.9
P-3600	n/a	$ 0.3	$ 1.2
Homes Now	n/a	$ 0.2	$ 2.5

1 Includes federal contribution.

Table 11
MCSS Spending on Supportive Housing and Total Units, by Program

Program	Total Program Spending	1991 ($in Millions) Total Supportive- Housing Spending	Total Units (1990)
Attendant Care	$ 45.1	$ 8.4	382
Home-Support Services for the Elderly	$ 58.2	$ 3.8	1,020
Halfway Homes and Alcohol- and Drug- Recovery Homes	$ 6.7	$ 1.0	181
Family Violence	$ 41.8	$ 4.3	545
Ministry Purchase of Counselling	—	$ 11.3	2,151
Adult Group Homes	—	$ 11.0	510
Supported Independent Living	—	$ 5.7	270
Community Residential Alternatives (program under development)	—	—	—

Program Descriptions

Attendant Care
(a) Support Services Living Units (SSLUs) provide services to persons with physi-cal disabilities living in ministry- sponsored living arrangements or integrated apartments (not necessarily non-profit) with on site staff available on a twenty-four-hour basis. Services include personal care, mobility, dressing, meal prepa-ration, cleaning, shopping, and laundry.
As of April 1991, there were 909 Support-Service Living Units serving 960 persons. The funds expended under this program were $29.7 mil-lion.

(b)Attendant Care Outreach Program provides services to persons with physical disabilities living outside designated housing units. The services available are similar to those services provided in SSLUs.

As of April 1991, there were 1,332 persons receiving Attendant Care Outreach; funds expended under this program were $13.1 million. In addition $2.2 million was spent on attendant care for brain-damaged persons.

Home Support Services for the Elderly
(a)This program provides a range of community support services to enable elderly persons and persons with physical disabilities to remain living in their own homes. Services include meals, transportation, home maintenance, care-giver relief, and home help.

As of August 1990, there were 469 home-support agencies operating 1,487 programs (e.g., meals, transportation, etc.). The number of persons served is not known.

Halfway Houses and Alcohol- and Drug-Recovery Homes
(a)This program provides services to adult ex-offenders, substance abusers, and "socially disadvantaged" persons. Support services include individual and group counselling and vocational-rehabilitation services.

Family Violence
(a)This program provides support services in transitional housing for assaulted women and their children.

Ministry Purchase of Counselling
(a)This program offers a wide range of support services to low- income socially disadvantaged adults in a wide variety of housing types.

Adult Group Homes
(a)Support services are provided to adults with developmental disabilities in group homes. Group homes with 794 units are funded as part of the Multi-Year Plan, in addition to those funded under supportive housing.

Supported Independent Living Program
(a)Support services provided to adults with developmental disabilities to assist them to live independently. Services include supervision, life-skills training, and assistance with daily living. Services are not tied to the housing site; individuals or very small numbers of individuals are served at any one site, often in apartments.

Approximately 665 units have been funded by the Multi-Year Plan since 1987.

Community Residential Alternatives
(a)This initiative was announced in 1989. It is designed to develop alternatives to institutional living for elderly persons who require daily-living supports but whose needs for nursing and professional support can be met satisfactorily on a visitation basis.

As of 1990–91, eleven projects have received operating funding and another fifteen projects are planned for 1991–92.

By 1995 funding is projected at $9 million for services to 1,051 units.

7 Again, owing to definitional discrepancies, this figure cannot be compared to the Ministry of Housing expenditure.

8 The term"'unit" refers to the number of people served.

9 Once again, it is difficult to present precise information because the MoH definition of supportive housing does not match that used by MCSS or Ministry of Housing. The data presented include funding for housing programs other than Ministry of Housing non-profit housing projects.

THE MINISTRY OF COMMUNITY AND SOCIAL SERVICES AND THE COMMUNITY HEALTH AND SUPPORT SERVICES DIVISION

Supportive housing is not a distinct program within MCSS and CHSSD. Rather, funding for support services to specific non-profit rental housing projects is committed by MCSS/CHSSD; the funds then flow through a number of MCSS or CHSSD programs (such as Attendant Care and Supported Independent Living (SIL) programs).

MCSS expenditures for its supportive-housing initiatives for adults totalled approximately $46.5 million in 1991.[7] In 1990, approximately $43 million was spent for support services for 5,058 units[8] in supportive housing.

Table 11 details MCSS/CHSSD total program spending, total supportive-housing spending (for 1991), and total supportive housing units (1990).

MINISTRY OF HEALTH

MoH, through its Community Mental Health Services, has a number of housing programs, most funded jointly with the Ministry of Housing's non-profit-housing funding. Most, though not all, of the housing is targeted at persons with psychiatric disabilities.[9]

According to the ministry, the support programs and services may provide life-skills training, resource linking (i.e., case management), counselling, crisis assistance, and other support as required.

The needs of residents range from twenty-four-hour-a-day support to weekly on-site visits plus on-call support and support for residents in boarding homes and self-contained housing units. These programs promote integration, stability, and consumer choice/needs for normalized living.

The Community Mental Health Services Housing Programs in MoH currently fund 2,035 beds. The total operating budget for services in 1990–91 was $22.1 million.

12 Professional and Human Resources

Most of this Report has been presented in the context of two interested parties: residents of rest homes (assisted by families and advocates), and operators (or owners/operators). There is, of course, a third group directly affected by the recommendations of this Commission: rest-home staff.

The Commission has heard from individuals and groups of employees, and we also received written submissions from the major unions in the field. Employees' concerns centred on the low standards and low levels of care found in some rest homes, and on their own role in these settings: poor pay; often poor training and inadequate preparation for assuming supervisory and care-giving responsibilities; and ongoing verbal and, occasionally, physical abuse by residents. The requests, not surprisingly, were for upgrading of status and wage levels and, in effect, for the development of new institutions to care for vulnerable adults.

The Commission is unable to accommodate the thrust of these requests. As we have indicated repeatedly, we do not intend to recommend the creation of more institutions for care-giving in Ontario. As community-based services are developed in future, they will replace many services at present provided in institutions. We recognize that the implications for employees and their unionization are potentially profound, and it will be necessary for all affected parties, including government, to work together to minimize the adverse consequences of these changes.

The Commission does recognize, however, that there is often a gap between employees' tasks and responsibilities, and their levels of compensation. As we have discussed earlier, we advocate a reduction of the expectations placed on staff while fostering the growth of outside community services.

We have also recommended that wage increases to low-paid staff in registered rest homes be added to the list of allowable expenses eligible for the "3 percent above-guideline" increases under rent control. This should encourage employers (at least at the upper end of the market) to increase pay levels, as it will be possible to pass on the costs.

In this chapter, we wish to examine the implications of our general approach to a number of other issues related to staffing: we first comment on the training of rest-home staff; we then examine coverage of rest homes under the *Hospital Labour Disputes Arbitration Act* (*HLDAA*) and Workers' Compensation; and, finally, we discuss in some detail the role of medical personnel with respect to rest-home residents.

The Staff in Rest Homes

This section is briefer than some persons and groups might have desired, because we place only a limited emphasis on education and training for care-giving staff in rest homes. This downplaying follows directly from the modest expectations we wish to place on rest-home staff and our view of rest homes as residential settings with only limited care-giving responsibilities.[1]

1 Had we endorsed a role for operators and staff as comprehensive-care providers, appropriately trained personnel would have been necessary.

ASSISTING WITH MEDICATIONS

One of the few areas in which training of staff is crucial is assisting residents with their medications. We assume the majority of rest-home residents are able and wish to administer their own medications; but, in some cases, assistance may be desired or needed.

In Part III, we recommended that all staff assisting with medications must be "competent." One empirical indicator of competence might be attendance at short workshops on medications; we recommend that all staff involved in this area participate. We suggest community agencies, such as St. John's Ambulance, be invited to develop such courses where they do not already exist.

> **RECOMMENDATION 128:** That community agencies, such as St. John's Ambulance, be encouraged to develop and deliver short workshops on assisting with medications to be attended by staff of rest homes.

Successful completion of such courses would be presumptive evidence of competence. The Commission does not wish to go beyond the criteria recommended: a higher standard would "professionalize" this service, an outcome we do not desire.

TRAINING AND RESIDENTS' RIGHTS

All persons potentially in a power relationship with residents—including owners/operators and staff who do not normally come into contact with residents—must become aware of the new relationships that will emerge in rest homes on implementation of the recommendations of this Report: a new set of priorities will stress residents' rights and autonomy. Staff must become informed about the residents' bill of rights and its practical implications. They must also be aware of the new protections set out in Part III of this Report and the implications of coverage under the *Landlord Tenant Act* (*LTA*). The new enforcement system and the Rest Homes Tribunal (RHT) must also be understood in terms of what is required, what is encouraged, and how individuals are protected against recriminations (in mandatory reporting of abuse, for example).

The necessary information is not overly complex and can be acquired in a brief workshop (perhaps of no more than a day). Such workshops may be organized by community-based agencies or educational institutions, with significant input from consumer and advocacy groups and the industry trade association. We do not wish to mandate a province-wide curriculum; we deem it sufficient if equal time is provided to consumer groups (such as the Ontario Psychiatric Survivors' Alliance) and advocacy groups, on the one hand, and industry representation, on the other. There should also be ample time for discussion and questions.

> **RECOMMENDATION 129:** That operators and staff participate in workshops to become familiar with the new rights-based protections in rest homes.

Various outside professionals—from police officers to local physicians—must also be informed of the existence of the rest homes within their community, the services provided therein, and the rights and protections available to residents.

> **RECOMMENDATION 130:** That information about rest homes be made available to professionals when the mandatory registration of rest homes begins.

Local hospitals (particularly their emergency departments), ambulance units, and police stations should have lists of area rest homes; hospital staff should be made aware of the distinction between these and high-care facilities, such as nursing homes.

2 For example, one Toronto-area institution has recently introduced a new educational program for the management of long-term-care systems; the greater need is for programs to assist individuals in deciding (and managing) their own long-term-care needs. One social-work program has recently refocused from practice skills to measuring and testing, the apotheosis of client disempowerment.

The law-enforcement and court systems should receive appropriate training with respect to abuse in rest-home settings and the implications of mandatory reporting.

It will also be necessary for educational programs, particularly in the "helping professions," to refocus on a more resident-centred approach to practice. Regrettably, some of the limited evidence we have seen suggests this is not always occurring.[2]

RETAINING STAFF

Many operators have complained that it is difficult to secure and retain properly trained (and motivated) staff. In the retirement-home sector, we are satisfied with a standard market analysis: better pay should attract better-trained staff and reduce turnover; higher wages should in part be passed along to consumers through higher prices. The preferences of consumers and their readiness to pay should determine the quality of staff in each home.

The problems are more complex at the other end of the spectrum, where there is little room for operators to pass through increased costs to consumers. The responsibilities assumed by staff will be restricted by the ability to pay of low-income consumers; limited responsibilities, in turn, will necessitate only limited training, which will be reflected in relatively low wages. Although care in rest homes should not require a work force with very specialized credentials, we endorse efforts by operators to train staff in the understanding of areas such as aging and disability. Particularly as a substantial proportion of front-line staff seem to be women and racial minorities, any general training is likely to be advantageous in a broader social sense, as well. We support any upgrading programs for staff in rest homes and we urge participation.

We recommend that local educational authorities be encouraged to develop short training courses suited to rest-home workers. Such courses should be scheduled to accommodate variable work shifts.

RECOMMENDATION 131: That local educational authorities develop short training courses with flexible schedules for staff in rest homes.

We do not, however, see anything that would warrant specific training subsidies directed only at the rest-home sector: problems of staff recruitment and retention are common throughout the low-wage sectors of the economy.

As staff become more qualified, they are likely to ask for higher wages or quit for more lucrative employment elsewhere (for example, in a hospital). Some may become overly trained for the limited responsibilities demanded of them in rest homes. From a broader public perspective, it is quite desirable that people upgrade their skills and then seek appropriate employment elsewhere. Indeed, high voluntary turnover can be a positive sign in the labour market.

From the perspective of individual employers, high turnover may be unfortunate but inevitable if they are unwilling or unable to pay higher wages to increasingly skilled staff.[3] At the same time, training new staff to work in a rest home does not involve much time, and most can be done on the job.

If employers desire a more stable work force, there may be opportunity to pay higher wages through organizational restructuring or lowering other costs. For example, better-paid staff may have less absenteeism, which might lower the frequency of costlier agency replacements (if these are used). High wages and good staff relations may also enhance the home's reputation in the market, leading to increased occupancy and higher profits. Obviously, there are many scenarios with differing outcomes and implications, but the general conclusion can only be that employers of low-paid, modestly trained staff must expect high turnover.

3 This assumes the acquired training is transferable, and not peculiar to the need of the specific employer.

Industrial Relations

HOSPITAL LABOUR DISPUTES ARBITRATION ACT

The *Hospital Labour Disputes Arbitration Act* (*HLDAA*) applies to "hospitals" as defined in paragraph (1)(1)(a) of the Act, which refers to "any hospital ... nursing home or other institution operated for the observation, care or treatment of persons ... and includes a home for the aged." Although labour relations in hospitals are governed primarily by the *Ontario Labour Relations Act* (*OLRA*), *HLDAA* provides for compulsory binding arbitration in the absence of a negotiated settlement.

HLDAA comes into force when hospital employers and unionized workers are unable to effect a collective agreement. The union will typically apply to the minister of Labour for binding arbitration under *HLDAA*, and the minister must decide whether the workplace constitutes a "hospital" within the meaning of the Act.

HLDAA coverage has been generally held as advantageous to the unions and employees, as binding arbitration often generates more favourable settlements than might emerge from a strike.

In part because of the largely unskilled work force, unionization of rest-home staff has been limited. However, those rest homes that employ unionized workers and unions themselves have complained to the Commission that *HLDAA* is applied inconsistently to rest homes: seemingly similar premises are accorded different treatment when *HLDAA* is requested. Indeed, decisions as to coverage under *HLDAA* are made on an individual basis, dependent on the facts of the case.

As rest homes become more akin to traditional accommodation-only premises with care services delivered from the community, it is probable that *HLDAA* will no longer apply. (This may be seen as an advantage to operators.) We do not deem it appropriate to make a specific recommendation about coverage of rest homes under *HLDAA* as the issue is decided on the facts at a given time, and over time we assume the *OLRA* will increasingly apply in these settings.

The move to community-based services, however, does create a problem. Care may be essential to the resident, but *HLDAA* would not apply, as a community-based care-giving agency would not meet the definition of "hospital" as set out in *HLDAA*. Agency-based community staff or employees of transfer-payment agencies—unlike hospital employees—are free to strike, to the detriment of vulnerable and dependent residents.

It is the view of this Commission that it is the essential nature of the service, not the designation of the building, that should determine whether staff may legally strike. Indeed, the entire *HLDAA* may be outdated and should be replaced by generic legislation dealing with essential care services, however and wherever delivered. In this way, vulnerable populations dependent on care would be protected, whether the care was delivered by an institution or by a community-based service agency.

> **RECOMMENDATION 132:** That the Ministry of Labour re-examine its definition of "hospital" under the *Hospital Labour Disputes Arbitration Act* with a view to replacing it with more general legislation dealing with essential care services, however and wherever delivered.

WORKERS' COMPENSATION

A second issue that affects the industrial-relations environment in rest homes is the rating for purposes of Workers' Compensation.

4 NRG 240 comprises industries in two Standard Industrial Classification (SIC) codes: SIC 8621—Homes for Personal and Nursing Care—are "establishments primarily engaged in providing personal care on a continuing basis with medical and professional supervision ... of residents with relatively stabilized chronic disease ... " SIC 8622—Homes for Physically Handicapped and/or Disabled—are "establishments primarily engaged in providing for the care of residents who are ambulant ... who have decreased physical capacity and who require supervision and assistance with activities of daily living."

5 The estimated assessment rate for NRG 241 is $1.53, reflecting the fact that hospitals have a much more favourable accident (cost) history than do nursing homes or homes for the aged.

There are 109 rate groups under Schedule 1 of the *Workers' Compensation Act*; each covered industry is placed in one of these. The assessment rate for each group is determined empirically and individually, based in part on the rate group's claims-cost experience during the prior three years. Rest and retirement homes are included in rate group 882, which also includes hospitals, nursing homes, and homes for the aged. The rate group is a relatively large one and covers a diversity of accident experience.

The Workers' Compensation Board (WCB) is currently reviewing the entire rate structure and has proposed a new system of rate groups (NRGs), to become operative January 1, 1993. Under this proposal, rate group 882 would be split into several new rate groups: "hospitals" would form a group on their own (NRG 241), and "homes for the aged and physically handicapped" would be in a different group (NRG 240).[4]

The current WCB assessment (based on 1990 figures) for rate group 882 is $1.97 per $100; a worker earning minimum wage, and working forty hours a week, fifty-two weeks a year, would have an annual assessment of $208.98. The estimated rate for NRG 240 is $3.86 per $100, which yields an annual assessment for the same worker of $409.47, nearly double the current figure.[5]

NRG 240, as envisaged, does not distinguish clearly between high and low levels of care, and between premises that operate with and without ongoing medical and professional supervision. The Ontario Long-Term Residential Care Association (OLTRCA) has argued that it is inappropriate to group institutions providing extended and nursing care with those that offer residential care only.

The Commission concurs. It is our view that if rest homes are to offer residential care, they ought not be grouped, for WCB or any other purpose, with premises that provide high levels of nursing care. Indeed, combining rest homes and nursing homes for WCB purposes would run directly counter to the thrust of this Report.

We therefore recommend that the WCB separate proposed NRG 240 into premises that do and do not provide nursing care, and that registered rest homes be included in the latter grouping.[6] Within each rate group, assessments will continue to be based in part on claims-cost history.

RECOMMENDATION 133: That the Workers' Compensation Board consider dividing its proposed new rate group 240 into two separate categories, distinguishing between premises that provide ongoing extended care and those that offer residential care (i.e., only limited nursing care). That registered rest homes be included in the latter grouping for assessment purposes.

The Medical Role

The most interesting comment on the medical role with respect to rest-home residents came not from a doctor but from a public-sector lawyer, who wondered about the legal ramifications for any doctor who agreed to be a "house doctor." Many rest homes have a designated house doctor, who in general terms agrees to be available to residents. The presence of a house doctor is often an effective marketing or advertising tool; however, the meaning and implications of such a relationship are ambiguous.

The definition and/or responsibilities of the house doctor are nowhere described. In many cases, it merely means that a doctor will see residents if they are referred by the operators; but there is no formal commitment to do so. In some cases, the house doctor visits the rest home weekly.

We do not know what the label of house doctor implies for the doctor, the owners/operators, the government, or the residents.[7] The role of the house doctor must be clarified, so

6 The WCB has indicated a readiness to consider the suitability of separate rate groups, provided that two conditions are satisfied: the memberships of the groups must be clearly defined and distinguishable; and the group must have had 550 lost-time injuries during the five-year period 1984–88. The first condition could be met by distinguishing between regulated and licensed nursing homes and homes for the aged on the one hand, and registered rest homes on the other. The second condition is problematic, as data are not currently available.

7 In chapter 6 we have expressed our concerns about potential conflict of interest if physicians own rest homes and serve as house doctor.

8 This information should also be provided as part of the information package that retirement homes may offer to prospective residents. It should also be given to every resident at the point of entry, on the public record, on-line, and in public libraries.

9 The issue is a broad one. The Commission has received information from the Alternative Funding Unit of MoH, Health Insurance Division, that operators of mobile X-ray services are seeking approval for new sites, including rest and retirement homes. As of mid-October 1991, requests were pending from thirty-one seniors' residences (including nursing homes). Some proposed weekly mobile X-ray service; others requested an annual chest X-ray. The reasons for the requests by the home operators included the age and frailty of residents, convenience, and cost savings (to the residents and operators), as staff time or ambulances would not be needed for accompanied travel to hospitals.

In the Commission's view, eligibility for this benefit, like home visits, should be on the same basis as for a person in a private residence. Most residents should be assisted to a clinic or hospital. Blanket referrals for all residents are fundamentally unacceptable, as cost savings to operators and residents translate into increased costs to OHIP.

that both buyer and seller of rest-home services be fully aware of what that term does, and does not, entail.

RECOMMENDATION 134: That the College of Physicians and Surgeons of Ontario develop a protocol describing the duties and responsibilities of "house doctors" in rest homes.

This protocol would presumably include an agreement to see any and all residents expeditiously. It should also contain an obligation for the house doctor to inform residents that they have the right to see their own doctors rather than the house doctor.

The name, address, and phone number of the house doctor, or notification that the home does not have a house doctor, should be clearly posted in every rest home.[8]

Informal conversations have identified a risk that any initiative to assign explicit obligations and responsibilities to house doctors may lead to the termination of this role. This is not necessarily an undesirable outcome.

Residents of rest homes are entitled to home visits by physicians under the same circumstances as other members of the community. The general presumption is that most people will go to a doctor's office or hospital clinic. This same presumption should operate with regard to residents of rest homes.

It is convenient for rest-home residents to see a doctor at home; there are also significant economies of scale for a doctor to make several home visits in one setting. However, these factors should not override the broader public interest: home visits are more costly to OHIP than are office visits. Physicians, as "gatekeepers" of the medical system, have an obligation to ensure that home visits are reserved for those who need them. Regular home visits should not be provided as a matter of course and convenience merely because residents live in a particular setting.[9]

The Commission is also concerned about descriptions given to us of assembly-line medical care. In one retirement home, we observed the elderly residents being brought from their rooms and lined up in the lobby, because this was the house doctor's day for visiting. The queue seemed more appropriate to a food bank than to frail seniors apparently about to receive quality medical care.

We recommend that the Ministry of Health (MoH) undertake a thorough investigation into the quality of medical care delivered by doctors in rest homes.[10] We also recommend that OHIP monitor and investigate billing practices of doctors who regularly claim for multiple and sequential home visits in rest homes.[11]

> **RECOMMENDATION 135:** That the Ministry of Health investigate the billing practices and quality of medical care delivered in rest homes by those physicians who regularly claim for multiple and sequential home visits in rest homes.

At present, there is a special-visit ("house-call") fee paid by OHIP to a doctor to offset travel time, etc., in addition to the regular fee for the examination. For each additional person seen in the same location, there is a reduced special-visit fee. On the face of it, we do not see the need for such additional special-visit fees, i.e., the premium for travel time need not be repeated.

> **RECOMMENDATION 136:** That the Ontario Health Insurance Plan consider paying the special-visit fee only once for multiple home visits in one physical location.

In some cases, however, suitable mechanisms do not exist to assist patients to get to physicians' offices or hospital clinics; as well, some residents who are truly immobile do not receive needed in-home medical care.

10 The mandate of the inquiry could be broadened to encompass all congregate living settings for vulnerable adults.

11 OHIP has an audit system for gross billing; they may question a doctor who claims for a large number of patients seen at one location. The medical reason for the visit could be requested as well as documentation of what was done (i.e., each patient must have a medical chart). In cases of inappropriate billing, OHIP can recover the money paid. Many comments to the Commission, particularly by persons with psychiatric histories, question the effectiveness of these audits.

12 Rest-home operators should not be compensated, on a per diem basis, to provide undefined care services, which might include assistance to attend a doctor's appointment. On the other hand, where alternative community resources are not readily accessible, it may be efficient to compensate operators, on a fee-for-service basis, for transportation.

It is necessary to build on existing community systems that assist vulnerable adults to travel in the community.[12] Special-purpose transportation vehicles, for example, or community resource workers can help people attend physicians' offices or dental appointments or any other needed service in the community.

To ensure that adequate in-home care is provided to those who are truly immobile is more difficult, yet the issue is crucial. If current pressure on acute- and chronic-care hospital beds is to be eased, medical care must be delivered to people in the community. For some, this care must be provided in their homes.

Some physicians appear reluctant or unwilling to make home visits, even to those who are unable to attend clinics; yet the right of people with severely limited mobility to adequate medical care is fundamental to the concept of universal access that underlies our medicare system.

The public interest requires that medical care be available in the community and, when necessary, at home, and we call on the government to ensure that this interest is served. As long-term-care reform develops, community-based and -delivered medical services must be widely and readily available.

We also recommend that MoH develop measures to ensure that persons unable to attend medical premises receive quality medical care at home, whether they are in the community or in rest homes.

RECOMMENDATION 137: That the Ministry of Health develop measures to ensure that persons who are unable to attend medical premises are able to receive medical care in their homes, which includes rest homes.

PRESCRIBING PRACTICES

We have heard repeatedly of persons receiving the same medications year after year, without reassessment. Prescribing physicians must take responsibility for the medications they prescribe; pharmacists must also have a professional role in this regard.[13]

Unless residents "doctor-shop"' and/or withhold information, it is the responsibility of the attending physician to ensure against contraindicated drugs, overmedication, inappropriate medication, etc. Pharmacists' professional responsibilities include evaluating the suitability of medications prescribed, recognizing possible drug duplication and multiple prescribing, and notifying physicians if there are concerns.[14] Should several doctors be prescribing simultaneously, a person's pharmacist may be the only source of comprehensive information on medications consumed.[15]

Under OHIP, all vulnerable adults can have their medication inventory reassessed at regular intervals. Once a year may be considered appropriate in many cases, but it can be done more frequently on request. Such reassessments reduce the likelihood that prescriptions will be added to previous automatically renewed prescriptions in a cumulative, expensive, and potentially dangerous manner.

RECOMMENDATION 138: That the Ministry of Health develop measures to improve the accountability of physicians with respect to the medications they prescribe to residents of rest homes. That the role and responsibilities of pharmacists in this area be clarified.

In its examination of "accountability," MoH should also take steps to ensure that vulnerable adults dependent on large amounts of medication have access to regular and complete prescription reassessments.

We also recommend that the MoH support resident initiatives, such as the establishment of peer self-help groups, to lessen dependence on medications.

13 Operators have an obligation—made explicit in the bill of rights—to ensure prescribed rules are followed, if they choose to assist with medications.

14 Ontario College of Pharmacists, *Guidelines for the Practice of Pharmacy*, June 1989. The text notes some limitations on this responsibility.

15 Though it is not formally in the *Guidelines*, pharmacists may refuse to fill a prescription if they feel it is not in the best interests of the patient. They would report such refusal to the College of Pharmacists and, perhaps, to the College of Physicians and Surgeons.

16 We assume these initiatives would be undertaken in partnership with consumer and advocacy groups, and not viewed as a problem amenable to a solely medical solution.

17 We note a parallel here to recent measures in Quebec, which considered the use of coercion to fill vacant medical positions in outlying regions of the province. The physicians' association was given twenty months to solve the understaffing problem; if it failed to do so, a legislated solution would be imposed. (Montreal *Gazette*, August 29, 1991)

RECOMMENDATION 139: That the Ministry of Health financially support resident initiatives to lessen dependence on drugs and medications.

Far too many cases have been reported to us of non-existent or inadequate medical care provided to residents of rest homes. It is the right and the responsibility of the government of Ontario to make meaningful the right to health care in this province. The Commission is aware that if it becomes necessary for government to intervene directly, such action will potentially infringe upon the self-governance of the medical profession and the entrepreneurial rights of individual physicians. We make these recommendations advisedly.

The College of Physicians and Surgeons of Ontario, acting under the authority of the *Health Disciplines Act*, has the responsibility "to serve and protect the public." The Ontario Medical Association, as part of its framework agreement with the government of Ontario, committed itself "to enhance the quality and effectiveness of medical care." We invite these bodies to co-operate with the government of Ontario to ensure that quality medical care is available to all residents of rest homes.[16]

In the final analysis, however, it is the obligation of the government of Ontario to ensure that the medical needs of residents are met. This responsibility cannot be privatized.[17]

Professional autonomy and self-governance are, in our view, neither ends in themselves nor absolute concepts never to be touched. Rather they represent a particular organizational arrangement through which the public interest is to be served. If this goal is not met, the arrangement must be questioned.

Our call for MoH to ensure that quality medical care is provided at home to those who cannot attend at clinics or physicians' offices has ramifications far beyond rest homes. It encompasses the future viability of community-based long-term care. If the self-governance arrangement for medical care does not produce results congruent with the broadly defined public interest in this area, we feel the government of Ontario must give thought to an alternative approach that would de-emphasize professional autonomy and entrepreneurial freedom in a monopoly context.

18 Community (general) hospitals offer a comparable service; however, the form and content vary from setting to setting, as these facilities operate on a decentralized basis.

Referrals and Placements to Unregulated Accommodation

Each of the populations of interest to this Inquiry experiences unique problems in locating suitable housing. Those with psychiatric histories often obtain accommodation with the assistance of a hospital-discharge planner. Persons with developmental disabilities have adult protective service workers (APSWs) to assist them, but critical problems arise when they leave the child-welfare system. Seniors or their families seeking appropriate accommodation may use the local Placement Co-ordination Service (PCS), if one exists.

We shall consider each group in turn.

PERSONS WITH PSYCHIATRIC HISTORIES

Each provincial (psychiatric) hospital is required to offer a discharge-planning service to oversee and implement appropriate services when patients are to be discharged.[18] Primary among patients' needs is housing; unregulated rest-home accommodation comprises much of the housing available to this population group.

Over the years, there have been no clear guidelines for discharge planners to follow. Some saw their mandate to be finding any housing, particularly for hard-to-serve clients, in tight markets; others viewed their role as locating suitable

19 The blacklisting has to be done informally, as there might be legal repercussions from a systematic exclusion of certain residential settings without clear criteria and a formalized due process.

20 The term "placement" is no longer officially used, though it still appears in common conversation.

21 *Discharge Planning: The Process*, Final report of the Discharge Planning Committee, MoH 1991.

housing. Ongoing lack of communication at times had unfortunate consequences: one planner might informally blacklist[19] a particular rest home because of unacceptable conditions there; meanwhile another discharge planner, sometimes in the same hospital, would continue referrals to the home, unaware of any problems. Even the verbs describing planners' activities were ambiguous: were they "referring" or "recommending," which implies approval? Were they "informing about"—a more neutral term—or "placing,"[20] which presumes limited, if any, choice for clients?

There has been recent activity among discharge planners to clarify their role. A small committee was formed by MoH to respond to issues raised during the Cedar Glen inquest; its work was subsequently extended to develop a discharge-planning protocol for use in "referring" patients to unregulated accommodation.

This committee based its work on an explicit statement of values that involved a commitment to community care as articulated in the Graham Report, and stressed the importance of self-determination, including "the right to make decisions that some might consider unusual or even bizarre."[21]

The committee of discharge planners was given the responsibility of developing standards for rest homes and of ensuring these are maintained. However, hospitals have no legal power to require any standards. We have noted earlier that standards without sanctions are merely voluntary guidelines, and guidelines are all the discharge planners could produce. Failure to comply with these guidelines might, after due warning, lead to the removal of a home from the recommended list; yet in a tight housing market, both planners and residents may have little choice but to accept the home, anyway. As well, planners would still be free to inform departing clients about non-approved housing.

Many persons leaving hospitals actively seek the least-regulated environment possible; for them the rest home is the accommodation of choice: little is demanded of them and their basic needs are taken care of. This wish must be respected, and attempts by discharge planners to direct people to "approved" housing will likely produce "green-garbage-bag departures" by patients (voluntary discharges from hospitals to desired but unapproved housing).

The Commission endorses the efforts of the discharge planners to identify "approved" housing in the community.

> **RECOMMENDATION 140:** That hospital discharge planners be supported in their efforts to draw up criteria to identify "approved" or "recommended" housing in their communities.

We also feel that communication and information among discharge planners must be shared more consistently and comprehensively than in the past. With on-line information networks widely available, data on every registered rest home can be instantaneously accessible to all discharge planners. We have also recommended that information on all penalties and sanctions imposed on operators of rest homes be in the on-line data base.

> **RECOMMENDATION 141:** That discharge planners continue to collect and share information on accommodation in the community; that discharge planners have all available information on rest homes on-line.

We encourage discharge planners from different hospitals to meet on a regular basis to share information about local housing conditions and to identify criteria that can be consistently applied in different communities.

There are two difficult questions, however: should discharge planners be prevented from giving patients being discharged information on illegal or unregistered or bootleg premises? Should they be prevented from giving information on premises not on an approved list but operating legally?

22 The debate fits within our earlier discussion of whether inadequate housing is better than no housing.

In some sense, the questions are moot, for it is difficult to prevent such information from being given. To deny the discharge planner the right to give full information about housing supply—both good and bad—would infantilize the individual, narrow the range of choices available, and perhaps prevent housing from being secured.

Nevertheless, it may be argued that discharge planners have an obligation not to give information about premises that are dangerous or harmful to the residents, i.e., rest homes that continue to operate in contravention of the law or without registration.[22]

> **RECOMMENDATION 142:** That discharge planners only give information to departing patients about rest homes that are registered with the municipality. That discharge planners be free to give information on "unapproved" but legal rest homes, while identifying the causes preventing "approved" status.

We also feel that whenever possible, discharge planners should personally visit any rest home not on the approved list that they may consider making referrals to, so full information can be provided to potential residents.

PERSONS WITH DEVELOPMENTAL DISABILITIES

We noted in chapter 2 that many adults with developmental disabilities have, in effect, two housing options if they do not reside with parents or relatives, in a group home, or in an integrated or independent living situation: they may reside in an unregulated rest home, or they can remain in a children's home.

The problems experienced by rest-home residents have been discussed at some length. However, for persons with developmental disabilities, there is even greater vulnerability. They are at particular risk of exploitation and abuse—verbal, physical, and sexual—from unscrupulous operators, staff, and other residents.

The other housing option is a children's residence. At least 120 adults are housed in these settings as of the February 1991 APSW data collection. These facilities are not necessarily suited to adults. Given the practical difficulties of having two sets of rules within a single home, adults who remain in the children's setting will likely be subject to child-appropriate rules and practices. (Sexual expression and interaction, to take but one example, require very different parameters for children and for adults.)

These settings are licensed by the Ministry of Community and Social Services (MCSS) as foster homes or other children's facilities, but there is no licensing or regulation for adult residents.[23] The accommodation is thus "unregulated" for adults within the Inquiry's terms of reference. Many of the residents have a "unique and difficult social situation," with extremely difficult behaviours and psychological diagnoses, including tendencies to self-abuse, etc., which require substantial—and costly—care. These adults may remain in the children's settings for several years, until they obtain a place in an adult-service residence, independent living arrangement, or other housing provided through the associations for community living: in some cases their needs may be too great even for most boarding homes.

The cost of housing adults with developmental disabilities in children's settings has never appeared in the budgetary estimates of MCSS. The cost forms part of the ministry deficit at the end of the fiscal year, and thus the spending is never authorized in advance by the legislature.[24]

The amounts involved are substantial: for 1991–92, some $6 million will be spent and covered through the ministry deficit at year's end.[25] The Commission has been shown copies of budgets approved by MCSS for privately supplied

23 Standards with respect to physical plant (Fire and Building codes) are often higher in children's facilities than in those for adults. Our concern is not with such standards but rather with standards of care and treatment.

24 The ministry explains this process as Exceptional Circumstance Reviews (ECRs), requested by Children's Aid Societies (CAS) as extended-care and maintenance agreements for Crown wards between the ages of eighteen and twenty-one. If there are additional eligible individuals for whom there was no budget approved, the CAS may apply to the ministry for additional funding. This will be given only when the number of clients exceeds that originally agreed to in the service plan, or when the ministry has approved increases above the economic adjustment for the residences.

25 Some $1–$2 million of this spending is formally funnelled through non-profit agencies to commercial operators who deliver the actual service. In practice, a substantial part of the funding is paid directly by the MCSS area offices to commercial operators, in contravention of the cost-sharing conditions of the Canada Assistance Plan, which preclude the use of commercial suppliers. Similar practices occur in a wide range of CAP-shared services.

services. In one case $370,000 had been approved for one commercial operator to supply care for one resident for one year beginning April 1990.

We cannot comment directly on the propriety of the specific amounts allocated to particular operators: the clients are hard to serve and may require twenty-four-hour supervision. We do, however, have two serious concerns. First, the spending is not approved in advance through departmental estimates. In addition, the accommodation, particularly in the commercial sector, is unregulated for adults; therefore, accountability is limited and appropriate-quality care may not be delivered.

RECOMMENDATION 143: That the Ministry of Community and Social Services clearly identify in advance, each year, the costs of providing accommodation for adults with developmental disabilities in children's facilities as part of the ministerial estimates.

RECOMMENDATION 144: That the Ministry of Community and Social Services accelerate its plans to remove all adults with developmental disabilities from children's residential accommodation; and that pending such removal, the ministry take steps to ensure that appropriate standards for adults and effective accountability mechanisms are in place in such residences.

THE FRAIL ELDERLY

Since 1970, MoH, under the *Ministry of Health Act*, has sponsored local placement co-ordination services (PCS), whose primary purpose is finding long-term care for the elderly. Provincial funding is 100 percent. The system is decentralized, and the twenty-three programs do not cover the entire province.

The original mandate of these services was to set priorities for admission to local high-care institutions. In practice, PCSs disseminate information and offer some information counselling. Some PCSs actively define local priorities and influence placements in nursing homes, homes for the aged, and chronic-care hospitals.

Some PCSs inform interested parties of local rest-home alternatives and explain what the homes do and do not offer. However, the information can be limited and even incorrect. A PCS may learn of a rest home by chance, by word of mouth, as a result of a complaint, or by other means; as well, it may never learn of the existence of some operations.

The Commission received a number of submissions from individual PCSs. These endorsed the official position of their provincial association that rest and retirement homes should be incorporated into institutional long-term care. If this were to occur, the submissions argue, admissions would be made only through service co-ordination agencies (SCAs), the gatekeepers of the institutional long-term-care system. Only persons requiring residential-level care would be referred to rest homes.[26]

The Commission is unable to endorse this recommendation. We see the rest home to be outside the institutional long-term-care system, as an alternative form of community residence.

RECOMMENDATION 145: That the role of local placement co-ordination services or service co-ordination agencies with respect to rest homes be solely one of providing information.

We endorse the information-provider role of PCSs or SCAs and encourage them to provide the fullest possible information—costs, prices, and price history, and other relevant data—about rest and retirement homes.[27]

26 The PCS function is likely to be subsumed within that of the SCAs once the latter are fully operational.

27 Mandatory registration will offer a complete listing of premises. We urge that standardized information about services in retirement homes be available on-line to all PCSs and SCAs.

13
Provincial-Municipal
Issues

A number of recommendations in this Report will have a significant impact on municipalities and their relationship with the government of Ontario. The most important of these recommendations are the phasing-out of domiciliary hostels; municipal registration of rest homes; and greater accountability with respect to local inspection and enforcement of fire, health, and building construction and occupancy standards.

Municipalities across the province have expressed concern lest this Commission impose on them added responsibilities without commensurate funding. With the decline in economic activity in Ontario, social-assistance claims and costs have risen dramatically. Municipalities feel they are unable to bear the rapidly increasing burdens—in particular, the 20 percent local share of General Welfare Assistance (GWA)—given their fixed or shrinking local property-tax bases.

The federal government's unilateral decision to impose a ceiling on its Canada Assistance Plan (CAP) contributions and to reduce its overall involvement in the social field has led to greatly increased financial pressure on lower levels of government. The comment is regularly made that the federal deficit is being fought on the backs of the provinces and, in turn, the municipalities, who are being given added burdens without added resources to carry them properly. The Commission has seen the data and endorses the legitimacy of these claims.

Many municipalities have also argued that the distribution of people requiring domiciliary-hostel accommodation across Ontario unfairly penalizes some communities. Rest homes, including hostels, often locate where land costs are low, even though residents may come from adjoining or even distant locations. The communities and neighbourhoods in which the provincial psychiatric hospitals are located have traditionally carried a disproportionate burden for those discharged. (At the same time, of course, rest homes contribute to local economies by paying local taxes and providing employment, particularly for low-skilled workers.)

Municipalities' grievances must be resolved in a broader context than that of rest homes. We are aware that the historic division of responsibilities, indeed the entire provincial-municipal relationship, is being re-examined through the Provincial-Municipal Social Services Review (PMSSR) and in broader contexts, as well. These are the appropriate venues in which to argue the disparities of responsibility and resources. We do not wish to put forward recommendations that will make more difficult any future rationalization of provincial and municipal roles and responsibilities; however, neither do we wish to leave unaddressed the concerns expressed by municipal governments.

We believe that municipalities should continue to exercise their current responsibilities to inspect and enforce fire and building standards. These are areas of traditional local expertise. A call for provincial funding of inspection and enforcement costs in rest homes, for example, would have implications far beyond this Report and could not be justified for rest homes alone.

1 Recommendation 242 of *Transitions* (p.483) stated: "Municipalities should be required to include a category for all boarding homes in their by-laws, to regulate such accommodation with respect to physical safety and public health standards, and then to enforce such bylaws."

2 We have previously noted the possible limitation of such by-laws imposed by the *Fire Marshals Act* and the *Building Code Act.*

3 Recommendation 22 of PMSSR states that municipalities should be given authority to regulate, license, and inspect rest homes if they choose to do so. (*Report of the Provincial-Municipal Social Services Review*, prepared for MCSS, Queen's Printer for Ontario, Toronto, 1990, p.111–112)

    The position of the Association of Municipalities of Ontario (AMO), as set out in their submission to this Commission, is that the PMSSR recommendation "should exclude 'regulation' on the basis that provincial regulations are necessary to establish standards for personal care across the province and therefore regulation should be a provincial responsibility. The association agreed the municipalities could then enforce the regulations." (p.3)

REST-HOME BY-LAWS

Many presentations to the Commission have urged that municipalities be required to adopt local by-laws dealing with matters of public health and safety in rest homes.[1] Some have suggested that the province draft a model by-law, which could be made available to municipalities.

We have considered existing and proposed provincial public health, fire-safety, and construction standards. In each case we have called for the identification of a category or categories of coverage appropriate to rest homes. If these recommendations are adopted, a clear provincial norm will exist in each of these areas; municipalities will have no role in setting these standards. (Municipalities may, of course, continue to set property standards for all local buildings to control their use and occupancy.)[2]

We also wish to comment on those municipalities that attempt to regulate standards of care through local by-laws. We have noted the prevalent legal opinion that, with the sole exception of Windsor's, those aspects of such by-laws that relate to care are probably illegal. Some submissions have requested that we recommend the "legalization" of such by-laws, that we call for specific municipal authority to regulate the standards of care in rest homes.[3] For the reasons indicated earlier, we must deny this request, and cannot recommend that the province pass the necessary enabling legislation.

DOMICILIARY HOSTELS

We agree with the common municipal viewpoint that most residents in domiciliary hostels would receive social assistance under the provincial GAINS(D) program were they not in hostels. There is no discernible justification for them suddenly to become municipal GWA clients when they enter a hostel. We endorse the position that in any restructuring of social assistance between the province and the municipalities, responsibility for funding the domiciliary-hostel system should be lodged with the jurisdiction generally responsible for assisting the client groups being served.[4]

RECOMMENDATION 146: That in any provincial-municipal restructuring, the level of government responsible for providing social assistance to a person should not alter by virtue of that person's residence in a hostel.

Our call to terminate the domiciliary-hostel system can represent a substantial saving for participating municipalities: their current 20 percent share of hostel costs could be eliminated entirely. We have also suggested that additional provincial funding could be made available to those municipalities who do not currently participate in the hostel system for the development of more services.

The Commission has been asked to recommend mandatory municipal participation in the domiciliary-hostel system; however, we are unable to do so. First, this would be operationally difficult without extensive direct provincial activity. More fundamentally, the Commission is unwilling to require expansion of the domiciliary-hostel program at the very time we recommend that the system be phased out in favour of portable service delivery. The many problems with domiciliary hostels that we have identified work against the expansion of the system. Indeed, those communities without domiciliary-hostel contracts are perhaps even in a favoured position for the development of portable services and individualized funding, as they have no structures and political interests to defend the status quo.[5]

One municipality has recently withdrawn from the domiciliary-hostel system and others are contemplating similar action. Abandoning the program has led to hardship for affected residents, as the monies available for their care and accommodation have dropped dramatically and rapidly. Although the

[4] We are not referring here to clients of the federal government or other agencies. We mean only that a client who is a Family Benefits responsibility under other circumstances should not suddenly fall under GWA when entering a hostel.

[5] As individualized funding and portable community services become more widespread, money will follow individuals; it will become irrelevant where individuals reside as the distinction between domiciliary-hostel and non-domiciliary-hostel communities vanishes.

Commission appreciates that municipalities are experiencing great financial pressure because of the rapid increase in GWA claimants, we regret that they are attempting to control expenditures by cutting back discretionary allocations to the most vulnerable members of the community. If municipal spending is to be cut back, the burden should be borne by those most able to do so, not by those least able to protest.

∧∧∧

The Last Word

This Commission began with the premise that government has an obligation to offer protection to vulnerable adults in rest, retirement, and boarding homes. There is too much evidence—impressionistic and case based at times, but ultimately compelling—that residents in these settings are daily at risk. Abuses—physical, verbal, sexual, and financial—occur with sufficient regularity and pattern that they cannot be dismissed as isolated events or singular occurrences.

The explicit goal of this Inquiry has been to suggest ways in which residents of rest homes can take control of their own lives—to decide, articulate, and act on their own needs, preferences, and wishes about how they live and with whom. Although it was a specific death that triggered the work of this Commission, our focus has been not on death, but on life—the quality of life of rest-home residents and how it can be improved. The problems we have observed and heard about, and their unacceptable outcomes, were rooted not in the errant behaviour of disturbed individuals but in the very structure of the rest-home system.

Resident empowerment is not a means to ensure a given set of outcomes or a particular quality of life for residents. Rather, empowerment is an end in itself: the right of residents to choose, and the means to act on their choices, are the goals of public intervention.

The Commission began quite agnostically concerning the form, nature, and extent of the most appropriate intervention, but the necessity for some intervention was clear. Given that the mandate of the Commission was to examine "unregulated accommodation," there was, perhaps, a presumption that the solution lay in regulation. However, the central goal was empowerment and protection of vulnerable adults; regulation was simply one means to be considered. Perhaps there were other, more effective, approaches.

In the early stages of the Inquiry, comprehensive regulation by government, like that of the nursing-home sector, was suggested as a model. Through the course of our consultation, it became clear there was a vast chasm between the nursing home as a day-to-day reality and as a conceptual system within which government funding and regulation could be used to attain public-policy goals.

Many presenters were attracted by the theoretical protections offered by nursing-home-type regulation, but woefully few could commend the effectiveness of such regulations or praise nursing homes as places to live in. The cost of the nursing-home system is high, and the quality of life often questionable.

The Commission's analysis of regulation stressed the threat of sanctions as necessary to produce desired behaviours and outcomes. Without credible sanctions, comprehensive regulation is fuelled only by voluntary compliance, and there can be no secure source of volunteers.

Indeed, we learned, relatively late in our research activity, that there has never been a single prosecution for violating the nursing-homes bill of rights. This one fact solidified our rejection of the comprehensive regulatory model.

At a time when virtually every trend in the social and health services is to deinstitutionalization (non-institutionalization), and to delivery of services to people living in the community, it seemed anomalous to promote the development of a new system of low-care, government-funded and -regulated, private-sector institutions. When institutions, including nursing homes, are expected to be de-emphasized through long-term-care reform, it makes no sense to use scarce public funds to create a new set of care-giving institutions. To formally incorporate into the system of long-term institutional care a new structure known as the "rest home," when the entire system itself is subject to fundamental restructuring, does not strike us as the proper way to proceed.

The alternative to comprehensive regulation that we promote in this Report speaks to the need for consumer empowerment within the community. Rather than a system of comprehensive regulatory intervention, we recommend that vulnerable adults be assisted to make decisions over their own lives, whenever, wherever, and to the maximum extent possible.

But empowerment of vulnerable persons is an elusive goal. For some, empowerment will always be constrained by restricted personal capability; for most, an effective system of advocacy and support can extend autonomous action and decision-making far beyond previously accepted limits.

We have devoted considerable attention in this Report to the goal of consumer/resident empowerment and involvement in decision-making. We have noted with approval the pending *Advocacy Act, 1991*, and we repeat our support of this initiative.

In these final pages of the Report, we return to the importance of community services. If these do not exist and are not developed rapidly, the approach put forward in this Inquiry will be jeopardized. The need for long-term community care and assistance to vulnerable adults is acute. The public-policy void that has allowed the creation of bootleg nursing homes and sleazy boarding homes cannot continue. Too many vulnerable people are at severe risk.

The option of community-based services is by far the pre-

1 It is to facilitate this transition that we particularly recommend that current spending on the domiciliary-hostel system be reallocated to more empowering community-based alternatives.

2 It has been pointed out to the Commission that community-based delivery of a service does not guarantee its acceptability to users. We see extensive involvement of users in service design and delivery to be essential to obviate such difficulties.

ferred approach from our perspective and that of virtually all residents we have met. But these services cannot be merely projected, planned or intended: they must be concrete community services, in place and available to those who need them. A system that articulates and promotes community services but does not actually provide them is no better, and possibly worse, than the status quo.

It is also our view that many community services need not be professionalized, "credentialized," and medicalized. For many post-psychiatric residents of rest homes, for example, the greatest community-based needs are for peer counselling and support services. "Experts" are not wanted, trusted, or, in many cases, helpful.

We do not know the full cost of comprehensive, community-based care, for no such system is in place. The transition from the status quo to a complete system of community care may well be more costly than the status quo, as elements of two systems will, for a time, co-exist, perhaps uneasily.[1] A fully mature system of long-term community care may not cost less, but will certainly deliver more.

We repeat our recommendation that the principles of community care put forward by the present and previous governments be endorsed and developed into concrete programs and services as a matter of great priority. We cannot emphasize too strongly the need for community-based services and care, particular programs actively involving peer-support systems.[2]

A PILOT PROJECT

Understandably, governments have traditionally been apprehensive about the possible costs associated with a fully comprehensive system of community-based services. The most common strategy has been to proceed incrementally, to phase in community services as resources permit. Although we support this general approach, we suggest that the government consider implementing one or more pilot projects, in which the development and implementation of relatively comprehensive community-based services take place in designated communities. The outcomes of such projects should be formally monitored and evaluated.

RECOMMENDATION 147: That the government consider implementing one or more pilot projects in which the development and implementation of relatively comprehensive community-based services will be accelerated in designated communities. These pilot projects should stress resident involvement in all stages of program design and delivery. That any such pilot program be formally evaluated as to outcome.

We recommend that Windsor be considered as a pilot site, in part because we find the current structure of rest homes in that community so disconcerting. As we have indicated earlier, the rest-home industry in Windsor is dominated by large physical premises: one home has some 450 beds and several others have more than 100 residents each.[3]

Even with the best will possible, structures of this magnitude cannot impersonate community living. Many residents have been "trans-institutionalized" from the provincial psychiatric hospital to the Windsor rest homes: deinstitutionalization—from an institution to the community—has never occurred.

We understand and commend the efforts of the Windsor Social Services Department to protect rest-home residents through active enforcement of that city's by-law;[4] moreover, we do not imply any improper motive on the part of rest-home owners or operators. What we find unacceptable are the large physical premises themselves, institutions built on the hospital model, with individual rooms off long corridors containing hospital-style beds.

3 At the same time, Windsor's uniquely large rest homes may lead to solutions that would be inapplicable in other communities where the average size of rest home is smaller. Thus Windsor should not be the sole location for a pilot project.

4 See above, chapter 4, concerning the Windsor by-law.

5 The jury's recommendations covered eleven general areas: public education; boarding homes; discharge planning; service agencies; advocacy; public health; fire safety; police forces; Crown attorneys' office; treatment in general hospitals; and coroner's system. We do not propose to comment in detail on the eighty-plus recommendations.

6 With *LTA* coverage, rest-home residents would have twenty-four-hour access to their premises.

RECOMMENDATION 148: That Windsor be considered as a site for any comprehensive community-care pilot program.

In Windsor, we find a ready match between a community that appears never to have really experienced deinstitutionalization and the need for a pilot venue to test and evaluate community-based services.

We do not propose here to detail the pilot project, for we feel it is essential that the residents and local community be involved at every stage. But it is clear that as residents leave the large rest homes, hostel funds will become available for reallocation to community-based services. Further interim provincial funding will be required to promote the development of community alternatives as well as to monitor and evaluate the project.

Would All This Have Prevented Cedar Glen?

We return to the most common question—and challenge—posed to this Commission: whether our recommendations would have prevented the death of Joseph Kendall at Cedar Glen. By implication, the question is broadened: can similar deaths, and situations in which vulnerable adults reside in appalling conditions, be prevented in future?

At the end of this Inquiry we return to the beginning: the recommendations of the coroner's report on the inquest at Cedar Glen.[5]

We are in general agreement with many of the recommendations of the jury. (Some we have strengthened or offered suggestions for implementation.) We reinforce their call for coverage of rest homes under the *Landlord and Tenant Act* (*LTA*) and rent control.[6] We also agree that:

1. receivers should be appointed for rest homes in circumstances where residents are at serious risk, and that a Rest

Homes Tribunal with the power to make such orders be created;

2. all operators and owners should be subject to a Canadian Police Information Centre check with respect to their criminal records and that owners/operators with certain serious criminal records not be involved in the rest-home business;

3. medications should be re-examined once a year (although we would prefer greater frequency);

4. a phone number for assistance should be posted prominently in rest homes;[7]

5. residents must receive their mail unopened; and

6. stricter enforcement of health and fire standards by inspectors is necessary.[8]

In some areas, we have explored the same ground but proceeded in a slightly different direction:

1. we concur with the need to enact a bill of rights, but have not chosen that in the *Nursing Homes Act* as a model, in part because of problems of enforcement; instead we call for a bill of rights enforceable by residents through a Rest Homes Tribunal;

2. our discussion of abuse has focused less on policing than on a requirement that such abuse be reported to the appropriate authorities;

3. we have recommended that the Ministry of Health, rather than the College of Physicians and Surgeons of Ontario, ensure that appropriate medical services are provided to rest-home residents; and

4. we endorse the jury's views on discharge planning, except that we do not believe it desirable that discharge planners limit referrals to subjectively "approved" housing.

In other areas, we and the jury differ in emphasis. We sense the jury is willing, as we are not, to regulate rest homes and

7 We have recommended that the phone numbers of the Rest Homes Tribunal and the Advocacy Commission be posted prominently in every rest home.

8 We have gone further, recommending a means for residents and their advocates to secure stricter compliance.

9 Direct comparisons are difficult because of the different mandates of an inquest and an inquiry and the associated length and detail of research.

10 The local Department of Health did find the water at Cedar Glen to be contaminated. Changes were "ordered," but there was no action taken by the operators.

create, in effect, a new set of nursing homes. For example, we view medical care in the home as a right of all persons who require that it be delivered there; the jury assigns a greater role to the house doctor. We have not called for regulation, as the jury did, but have presented an alternative that we believe will be more effective overall.

Certain recommendations of the jury have already been acted on by the Ontario government: the most important of these is legislation to establish an advocacy program and to provide advocates with access to rest homes. We have reinforced the right of advocates and community-service providers to enter rest homes.

We feel we have responded to the major inquest recommendations that fall within our terms of reference.[9] Certainly, many of our recommendations, or indeed those of the jury—had they been in place—would have significantly reduced the likelihood of a Cedar Glen occurring:

1. the requirement for rest homes to register would have drawn the existence of such homes to the formal attention of the local inspection bodies;

2. a CPIC check would have precluded abusive owners/operators from being involved in the rest-home industry;

3. a right of access for advocates, as well as regular visiting and entry to the premises by others—assured through coverage under the *LTA* and our proposed bill of rights—would have brought the problems to light and promoted an earlier response;

4. the Rest Homes Tribunal would have provided a convenient forum in which the multiple violations of the bill of rights could have been addressed;

5. residents' use of buckets as toilets would presumably have been reported by any number of visitors or staff, and public-health officials would have become actively involved early;[10] and

6. the right to place a home in temporary receivership and to suspend the operators from the industry would have offered a ready remedy.

Undoubtedly there would have been other positive responses, as well.

Our recommendations should markedly improve both the quality of residents' lives and their control over their lives in rest homes. Residents should not have to endure the appalling conditions of life—and death—experienced at Cedar Glen.

And this, in the final analysis, is what this Commission of Inquiry has been all about.

1 *Redirection of Long-Term Care and Support Services in Ontario*, p.32.

APPENDIX:
Aspects of Long-Term Care

The Commission is encouraged by the government's awareness of the need to shift from excess reliance on institutions to community care. This general approach is reflected in the important document *Strategies for Change*, and the 1991 public consultation paper *Redirection of Long-Term Care and Support Services in Ontario*.

We are, however, concerned at the modest pace at which the shift from institutions is taking place. We recognize the budgetary dilemma involved in funding two systems during the transition from institutional to community-based care. We stress the obvious point that resources devoted to reinforcing the system of institutional care are resources that cannot, by definition, develop community-based alternatives.

Per diem funding for nursing homes in Ontario, as proposed by the long-term-care project, is to be divided into three separate components: nursing and personal care; program; and accommodation.

Operators will be reimbursed for the first two elements, based on actual expenditures: that is, costs will be passed through, but there will be no direct profit. With respect to accommodation—the so-called "hotel" costs—facilities "will be permitted to keep any surpluses they can achieve through efficiencies in the accommodation budget."[1]

The strength of this general approach is that it begins the separation or delinking of accommodation from care. The nursing and program roles could be shifted from operators to community-based agencies as the latter develop. (As costs in these areas are to be passed through directly, some operators may welcome release from a responsibility for which they receive no profit.)

The next step in long-term-care reform, in the Commission's view, would be to promote actively the devolution of responsibilities for nursing care and programming from nursing-home operators to community agencies. Such a shift, even if gradual, would enhance and solidify the funding and service-delivery base of community services through a reallocation of existing spending. Such community-based services would undoubtedly be more empowering to residents, and to their families, than is the current operator-driven mode of service provision.

The separation of accommodation from care, associated with community-based services, is being advocated for use in nursing homes in the United States. A recent article in the *New York Times* by two well-known researchers in the field gives added credibility and might well accelerate the acceptance of delinking.[2]

This Commission endorses the general approach of delinking accommodation from care in nursing homes and urges the government of Ontario to implement this approach as quickly as possible.

THE FUNDING DIFFERENTIAL

In Part I of this Report, we cited the provincial auditor's findings concerning compliance with standards in nursing homes. It is in this context that we wish to express our serious concerns about the government's plan to eliminate the historical differential in funding between nursing homes and homes for the aged.[3]

We make no direct comment on the general desirability of eliminating this differential in funding; our short-term concern is that scarce resources are being directed towards nursing homes without adequate assurance of effective enforcement mechanisms.[4] The goal, to our mind, is equal quality of care and equal quality of life for residents; equality of funding is no more than a means to this end. Without an effective system that ensures that benefits pass through to residents,

2 See, for example, R. A. Kane and R. L. Kane, "Time to Rethink the Nursing Home," *New York Times*, August 18, 1991.

3 Strictly speaking, the differential per se is not being eliminated. As the funding basis shifts to levels of client need rather than type of institution, the effect will be to eliminate the differential.

4 The government has allocated an additional $30.9 million to nursing homes to the end of 1992, to enhance services and programs to residents.

5 Some observers suggest that a rate of 5 percent represents a reasonable target. Lower targets may be technically possible, but the costs of meeting care needs in the community may be excessive. Others argue that even 5 percent is too high a rate.

The bed rate can also be calculated for an older population—for example, people seventy-five and older—on the assumption that care needs for the younger elderly can be more easily met in the community. Such an approach would significantly reduce the projected bed requirements.

equality of funding itself becomes the goal, and this is not a goal that we can endorse. To increase funding to particular institutions without first ensuring that adequate and appropriate compliance requirements are operational places the financial interests of operators above the needs of residents.

The object should not be to eliminate the funding gap between nursing homes and homes for the aged, but rather to ensure quality care for vulnerable adults in all settings. It is our view that this cannot come to pass without the development of a compliance system that maximizes consumer empowerment.

We therefore urge that the government delay its plan to eliminate the funding gap between nursing homes and homes for the aged pending the implementation of effective compliance mechanisms to ensure the centrality and empowerment of residents.

COSTS OF INSTITUTIONAL CARE FOR AN AGING POPULATION

We are also concerned that eliminating the historical funding differential between nursing homes and homes for the aged will necessitate scarce resources being unduly directed towards institutional care. We feel that a substantial portion of these funds could be better devoted to accelerating the development of community-based alternatives.

The Commission has estimated that if the current 5.9 percent institutionalization rate of people sixty-five and over is maintained, it will be necessary to create some 53,000 additional extended-care beds by the year 2010. If the rate were decreased to 5 percent, more than 20,000 new beds will be needed.[5]

The cost of these new places will be substantial: if we take a conservative figure of $70 per bed per day, the new or additional operating cost (in 1991 constant dollars) will be between $1.4 million and $3.7 million per day.[6] This is a stag-gering figure in the Commission's view, and a clear indicator that purely in fiscal terms, the current rate of institutionaliza-tion of Ontario's seniors simply cannot continue.

It is our view that much of this new spending, in real terms at least, should be devoted to developing and enhanc-ing community-based in-home care.

The issue has immediate relevance for the mandate of this Commission of Inquiry. We assume that extra needed money will not be readily available from the public sector or from consumers paying user fees in times of fiscal crisis and eco-nomic weakness. The inevitable result will be the further spread of private rest homes, where care is based not on need but on ability to pay. We will, in effect, accelerate the privati-zation of care for the seniors of Ontario, creating a system in which income and wealth become primary determinants of care received.

Few people *want* to be in institutions as they age; yet in the absence of community-based care, they will have no real alternative, as Ontario's rest and retirement homes inevitably—and speedily—develop into a powerful new tier of institutional care.

6 In addition, there will be capital costs to create new beds.

~~~~~~

Commission's Recommendations

Chapter 1: An Introduction

RECOMMENDATION 1:

That a "rest home" be defined as any residential premises in which three or more persons unrelated to the owner/operator reside, and in which one or more of the following conditions is satisfied:

> 1. the operator is paid for caring for residents, whether or not this care is actually received;
> 2. the operator makes public or gives others, such as hospital discharge planners, to understand that care to residents is provided by the operator; and/or
> 3. care is regularly provided by the operator to residents.

Chapter 3: Residents Must Be Central

RECOMMENDATION 2:

That the rest home's primary function be viewed as the provision of residential accommodation in which some element of care is also provided.

RECOMMENDATION 3:

That the government of Ontario expand, as a matter of priority, community services that enable people to remain in their own homes.

RECOMMENDATION 4:

That the rest home be viewed as an alternative form of accommodation in the community, and not as the first stage in a continuum of institutional care.

RECOMMENDATION 5:

That the Community Health and Support Services Division develop a precise legal definition of a "nursing home" so that it is clear which premises offering "nursing care" require a licence.

RECOMMENDATION 6:

That no rest-home operator be permitted to sell more than the threshold amount of nursing care to any resident of that rest home.

RECOMMENDATION 7:

That the reform of long-term care ensure that admission to a nursing home is not influenced by a person's prior residence in a rest home.

RECOMMENDATION 8:

That the *Nursing Homes Act* or its successor prevent licenced nursing homes from having a rest home on the same premises.

Chapter 4: The Regulatory Dilemma

RECOMMENDATION 9:

That the rest-home industry consider a system of voluntary accreditation similar to the star rating used in the hotel industry.

RECOMMENDATION 10:

That standards (physical and care) above the minima recommended by the Commission be achieved through contracts with operators.

Chapter 5: The *Landlord and Tenant Act* and Rent Control

RECOMMENDATION 11:

That the government of Ontario accept as a principle the desirability of certainty concerning coverage of all residential accommodation for vulnerable adults under the *Landlord and Tenant Act* and the proposed *Rent Control Act, 1991* and that these statutes be amended to this effect.

RECOMMENDATION 12:

That rest homes be subject to Part IV of the *Landlord and Tenant Act.*

RECOMMENDATION 13:

That the *Landlord and Tenant Act* be amended to delete the phrase "or for the purposes of receiving care" from clause 1(c)(ix).

RECOMMENDATION 14:

That the Ministry of the Attorney General and other affected ministries define specific criteria for qualifying under the "rehabilitative or therapeutic purpose" exemption from the *Landlord and Tenant Act* [clause 1(c)(ix)]. These criteria should then be given legal effect through an appropriate amendment to the *Landlord and Tenant Act* or its regulations.

RECOMMENDATION 15:

That the Ministry of the Attorney General delete from the

Landlord and Tenant Act the exemption for accommodation subject to fourteen listed statutes [clause 1(c)(viii)]; and that the Ministry of the Attorney General, in conjunction with affected ministries, identify in the *Landlord and Tenant Act* or its regulations clear criteria for exempting premises accountable to the government. These criteria are to include the following:

1. the accommodation is not intended to be permanent accommodation; or

2. protection against arbitrary and/or economic eviction, due process for evictions, and protection of basic rights through an enforceable bill of rights are provided for residents in the relevant legislation.

RECOMMENDATION 16:

That any accommodation exempt from the *Landlord and Tenant Act* on the grounds that it meets the criteria for "accommodation occupied ... for rehabilitative or therapeutic purposes" [clause 1 (c)(ix)] or based on the criteria to replace the exemption for accommodation subject to fourteen listed statutes [clause 1 (c)(viii)], or provided as short-term emergency shelter, be excluded from the definition of "rest home" as set out in this Report.

RECOMMENDATION 17:

That the *Landlord and Tenant Act* be amended to provide that landlords of registered rest homes may apply for an order requiring a resident to temporarily vacate a rest home until a pending application to terminate the tenancy is heard in situations in which paragraphs (a), (c), or (d) of subsection 109(1) of the *Landlord and Tenant Act* applies and in which the time required to proceed with the application for termination would likely result in serious harm to the person or property of other tenants or the landlord.

RECOMMENDATION 18:

That rest homes be subject to rent control. That paragraph 3(1)(e) of the proposed *Rent Control Act, 1991* (Bill 121) be amended to remove the phrase "or for the purpose of receiving care."

RECOMMENDATION 19:

That any accommodation exempted from *Landlord and Tenant Act* coverage on the basis of a court determination that it is occupied for "rehabilitative or therapeutic purposes" [clause 1(c)(ix)] or on the basis of the criteria that will replace clause 1(c)(viii) also be exempt from rent control.

RECOMMENDATION 20:

That any care service sold on a mandatory basis in a rest home be subject to rent control in the same manner as the basic accommodation.

RECOMMENDATION 21:

That charges for accommodation and mandatory care services in rest homes be subject to the same annual guideline increase as charges for other accommodation subject to the *Rent Control Act, 1991*.

RECOMMENDATION 22:

That the costs of any meals provided as part of the mandatory package in rest homes be subject to rent control in the same manner as the basic accommodation.

RECOMMENDATION 23:

That wages of low-paid staff in registered rest homes be treated as an extraordinary operating cost under the *Rent Control Act, 1991* and as such may constitute the basis of an application for rent increases above the annual guideline.

Chapter 6: Life at the Top

RECOMMENDATION 24:
That subsection 1(1) and section 31 of the proposed *Rent Control Act, 1991* be amended to indicate, respectively, that in a registered rest home, charges for optional care services are not "rent" and that the purchase of care services as part of a mandatory package of accommodation and care services does not constitute an illegal "additional charge."

RECOMMENDATION 25:
That registered rest homes be permitted to sell any mandatory package of accommodation and services they wish, provided that the same mandatory package be sold to all residents.

RECOMMENDATION 26:
That section 18 of the proposed *Rent Control Act, 1991* be amended to exclude personal-care services, in order to ensure that the same mandatory package is available to all residents.

RECOMMENDATION 27:
That comprehensive information be provided in writing to each prospective resident of a rest home, covering the following:
1. services available as part of the mandatory package, identifying any limitations on their use, and the price of the mandatory package;
2. optional services available from the operators, identifying any limitations on their availability, and the price of each such service;
3. minimum staffing levels, and qualifications, if any, of staff;
4. details of the emergency-response system, if any, or an indication that none is available; and
5. internal procedures, if any, for dealing with complaints.

RECOMMENDATION 28:

That the lease include a prescribed standard list on which information is provided as to whether each enumerated care service is included in the mandatory package, identifying any limitations on its use.

RECOMMENDATION 29:

That detailed information on the emergency-response/call system, if any; minimum staffing level on each shift; and qualifications of staff be provided as part of the lease, or a statement be provided that no commitment beyond any legal requirement is made with respect to standards for these services.

RECOMMENDATION 30:

That information about and prices for optional services provided by operators be readily available on a prescribed standard form list. This list, completed by the operator, must be posted publicly in the rest home or available on request.

RECOMMENDATION 31:

That operators not be permitted to withhold any optional service or its posted price or charging method from individual residents.

RECOMMENDATION 32:

That the price list include details of price increases for each optional service during the previous two years.

RECOMMENDATION 33:

That each resident shall sign a receipt for each optional service and shall receive on a weekly basis an enumerated statement of optional or additional charges incurred during the preceding seven days.

RECOMMENDATION 34:

That price changes to the list of optional services be permitted only at six-month intervals. In addition, optional services may be withdrawn from all residents only at six-month intervals. Tenants must be notified in writing ninety days in advance of any increase in optional service prices or of termination of any optional service.

RECOMMENDATION 35:
That the *Landlord and Tenant Act* contain an "escape clause" for residents of rest homes permitting them to terminate fixed-term leases with notice if an optional service that they use is withdrawn or the price of an optional service they use is increased during the term of the lease.

RECOMMENDATION 36:
That costs incurred in providing new or enriched care services in the mandatory package of registered rest homes be allowable expenses in calculating the "3 percent above guideline" increase under the proposed *Rent Control Act, 1991.*

RECOMMENDATION 37:
That appropriate community information services be funded by the government to collect and distribute information on the availability of community-based services for vulnerable adults.

RECOMMENDATION 38:
That operators not be permitted to deny or impede access to the rest home by any outside service providers requested by the resident, that use of the premises must be given on terms no less advantageous than those under which the operators deliver the same or similar services, and that no fee be charged to outside suppliers for entry, except to defray or off-set direct costs to the operators.

RECOMMENDATION 39:
That no residents be required or coerced to purchase optional

services from any named service provider (including the operators or the house doctor) over suppliers of their own choice.

RECOMMENDATION 40:

That Home Care and other community-based agencies consider residents of rest homes to be equally eligible for their services as anyone else in the community, i.e., they may not discriminate against individuals on the basis of their residence in a rest home.

RECOMMENDATION 41:

That rental of the first unit of the type vacated by a departing resident ends the financial liability of the departing tenant or estate.

RECOMMENDATION 42:

That no lawyers, social workers, or persons regulated under the *Regulated Health Professions Act, 1991* be permitted to have any professional relationship with residents in a rest home in which they have or their immediate family has a financial interest.

RECOMMENDATION 43:

That subsection 10(2), section 24 and subsection 54(1) of the proposed *Substitute Decisions Act, 1991* be amended to exclude the immediate family of rest-home operators from being witness to a continuing power of attorney by a rest-home resident, and from being appointed by a court as the guardian of the person or property of an incapable person who resides in the rest home.

RECOMMENDATION 44:

That informal mediation be pursued as a "first-line" response to disputes within a rest home whenever possible.

RECOMMENDATION 45:

That the rest-home industry consider adoption of an ombuds-man system for fast and informal resolution of disputes.

RECOMMENDATION 46:

That operators indicate in writing in advance any voluntary adjudicative procedures they are prepared to adopt.

Chapter 7: Life Near the Bottom

RECOMMENDATION 47:

That current initiatives to increase the adequacy of social-assistance payments, to vulnerable adults in particular, continue at the maximum speed possible.

RECOMMENDATION 48:

That the domiciliary-hostel program with its per diem funding of operators be phased out as soon as possible, and that the provincial government commit itself to end the domiciliary-hostel system within a fixed period.

RECOMMENDATION 49:

That as the phasing-out of the domiciliary-hostel program proceeds, funds currently spent on the hostel system be made available for reallocation to accommodation (with or without meals), and to care services.

RECOMMENDATION 50:

That the Ontario government fund non-profit housing agencies to assist in arranging housing alternatives for those residents of rest homes who wish to leave domiciliary hostels and desire assistance to go onto other forms of social assistance.

RECOMMENDATION 51:

That the Ontario government fund non-profit agencies and groups of current or former rest-home residents to assist residents, as desired, to identify their own care needs and arrange for these to be met in ways acceptable to themselves as they leave domiciliary hostels and go onto other forms of social assistance.

RECOMMENDATION 52:

That all community-based agencies involved with housing or service provision in the move away from the domiciliary-hostel system have an explicit commitment to involve consumers actively in all aspects of decision-making to the maximum extent possible.

RECOMMENDATION 53:

That all new and reallocated funding of services for residents of hostels be directed towards non-profit community-based suppliers whenever possible.

RECOMMENDATION 54:

That groups of consumer/survivors be utilized as paid first-line emergency-response teams in the event of resident crises in rest homes whenever possible.

RECOMMENDATION 55:

That the provincial government allocate new funding of about $1,000 per year for the provision of community-based services for each resident who leaves domiciliary-hostel accommodation for another social-assistance status in the community. This funding is to be in addition to the reallocated hostel funding.

RECOMMENDATION 56:

That in the reallocation of domiciliary-hostel funding, the "care services" portion be funded 100 percent by the Ontario government.

RECOMMENDATION 57:

That residents funded under the domiciliary-hostel system be involved in negotiating the agreements for their accommodation and care between operators and municipalities.

RECOMMENDATION 58:

That a variable per diem, with two or, perhaps, three levels of remuneration be used by municipalities, as both incentive and deterrent to operators.

RECOMMENDATION 59:

That increased per diem funding for operators not be viewed as the appropriate way to improve the quality of life for rest-home residents, and that operators of domiciliary hostels be encouraged to move towards a role that approximates that of landlords as closely as possible.

RECOMMENDATION 60:

That no increases in the level of per diem funding to operators (in real terms) be considered at present.

RECOMMENDATION 61:

That the domiciliary-hostel payment system from municipalities to operators be modified so as to involve residents directly.

RECOMMENDATION 62:

That the *General Welfare Assistance Act* Regulations be amended to specify that no municipal hostel agreement with operators can exceed one year. Such contracts may be renewed annually.

RECOMMENDATION 63:

That the *General Welfare Assistance Act* Regulations permit hostel funding only to residences below a provincially determined maximum resident capacity.

RECOMMENDATION 64:

That the *General Welfare Assistance Act* Regulations be amended to require that all domiciliary-hostel agreements include a requirement that the operators provide, without additional charge, all needed supplies of soap, toilet paper, and hygienic pads.

RECOMMENDATION 65:

That if rest-home operators choose to offer a "canteen service," they may not charge prices above those prevailing in the neighbourhood.

RECOMMENDATION 66:

That owners/operators/staff of rest homes shall neither dispense nor trustee a personal-needs allowance, under any circumstances.

RECOMMENDATION 67:

That the personal-needs allowance be paid separately from other social-assistance payment to recipients who qualify for it.

RECOMMENDATION 68:

That the Ministry of Community and Social Services arrange with suitable outside non-profit agencies to serve as trustee for those residents who wish such a service. That where a trustee is appointed under Family Benefits legislation, the social-assistance recipient should be permitted to appeal the appointment to the Social Assistance Review Board. That the regulations to the *Family Benefits Act* prohibit the appointment of rest-home owners/operators/ staff as trustees for rest-home residents.

Chapter 9: A Residents' Bill of Rights

RECOMMENDATION 69:
That a bill of rights for residents of rest homes be enacted as a matter of priority.

RECOMMENDATION 70:
That the residents' bill of rights include rights in the following general areas: respect for the basic human dignity of the residents; a safe, secure, and clean living environment; personal rights; confidentiality; sexuality; religion; consent to treatment; restraint and seclusion; freedom from abuse; advocacy and other outside supports.

RECOMMENDATION 71:
That there be a legal requirement to report abuse of residents of rest homes. That there be a legal prohibition of sanctions or retaliation by operators and staff against the allegedly abused resident and any person who reports the abuse of a resident in a rest home.

RECOMMENDATION 72:
That a Rest Homes Tribunal be created. That the Rest Homes Tribunal assume administrative, mediative, and adjudicatory responsibilities with respect to the rest-homes residents' bill of rights.

RECOMMENDATION 73:
That in dealing with the bill of rights, the Rest Homes Tribunal staff first offer an informal mediation process, followed by a second adjudicatory stage if necessary.

RECOMMENDATION 74:
That rest-home residents have access to advocates under the proposed Advocacy Commission and, if eligible, access to

legal representation under the Legal Aid Plan to pursue complaints before the Rest Homes Tribunal.

RECOMMENDATION 75:

That there be legal prohibition of sanctions or retaliation by the operators, employers and staff against residents and staff persons who make complaints to the Rest Homes Tribunal.

RECOMMENDATION 76:

That there be an 800 telephone number, staffed continuously, for easy and rapid access to the Rest Homes Tribunal.

RECOMMENDATION 77:

That printed signs with the 800 number be posted in every rest home and that literature concerning the Rest Homes Tribunal be readily available in all rest homes.

RECOMMENDATION 78:

That the Rest Homes Tribunal have available a wide range of penalties and remedies appropriate to the severity of a violation.

RECOMMENDATION 79:

That the Rest Homes Tribunal possess the capacity to order emergency responses and interventions, including the power to order the temporary takeover of a residence, when the Rest Homes Tribunal believes that the rest home is being operated in a manner that presents a serious risk to the health of residents or a serious risk of physical injury to residents.

RECOMMENDATION 80:

That all decisions and penalties of the Rest Homes Tribunal be widely and easily available to the public at large.

RECOMMENDATION 81:

That a complaints register that is readily accessible to the public be maintained by the Rest Homes Tribunal.

RECOMMENDATION 82:
That the Ministry of Citizenship be vested with responsibility for the administration and funding of the Rest Homes Tribunal.

RECOMMENDATION 83:
That the Advocacy Commission consider identifying settings in which the receipt of advocacy services will be deemed a priority. Rest homes as defined by this Commission should be one such setting.

RECOMMENDATION 84:
That the Advocacy Commission ensure operational procedures are in place so that empowerment of the individual remains the central goal of the program.

RECOMMENDATION 85:
That church, community, and other voluntary groups be encouraged to visit rest homes regularly, thereby serving as informal advocates. That limited funding be available to such groups to defray direct costs in connection with such visiting.

RECOMMENDATION 86:
That the Good Neighbours initiative promote awareness of the needs of rest-home residents.

Chapter 10: Safety Standards

RECOMMENDATION 87:
That the principle of a minimum standard for housing quality for rest homes based on protecting the lives and safety of residents be adopted, and that no operator be permitted to offer accommodation that fails to meet this minimum.

RECOMMENDATION 88:

That a system of mandatory registration for all rest homes be introduced as soon as possible. That all rest homes be required to register with the municipality in which they are located. That municipalities be permitted to charge a modest fee for registration.

RECOMMENDATION 89:

That any owner or operator seeking registration for a rest home shall be required to produce the following documents to the municipality in which the dwelling is located:

1. a certificate from the fire inspector attesting to compliance with the relevant sections of the Fire Code, or noting all outstanding work orders;

2. a certificate from the building inspector attesting to compliance with the relevant sections of the Building Code and applicable local property standards by-laws, or noting all outstanding work orders; and

3. a certificate from the local board of health attesting to compliance with the applicable sections of the *Health Protection and Promotion Act*, or noting all outstanding orders;

4. a certificate from the local police containing the results of a Canadian Police Information Centre check on the operators;

5. a certificate from the Rest Homes Tribunal that affirms the operators are not at present banned from the industry and that the Rest Homes Tribunal holds that any convictions indicated by the Canadian Police Information Centre check do not constitute a bar to involvement in the industry.

RECOMMENDATION 90:

That every person seeking registration as owner/operator of a rest home be required to undergo a Canadian Police Information Centre check prior to registration.

RECOMMENDATION 91:

That if an applicant has previous criminal convictions, the Rest Homes Tribunal determine the suitability of the applicant to own or operate a rest home and whether the applicant shall be permitted to register the rest home.

RECOMMENDATION 92:

That full information on the names, addresses, and phone numbers of all owners and operators holding more than a specified minority interest accompany an application for registration of a rest home and subsequently be posted prominently in the home.

RECOMMENDATION 93:

That registration be obtained upon any change of ownership and renewed annually.

RECOMMENDATION 94:

That all municipal inspection and enforcement bodies be encouraged to keep all information about rest homes in such a manner that it can be easily shared. That these bodies share the information on a regular basis.

RECOMMENDATION 95:

That all rest homes be given a six-month period to register after the enactment of the legal requirement to do so.

RECOMMENDATION 96:

That there be a range of penalties for a rest home that operates without registration, including an order by the Rest Homes Tribunal to close the premises with the cost of relocation of the residents chargeable to the operators.

RECOMMENDATION 97:

That staff in rest homes be viewed as serving a safety rather than a care-giving function.

RECOMMENDATION 98:

That a minimum staff-to-resident ratio be mandatory in all rest homes at all hours. That only adults over the age of sixteen count in meeting this ratio.

RECOMMENDATION 99:

That administrative responsibility to ensure staff ratios in rest home are met be given to municipal fire inspectors.

RECOMMENDATION 100:

That any staff person who is involved in any aspect of assisting residents to take medications must be "competent" to do so. In assisting a resident in taking medications, "competence" means, at a minimum, that assistance can be provided only by someone who is:

1. sixteen years of age or older;
2. able to read and follow the directions on the bottle or package; and
3. able to identify, recognize, and communicate with the resident.

RECOMMENDATION 101:

That any operator providing assistance with medications be responsible to ensure that the medications, as prescribed, are delivered to the correct person in the prescribed dosage at the prescribed frequency.

RECOMMENDATION 102:

That operators be required to offer a secure locked area for the storage of medications.

RECOMMENDATION 103:

That the Ministry of Health develop relevant standards and guidelines for the regular inspection of rest homes, as defined by the Commission, under section 10 of the *Health Protection and Promotion Act.*

RECOMMENDATION 104:

That the duty to inspect food premises under section 10 of the *Health Protection and Promotion Act* include regular inspections of all rest homes serving food to ten or more residents.

RECOMMENDATION 105:

That the Ministry of Health consider the development of guidelines that would apply to all premises serving food to three or more and fewer than ten persons.

RECOMMENDATION 106:

That rest-home residents be recognized as a special group for the purpose of equal access to mandatory public-health programs under the "General Standard—Equal Access" in *Mandatory Health Programs and Services Guidelines* under the *Health Protection and Promotion Act.*

RECOMMENDATION 107:

That public-health officials, in conjunction with the Ontario Dietetic Association, explore appropriate minimum nutritional standards for residents of rest homes.

RECOMMENDATION 108:

That public-health nurses and nutritionists offer nutritional services to rest-home residents and operators as part of their mandatory provision of health services. This requirement should be incorporated into the "Program Standard—Nutrition Promotion" in the *Mandatory Health Programs and Services Guidelines* under the *Health Protection and Promotion Act.*

RECOMMENDATION 109:

That public-health nurses offer assistance to rest-home operators in developing appropriate systems for assisting residents with their medications, and that they offer training to meet rest-home staff in utilizing an appropriate system.

RECOMMENDATION 110:

That as a matter of general policy, residents of rest homes should have the same protections under the Fire Code as are provided to persons in rooming houses.

RECOMMENDATION 111:

That the standards required of rooming houses as set out in section 9.3, and draft sections 9.5 and 9.6 of the Fire Code be required of rest homes.

RECOMMENDATION 112:

That the exclusionary reference to premises in which the residents "do not require care or treatment" in section 9.3 of the Fire Code be eliminated, and that the terms "boarding, rooming and lodging accommodation" as used in section 9.3 and draft sections 9.5 and 9.6 be interpreted to include rest homes as defined by this Commission.

RECOMMENDATION 113:

That the fire marshal explicitly recognize the possible adverse effect on the rest-home stock of any higher standards under consideration.

RECOMMENDATION 114:

That community housing groups be involved in any decision-making process concerning higher fire-protection standards for rest homes.

RECOMMENDATION 115:

That the Low Rise Rehabilitation Program of the Ministry of Housing permit that funding be made available to operators of rest homes for upgrading purposes, including meeting retrofit fire-safety standards.

RECOMMENDATION 116:

That where a municipality desires higher standards in a domiciliary hostel than those contained in the Fire Code, they should be negotiated on a contractual basis between the municipality and operators of the rest homes.

RECOMMENDATION 117:

That whatever new fire-safety standards may emerge from the Rupert Hotel inquest apply not only to rooming houses, such as the Rupert Hotel, but also to rest homes as defined by this Commission.

RECOMMENDATION 118:

That rest homes, as defined by the Commission, be included in the list of examples of "residential occupancies" in Appendix A (at A-3.1.2.A.) of the Building Code.

RECOMMENDATION 119:

That the Building Code be endorsed as a single provincial construction standard, and that municipalities not be permitted to impose higher standards for the occupancy and/or maintenance of rest homes than those required by the "residential" standard of the Building Code.

RECOMMENDATION 120:

That all inspection visits to rest homes be conducted on an unannounced or surprise basis.

RECOMMENDATION 121:

That the ministry responsible for rest homes ensure an effective and speedy appeal procedure is in place with respect to inaction or decisions by public inspection authorities responsible for minimum standards in rest homes.

RECOMMENDATION 122:

That in matters within the jurisdiction of Fire Code Commission, the Building Code Commission, and the Public Health Appeal Board, any residents or their advocates shall have the same formal standing as is given to the owner/operators.

RECOMMENDATION 123:

That the mandates of the appropriate appeal tribunal or provincial inspectorate be extended to include non-response and untimely responses on the part of front-line inspectors.

RECOMMENDATION 124:

That persons familiar with residential tenancies, including residents, be appointed to the Fire Code Commission, Building Code Commission, and Health Protection Appeal Board.

Chapter 11: Housing: Supply and Choice

RECOMMENDATION 125:

That current efforts at co-ordination among the ministries responsible for supportive housing be intensified, and that they develop a single, common definition of "supportive housing."

RECOMMENDATION 126:

That the ministries involved with supportive housing recognize the importance of delinked service provision to such housing.

RECOMMENDATION 127:

That the Ministry of Housing amend the *Planning Act* to make accessory apartments and rooming, boarding, and lodging houses an as-of-right use in all zones where residential uses are permitted.

Chapter 12: Professional and Human Resources

RECOMMENDATION 128:

That community agencies, such as St. John's Ambulance, be encouraged to develop and deliver short workshops on assisting with medications to be attended by staff of rest homes.

RECOMMENDATION 129:

That operators and staff participate in workshops to become familiar with the new rights-based protections in rest homes.

RECOMMENDATION 130:

That information about rest homes be made available to professionals when the mandatory registration for rest homes begins.

RECOMMENDATION 131:

That local educational authorities develop short training courses with flexible schedules for staff in rest homes.

RECOMMENDATION 132:

That the Ministry of Labour re-examine its definition of "hospital" under the *Hospital Labour Disputes Arbitration Act* with a view to replacing it with more general legislation dealing with essential care services, however and wherever delivered.

RECOMMENDATION 133:

That the Workers' Compensation Board consider dividing its proposed new rate group 240 into two separate categories, distinguishing between premises that provide ongoing extended care and those that offer residential care (i.e., only limited nursing care). That registered rest homes be included in the latter grouping for assessment purposes.

RECOMMENDATION 134:

That the College of Physicians and Surgeons of Ontario develop a protocol describing the duties and responsibilities of "house doctors" in rest homes.

RECOMMENDATION 135:

That the Ministry of Health investigate the billing practices and quality of medical care delivered in rest homes by those physicians who regularly claim for multiple and sequential home visits in rest homes.

RECOMMENDATION 136:
That the Ontario Health Insurance Plan consider paying the special-visit fee only once for multiple home visits in one physical location.

RECOMMENDATION 137:
That the Ministry of Health develop measures to ensure that persons who are unable to attend medical premises are able to receive medical care in their homes, which includes rest homes.

RECOMMENDATION 138:
That the Ministry of Health develop measures to improve the accountability of physicians with respect to the medications they prescribe to residents of rest homes. That the role and responsibilities of pharmacists in this area be clarified.

RECOMMENDATION 139:
That the Ministry of Health financially support resident initiatives to lessen dependence on drugs and medications.

RECOMMENDATION 140:
That hospital discharge planners be supported in their efforts to draw up criteria to identify "approved" or "recommended" housing in their communities.

RECOMMENDATION 141:
That discharge planners continue to collect and share information on accommodation in the community; that discharge planners have all available information on rest homes on-line.

RECOMMENDATION 142:
That discharge planners only give information to departing

patients about rest homes that are registered with the municipality. That discharge planners be free to give information on
"unapproved" but legal rest homes, while identifying the causes preventing "approved" status.

RECOMMENDATION 143:

That the Ministry of Community and Social Services clearly
identify in advance, each year, the costs of providing accommodation for adults with developmental disabilities in children's facilities as part of the ministerial estimates.

RECOMMENDATION 144

That the Ministry of Community and Social Services accelerate
its plans to remove all adults with developmental disabilities
from children's residential accommodation; and that pending
such removal, the ministry take steps to ensure that appropriate standards for adults and effective accountability mechanisms are in place in such residences.

RECOMMENDATION 145:

That the role of local placement-co-ordination services and
service co-ordination agencies with respect to rest homes be
solely one of providing information.

Chapter 13: Provincial-Municipal Issues

RECOMMENDATION 146:

That in any provincial-municipal restructuring, the level of
government responsible for providing social assistance to an
person should not alter by virtue of that person's residence in
a hostel.

The Last Word

RECOMMENDATION 147

That the government consider implementing one or more pilot projects in which the development and implementation of relatively comprehensive community-based services will be accelerated in designated communities. These pilot projects should stress resident involvement in all stages of program design and delivery. That any such pilot program be formally evaluated as to outcome.

RECOMMENDATION 148:

That Windsor be considered as a site for any comprehensive community-care pilot program.

List of Written Submissions

Addiction Research Foundation
Toronto
Mark Taylor, President

Adult Protective Services
Peterborough
Maria Van Hoeve

Adult Protective Services
Perth
Jeff Nault

Advocacy Centre for the Elderly
Human Rights Committee
George T. Monticone

Alert Care Corporation
Richmond Hill
Avril Davies, Regional Manager

Algoma Community Legal Clinic Inc.
Sault Ste. Marie
Gayle Broad, Community Legal Worker

Algoma District Health Council
Sault Ste. Marie
Marie Price, Chairperson

Algoma Health Unit
Sault Ste. Marie
Jane Harbour, Director of Nutrition

Alzheimer Association of Ontario
Toronto
John Ellis, Executive Director

Alzheimer Society of Kingston
Lyn Hall

Alzheimer Society of Kingston
Jane Kelly

Alzheimer Society of Sudbury-Manitoulin
Sudbury
Joyce M. Tovey, Executive Director

Anglican Houses Serving People
Toronto
Julie Mancuso, Manager Adult Programs

Anglican Houses Serving People
Toronto
Terry McCallum, M.S.W., C.S.W.

Apartments for Living for Physically Handi-
capped
Windsor
Mrs. Simko-Hatfield, Administrator

Archway
Toronto
Maria Arruda

Association of Municipalities of Ontario
Toronto
John Harrison, President

Association of Supervisors of Public Health
    Inspectors of Ontario
M. R. Bragg, B.A., C.P.H.I.(C), President

Brant Community Social Planning Council
Robert K. Van Louwe, Executive Director

Brant County Community Legal Clinic
Carol Burns, Community Legal Worker

Brant County Health Unit
Dr. Ian Cunningham, Medical Officer of Health

Brant County Social Services
Ms Margaret Hughes

Brant District Health Council
Brantford
Tessa Kane, Chairman

Brant Family Counselling Centre
Brantford
Marie Friesen

Brant Family Counselling Centre
Brantford
Colleen Heer, B.A.

Brant Family Counselling Centre
Brantford
Maxine Lean, B.A.

Brantford Ethnoculturefest
Lillina Petrella, Executive Director

Brantford Ethnoculturefest
Elfrieda Neumann, Seniors Health Counsellor

Brockville Psychiatric Hospital
Peter K. Carter, M.S.W., M.P.A.

Brockville Psychiatric Hospital
Dr. H. Lafave

Brockville Psychiatric Hospital
P. A. Lee, Administrator

Brown, Mrs. Flora
Nepean

Browne, Angela
St. Catharines

Buckingham Manor
Stouffville
Manil Simon, C.A.

Cambridge Active Self Help
Annette Bauman, Program Coordinator

Cambridge Memorial Hospital
Grandside Psychogeriatric Clinic
Jane Grieve, M.S.W, Co-ordinator

Campbell, Lilian
Chesley

Canadian Association of Retired Persons
Toronto
Lillian Morgenthau, President

Canadian Institute of Public Health Inspectors
Ontario Branch
Klaus Seeger, President

Canadian Mental Health Association
Brockville
A. Pinkney, Executive Director

Canadian Mental Health Association
Durham Branch
Virginia Colling, President

Canadian Mental Health Association
Kent Branch, Chatham
Sandra Adie

Canadian Mental Health Association
Lambton County Branch
Colleen Zakoor, C.I.P. Co-ordinator

Canadian Mental Health Association
North Bay
J. Richard Christie, Executive Director

Canadian Mental Health Association
Ontario Division, Toronto
Carol Roup

Canadian Mental Health Association
Ottawa
Marnie Smith, Community Programs

Canadian Mental Health Association
Sudbury Branch
Mary Ann Quinlan, Executive Director

Canadian Mental Health Association
Windsor-Essex County Branch
Pamela G. Hines, Executive Director

Canadian Pensioners Concerned
Ontario Division
Gerda Kaegi

Canadian Union of Public Employees
Ontario Division
Ruth Scher

Caregard Management Inc.
Robertson House, Nepean
J. M. Tate, Vice-President

Catulpa-Tamarac, Community Services
Orillia
Lyn Tyerman, Manager

Centenary Hospital, Scarborough
Marjorie Lennox, Director of Social Work

Centre for Independent Living in Toronto
    (C.I.L.T.) Inc.
Sandra MacEachern, Peer Advocate

Chatham Public General Hospital
Dr. B. D. Sood, Chief of Psychiatry

Christian Labour Association of Canada
Mississauga
Ed Vanderkloet

Clark, Lynn G.
Chatham

Coalition for the Protection of Roomers and
    Rental Housing
Toronto
Lenny Abramowicz

Community Occupational Therapy Associates
Toronto
Nancy Sidle, O.T.(C)

Cotton, Evelyn
Arthur

Dawn House Women's Shelter
Kingston
Joanne Mcalpine, Administrator

Duncan, Dr. Lucy
Sarnia

Durham Region Placement Co-ordination
    Service
Diane Bennett, Director

Durham, Regional Municipality of
Environmental Health Services
Brian Devitt, C.P.H.I.(C), Director

Durham, Regional Municipality of
Dr. Robert Kyle, Medical Officer of Health

Eastern Ontario District Health Council
Donald R. St-Pierre, Executive Director

Eastern Ontario Health Unit
Dr. Robert Bourdeau, Medical Officer of Health

Eldridge, Elizabeth
Durham

Etobicoke, City of
Dr. A. Egbert, Medical Officer of Health

Etobicoke, City of
Ronald S. Gillespie, City Clerk

Etobicoke Council of Consumers/Survivors
E. L. Grosvenor

Family and Friends of the Mentally Handi-
    capped
Windsor
Bertha Lott, President

Family Counselling Centre of Brant
Sonia Pouyat, M.S.W., C.S.W., Executive
    Director

Family Home Program
Pembroke
Mary McBride

Family Services Centre of Sault Ste. Marie
David B. Rivard, M.S.W., C.S.W.

Federation of Ontario Facility Liaison Groups
Margaret Paproski, President

Friends and Advocates
Toronto
Elizabeth Fowler

Friends and Advocates
Toronto
Murray Saul

Galbraith, Mrs. Carla
Fort Frances

Gerstein Centre
Toronto
Pat Capponi, Leadership Facilitator

Good Neighbours Club
Toronto
Gary H. Corlett, Chairman

Goveia, Dorothy B., C.S.W.
Kingston

Grant, Gail C.
Gore's Landing

Habitat Services
Toronto
Mary Ellen Polak, Director

Haldimand-Norfolk District Health Council
Lynn Bowering

Haldimand-Norfolk Regional Health Dept.
Dr. William E. Page, Acting Medical Officer of
    Health

Haliburton, Kawartha and Pine Ridge District
    Health Council
Anne Gallant, Health Planner

Haliburton, Kawartha, and Pine Ridge District
    Health Unit
Dr. D. E. Mikel

Halonen, Eric
Windsor

Halton District Health Council
Oakville
Jane Sanders, Assistant Executive Director

Halton, Regional Municipality of
Social Services Department
Bonnie Ewart, Commissioner

Hamilton, City of
A. L. Georgieff, Director of Local Planning
    Dept.

Hamilton Psychiatric Hospital Clinical Services
Len May, Assistant Administrator

Hamilton-Wentworth District Health Council
Dr. Robert G. Kirby

Hamilton-Wentworth Placement Coordination
    Service
Joyce Caygill, Director

Hamilton-Wentworth, Regional Municipality of
Health and Social Services Committee
Dominic Agostino, Chairman

Hamilton-Wentworth, Regional Municipality of
R. J. (Reg) Whynott, Regional Chairman

Hamilton-Wentworth, Regional Municipality of
Nancy Voorberg, B.Sc.N., R.N., Supervisor,
Lodging Home Program

Haxton's Senior Lodge
Brantford
Pierre Jolicoeur, Administrator

Hearst, Kapuskasing and Smooth Rock Falls
    Counselling Services
André Marcel, Executive Director

Hearst, Kapuskasing and Smooth Rock Falls
    Counselling Services
Michel Lamontagne, Manager

Helpmate Community Information
Richmond Hill
Betty Forward, Executive Director

Henhoeffer, Linda
Gorrie

Hewett, Peter, R.N., B.Sc.
Peterborough

Highland Manor
Fergus
Margaret Middleton, Administrator

Holt, Peter
Ward's Island, Toronto

Homestead Residential and Support Services
Hamilton
R. DeVries, Co-ordinator

Honeyman, Madeleine
Ottawa

Hotel Dieu Hospital
St. Catharines
Frank Vetrano, Executive Director

Johnston, Anne, Metro Councillor
Toronto
North Toronto Ward

Kent County
M. E. Kuchta, Administrator, Community and
    Social Services

Kent County District Health Council
Diana J. Overholt, Assistant Executive Director

Kingston Friendship Homes Inc.
Vicky Schenk

Kingston, Frontenac and Lennox Addington
    District Health Council
Judith Mackenzie, Senior Planner

Kingston Psychiatric Hospital Community
    Development Services
Raymond D. Tremblay, Co-ordinator

Kitchener-Waterloo Social Planning Council
Ernie Ginsler, Executive Director

Lambton District Health Council
Dr. P. Englert, Chairman

Leduc, Roland
Chelmsford

Leeds and Grenville Developmental Services
R. G. McMullen, M.A., M.S.W.

Leeds, Grenville, and Lanark District Health
    Unit
Dr. A. B. Allen, Medical Officer of Health

Leeds, Grenville and Lanark District Health Unit
Catherine Woolham

Leeds, Grenville and Lanark District Health Unit
Dave Hart, Program Manager

Leeds, Grenville and Lanark Placement
        Co-ordination Service
Mrs. Jean Macintosh, Director

Listowel Memorial Hospital
James Van Camp, Administrator

London, City of
Mary Lynn Metras
Councillor, Ward 2

London Psychiatric Hospital
M. T. Mercer, Administrator

Marshall, Louise
Nepean

McKinnon, Kim
Toronto

McNeill, Wilma
Sarnia

Mental Health Coordinating Group of
    Scarborough
Freida Chavez

Metropolitan Toronto
Lea Caragata, Policy Development Officer

Metropolitan Toronto Home Care Program
Marie Lund, President

Metropolitan Toronto Housing Authority
Jean Augustine

Muskoka–Parry Sound District Health Council
Peter Deane, M.P.H., Executive Director

Muskoka–Parry Sound Health Unit
Dr. J. Walter Ewing, Medical Officer of Health

National Pensioners and Senior Citizens
    Federation
Les Batterson, President

Network North, Sudbury
The Community Mental Health Group
Michael Park, Chief Executive Officer

Niagara, Regional Municipality of
Senior Citizens Department
D. H. Rapelje, Director

Niagara District Health Council
Gary N. Zalot, Executive Director

Niagara Falls Social Planning Council
Mrs. Julie A. Darnay

Niagara Health Services Department
Marilyn Spadafore, Community Mental Health
    Program Manager

Niagara Health Services Department
Laurie Columbus, Adult Health Program
    Manager

Niagara Placement Co-ordination Service
Nancy McDonald, Executive Director

North Bay Psychiatric Hospital
Jack Menzies, Administrator

Ojibway Tribal Family Services
Kenora
Colin Wasacase, Executive Director

Ontario Advisory Council for Disabled Persons
Bob Loveless, Chairman

Ontario Association for Community Living
Nancy Stone, President

Ontario Association for Community Living
Don Mills
Rod Walsh

Ontario Association of Non-Profit Homes and
    Services for Seniors
Janice E. Mills, President

Ontario Association of Professional Social
    Workers
Doreen Cullen, M.S.W, C.S.W, President

Ontario Association of Residents' Councils
Toronto
Mary Ellen Glover, Co-ordinator

Ontario Dietetic Association
Toronto
Carol Poduch, R.P.Dt., President

Ontario Friends of Schizophrenics
Metro Toronto Chapter
Claire McLaughlin, President

Ontario Friends of Schizophrenics
Thunder Bay Chapter
Helen Schumacher

Ontario Friends of Schizophrenics
Toronto
June Conway Beeby, Executive Director

Ontario Gerontology Association
Concord
Annabel Sissons, President

Ontario Long Term Residential Care Association
Oakville
Rick Winchell

Ontario Nurses' Association
Glenna Cole Slattery, M.P.A.
Chief Executive Officer

Ontario Social Development Council
Toronto
Diane Mandell, Acting Executive Director

O'Shea, Isabelle
Hope Island
The Thousand Islands

Ottawa-Carleton, Regional Municipality of
Arthur J. Pope, Commissioner

Ottawa-Carleton, Regional Municipality of
Luc Legault
Director, Residential Services

Ottawa-Carleton Council on Aging
Margaret Wade Labarge, President

Ottawa-Carleton Health Department
Seniors' Co-ordinating Committee
Mary McNamara, Chairperson

Owen Sound Community Network Support
    Team
Jim Mulvale, Director

Palmerston and District Hospital
Dr. C. F. Cressey

Parkdale Activities and Recreation Centre
Toronto
Marc La Fontaine

Parkdale Activities and Recreation Centre
Toronto
David Littman

Peel, Regional Municipality of
Home Care and Community Services
Linda Instance, Director

Penetanguishene Mental Health Centre
George Kytayko, Administrator

Peterborough County-City Health Unit
Donna Evertsen, Public Health Nurse

Peterborough County-City Health Unit
Ann McLeod, Public Health Nurse

Peterborough Senior Citizens Council
Elizabeth A. Wright, President

Pinnock, Mrs. Stella
Scarborough

Plummer Memorial Public Hospital
Sault Ste. Marie
Lois C. Krause, Vice-President

Porcupine Health Unit
Timmins
JoAnne Stark, Director, Home Care

Portal Village Retirement Home
Port Colborne
Helen E. Baddeley, Administrator

Psychiatric Patients Advocate Office
Toronto
Duff Warring

Psychiatric Rehabilitation Case Management
  Interest Group
Rawle Elliott, President

Queen Street Mental Health Centre
Community Support and Research Unit
Toronto
John Trainor, Director

Reinke, Ellen
Hamilton

Queenchester
St. Catharines
Ruth Thiessen, R.N.

Residence on the St. Clair
Sarnia
Mrs. Carolyn L. Harris, Administrator

Rideau Valley District Health Council
Smiths Falls
Stella Turner, Chairperson

Royal Ottawa Hospital
Anne M. Huot, M.S.W., C.S.W., Director of
  Social Work

Royal Ottawa Hospital
Jane McLean, M.S.W., C.S.W., Community
  Social Worker

Ryerson Polytechnical Institute
School of Nursing
Linda M. Latham, B.A., R.N.

St. Catharines General Hospital
Community Mental Health Program
Mary Krajewski

St. Mark's Anglican Church
Brantford
K. Duning, Outreach Group

St. Thomas Psychiatric Hospital
Robert E. Cunningham, Administrator

Sarnia Community Legal Assistance
Margaret Capes, Staff Lawyer

Sarnia-Lambton Placement Co-ordination
  Service
Mrs. Anne Evans, Director

Sault Ste. Marie, City of
L. A. Bottos, City Solicitor

Sharbot Lake Seniors Home
Dr. Peter Bell

Sharon House
Toronto
Mrs. Lyn Zacher

Sherman, Helen
Richmond Hill

Simcoe County District Health Unit
Dr. David Butler-Jones

Slade, Betty
Marmora

Sudbury and District Health Unit
Dr. R.. J. Bolton, Medical Officer of Health

Sudbury Community Service Centre
Anne McGlade

Sudbury Community Service Centre
Lynn Wright

Sudbury General Hospital Crisis Intervention
    Program
G. R. Rasi, Co-ordinator

Supportive Housing Network
Kingston
Tom Greening, Co-chair

Thames Valley Placement Coordination Service
London
J. Payne, R.N., B.N., M.Ed., Director

Theunnissen, Mrs. Dianne
Beaverton

Thiessen, Isabel
Ottawa

Tilbury Manor Nursing Home
Tilbury
Jorge Tangkengko, Administrator

Toronto Mayor's Committee on Aging
Harriet H. Smith, Chair

Toronto, City of
Fred Breeze, Director of Inspections

Town and Country Homemakers
Wingham
Jean Young, Executive Director

United Senior Citizens of Ontario
Toronto
Jane Leitch, President

United Steel Workers of America
Sault Ste. Marie
Leo Gerard, District Director

Versa-Care Limited
Rick Willis, President

Veterans Affairs Canada
Hamilton District Office
Myron Kramar, Chief, Client Services

Victorian Order of Nursing
York Branch, Placement Co-ordination Service
Newmarket
Bev Lamont

Waterloo, Regional Municipality of
John Current, A.M.C.T., Deputy Regional Clerk

Waterloo, Regional Municipality of
Maggie Weidmark, Acting Director of Nursing

Waterloo Region Placement Co-ordination
    Service
Miss Millie Rider, Director

Wellington County Placement Coordination
    Service
Mrs. Joanne Weiler, Director

Wellington-Dufferin-Guelph Health Unit
Dr. R. M. Aldis

Wellington-Dufferin Homes for Psychiatric
    Rehabilitation
Alistair Moodie, Program Director

West Nipissing Association for Community
    Living
Sturgeon Falls
Denise Gignac, Executive Director

Whitby Psychiatric Hospital
John Anderson, Chairman

Whitby Psychiatric Hospital
Ronald Ballantyne, Administrator

Whitby Seniors' Programs
Fay McCorkell, Manager

Wilcox, Helen
Bridgenorth

Windsor, City of
Dana Howe, Commissioner of Social Services

Windsor, City of
Thomas W. Lynd, M.A., A.M.C.T., City Clerk

Windsor YMCA Residence Inc.
Marie Turek

York Central Hospital
Richmond Hill
Judy Raitt

York Community Services
Toronto
Elizabeth Wangenheim

York Heights Residents Association
Don Mills
Bruce Bokhout

York Region Mental Health Services
Doug Rankmore, Executive Director

York, Regional Municipality of
Dr. K. Helena Jaczek, Medical Officer of Health

York Support Services Network
Newmarket
Penny Hubbert, President

York Support Services Network
Newmarket
Marie Lauzier, Program Manager